MONOGRAPHS OF THE
SOCIETY FOR RESEARCH IN
CHILD DEVELOPMENT

Serial No. 238, Vol. 58, No. 10, 1993

VOCABULARY DEVELOPMENT:
A MORPHOLOGICAL ANALYSIS

Jeremy M. Anglin

WITH COMMENTARY BY
George A. Miller and
Pamela C. Wakefield

AND A REPLY BY THE AUTHOR

MONOGRAPHS OF THE SOCIETY FOR RESEARCH IN CHILD DEVELOPMENT
Serial No. 238, Vol. 58, No. 10, 1993

CONTENTS

ABSTRACT

ANGLIN, JEREMY M. Vocabulary Development: A Morphological Analysis. With Commentary by GEORGE A. MILLER and PAMELA C. WAKEFIELD; and a Reply by JEREMY M. ANGLIN. *Monographs of the Society for Research in Child Development*, 1993, **58**(10, Serial No. 238).

The purpose of this research was to investigate the growth of recognition vocabulary during the early and middle elementary school years in relation to the development of morphological knowledge. Six-, 8-, and 10-year-old children from grades 1, 3, and 5 (32 children at each age/grade level) were tested for their knowledge of a relatively large sample of main entry words drawn from a recent unabridged nonhistorical dictionary of the English language. Analyses of the sample of words indicated that it was reasonably representative of the main entry words in the entire dictionary in terms of frequency of occurrence and in terms of the distribution of the words according to morphological type. The children were tested on the words by means of definition, sentence, and multiple-choice questions. By multiplying the proportion of known words in the sample by the number of main entry words in the dictionary, estimates of total main entry recognition vocabulary knowledge were derived suggesting remarkable growth of vocabulary knowledge during the early and middle elementary school years.

The focus of the present study, however, was on the contribution made by different morphologically defined word types and by knowledge of morphology and word formation to total recognition vocabulary at different age and grade levels. It was found that comprehension of derived words in particular improved dramatically between grades 1 and 5, contributing relatively little to total recognition vocabulary in grade 1, but contributing more to such knowledge than any other morphologically defined type of word by grade 5. Moreover, it was found that multimorphemic words—words consisting of three or more morphemes—were also associated with particular growth, being not well known in grade 1 but being relatively much better known by grade 5. This is interpreted as supporting the view that lexical development can be characterized in terms of increasing morphological complexity. Further, it was found that the proportion of known complex words for which there was evidence that children figured them out by analyzing their morphological structure increased with age and grade. Qualifications regarding this latter finding are discussed, but it is argued that the data indicate the importance of making a distinction between knowing words because they have been previously learned and knowing them by means of morphological analysis and composition, particularly when trying to interpret the dramatic growth in recognition vocabulary suggested by this and related studies.

I. INTRODUCTION

Language acquisition is an important topic for research because it is a uniquely human process that influences in a powerful way the course of both social-communicative development (e.g., Bruner, 1983) and cognitive development (e.g., Vygotsky, 1986). Moreover, it is exciting because the speed and complexity of children's learning of a first language are truly impressive. Perhaps especially well documented is the rapid pace at which children acquire the grammatical rules that enable the production and comprehension of sentences during the preschool years (e.g., Bowerman, 1979; Brown, 1973; Brown & Hanlon, 1970; Slobin, 1973; see also Chomsky, 1965, 1975). No less dramatic, however, is the child's swift mastery of the sound pattern of speech in the first 4 or 5 years of life (e.g., Ingram, 1986). Children's progress in communicative and conversational development is also quite remarkable, beginning well before the acquisition of speech per se (Bates, 1976; Bruner, 1983; Trevarthen, 1980), and with considerable proficiency being attained during the first few years of linguistic growth (e.g., Bates, 1976; Brown, 1980; Dore, 1979). However, whereas the basics of syntax and phonology are largely mastered during the preschool years, communicative and conversational skills—such as maintaining the topic of discourse; expressing one's intentions felicitously, politely, and persuasively; producing unambiguous messages; and comprehending ambiguous messages as such—manifest a more protracted development that extends well beyond the early school years (e.g., Brinton & Fujiki, 1984; Flavell, Botkin, Fry, Wright, & Jarvis, 1968; Flavell, Miller, & Miller, 1993, pp. 295–300; Owens, 1992; Piaget, 1926). The research presented in this *Monograph* on the growth of vocabulary knowledge, another important aspect of language development, suggests that children's achievements in this domain are also quite remarkable. But, somewhat like the acquisition of communicative and conversational skills, vocabulary development appears to be relatively protracted, becoming in some respects even more impressive after the child has entered school than before.

It is likely that all languages have a vocabulary, a set of words that are the basic building blocks used in the generation and understanding of sentences (Miller, 1991). Without some knowledge of that vocabulary, neither language production nor language comprehension would be possible. Thus, the growth of vocabulary knowledge is one of the essential prerequisites for language acquisition. Vocabulary development has been shown by psychologists to be strongly related both to cognitive development (as measured, e.g., by tests of intelligence; see Anderson & Freebody, 1981; Terman, 1918; Wechsler, 1949) and to the acquisition of competence in reading (see Anderson & Freebody, 1981; Beck, McKeown, & Omanson, 1987; Graves, 1986; Miller, 1988; Nagy & Anderson, 1984; Nagy & Herman, 1987; Stanovich, 1986); the latter is, in turn, critical for success in school (e.g., Miller, 1988; Stanovich, 1986). These reasons alone would be sufficient to justify detailed investigations of the growth of vocabulary knowledge by developmental psychologists. However, what has most directly motivated the present research is a desire to confirm or disconfirm—and, if verified, to illuminate—the evidently rapid and large-scale acquisition by children of vocabulary knowledge. Several studies have suggested that schoolchildren acquire words at a rate of not hundreds but rather thousands per year, of not several per week but rather several per day (e.g., Miller, 1977, 1991; Miller & Gildea, 1987; Nagy & Anderson, 1984; Nagy & Herman, 1987; Smith, 1941; Templin, 1957). The research reported in this *Monograph* was conducted to see whether vocabulary really develops at such a rapid rate and, if it does, to clarify the nature of this apparently astonishing developmental process.

Vocabulary acquisition, semantic development, and the growth of word knowledge are currently being studied in several interesting ways. However, few recent studies have allowed the estimation of vocabulary size in children beyond the earliest years or the characterization of the quality of children's word knowledge and semantic development for representative samples of their entire vocabulary. Some earlier investigations (e.g., Seashore & Eckerson, 1940; Smith, 1941; Templin, 1957) and a few more recent ones (e.g., D'Anna, Zechmeister, & Hall, 1991; Dupuy, 1974; Goulden, Nation, & Read, 1990) have made some important progress in these directions, but each is associated with limitations of various kinds. The research presented here is meant to overcome some of these limitations and is the first in a series of related studies by means of which my students, my colleagues, and I hope to illuminate these issues further.

Beyond the earliest years of language learning, it becomes impossible to keep track of the many words that children learn and understand. However, it is possible to estimate vocabulary size at later points in development by taking a representative sample of words from an unabridged dictionary, testing children on them, and then multiplying the proportion of words in the sample known by the children by the total number of words in the dictionary. For example, if a child knows 10% of the words in such a sample taken from a dictionary with 250,000 entries, one's best guess is that he or she knows about 10% of 250,000, or about 25,000 words in total. One can use related methods to illuminate the quality of the child's vocabulary. For instance, to choose an example that is pertinent to this study, if 25% of the words known by a child in a representative sample taken from an unabridged dictionary are root words (monomorphemic single words with no affixes, like *happy* as opposed to *unhappy, happiness, happiest,* or *happy hour*), one's best estimate is that about one-quarter of *all* the words that he or she knows are root words as well. This method of dictionary sampling and estimation is the basic procedure used in the research reported in this *Monograph*. Thus, in the study presented here, children from grades 1, 3, and 5 were interviewed and tested in order to ascertain the extent of their knowledge of a relatively large representative sample of words taken from a recent unabridged dictionary of English. The results were then analyzed to generate estimates of vocabulary size in children at different age and grade levels and to elucidate the quality of their vocabulary, particularly with respect to morphological characteristics (see below).

To avoid seriously underestimating vocabulary knowledge using this method, it is important to sample from an unabridged dictionary (e.g., Miller, 1977, 1991; Seashore & Eckerson, 1940). No dictionary contains all the words of a language, but unabridged dictionaries come closer to this ideal than others. For this reason, *Webster's Third New International Dictionary of the English Language* (1981) was chosen as the source from which a sample of words was drawn for this research because it was the largest unabridged nonhistorical dictionary of present-day English vocabulary available when the study was begun (Landau, 1984; see also Goulden et al., 1990).[1]

Once words from this dictionary were sampled and examined, it soon became obvious that the main entries (boldfaced entries flush to the left-hand margin) in it included several types of words that differed in their morphological structure. In addition to root words such as *priest, happy,* and *define,* there were many derived words such as *priesthood, happiness,* and *redefine.* There were also many compound words, including some whose meanings can be literally interpreted in terms of their constituent words (e.g., *live-born, seabound, birthday*), and some whose meanings are idiomatic in the sense that they cannot be correctly construed through a literal interpretation of their constituent words (e.g., *dead heat, red herring, softheaded*). It was also found that some main entries were inflected words (e.g., *changed, reports, sourer*), although most such words were listed as subentries (bold-

---

[1] The reader should note that, unless the 1961 ed. is specified, subsequent citations of *Webster's Third* refer to the 1981 ed. For an explanation of our choice of the 1981 over the 1961 ed., see the beginning of Chap. IV below.

faced entries occurring within the definition of a main entry). When other dictionaries were checked, they were also found to include these various types of lexical entries. For example, Funk and Wagnalls's (1937) *New Standard Dictionary of the English Language* (unabridged), which had been used by Seashore and Eckerson (1940), Smith (1941), and Templin (1957) in their studies of recognition vocabulary size in adults and children, contains as main entries many derived words, many literal and idiomatic compounds, and some inflected words. Moreover, derived and compound main entries in particular varied in terms of morphemic complexity. For example, although many derived words were bimorphemic, consisting of a root and a single derivational affix (e.g., *stillness, modernish, redefine*), others were multimorphemic, consisting of a root and two or more affixes (e.g., *incomparable, hopelessness, despiritualization*). And, although compound words were sometimes bimorphemic, consisting of two root words (e.g., *live-born, low-level, cardinal flower*), others were multimorphemic, consisting of three or more root words (e.g., *whole wheat flour, get-rich-quick, northwest coast indian*) or of two or more words, some of which were derived or inflected (e.g., *western saddle, bare-eyed cockatoo, exhaust-gas-analyzer*).

Once this morphological heterogeneity in the composition of the English lexicon (as it appears in authoritative dictionaries) was discerned, it was decided to make children's knowledge of different morphologically defined categories of words a special focus of the present research for two reasons. First, there is a large and growing literature on the acquisition of the rules of inflectional morphology, derivational morphology, and compound formation that, taken together, suggests that certain types of morphologically defined words might be acquired somewhat later than others. For example, previous research suggests that derived words might in general be acquired somewhat later than inflected and compound words (e.g., Berko, 1958; Clark & Hecht, 1982; Derwing & Baker, 1979; Wysocki & Jenkins, 1987) and that morphologically more complex words might in general be acquired later than morphologically simpler words (e.g., Brown, 1973; Clark & Berman, 1987; Clark, Hecht, & Mulford, 1986). A study such as the one reported here, in which children at different age and grade levels are tested for their knowledge of a large, representative sample of words varying in morphological type and complexity, provides an excellent opportunity to examine vocabulary growth functions for different morphologically defined categories of words. Besides being of interest in their own right, such growth functions could then be examined to see if they verify or disconfirm trends suggested by the recent literature on morphological development.

Second, because many entries (in particular, the derived, inflected, and literal compound words) in *Webster's Third,* and in the representative sample drawn from it for the research reported in this *Monograph,* are morphologically complex words whose meanings could possibly be figured out through knowledge of their corresponding root words and the rules of morphology and word formation, it was deemed especially important to pay attention to children's responses to such words to see if there was evidence that they were constructing meanings for them through such knowledge. If there were to be evidence suggesting that a large proportion of credited words were figured out through morphological knowledge, then morphological analysis and composition—or what I will call *morphological problem solving*—would loom as a potentially important part of the explanation for the seemingly large estimates of vocabulary size and of rate of vocabulary development suggested by previous research. Such a finding would also suggest the importance of distinguishing between what I will call *psychologically basic words*, which are known because they have been previously learned and stored as distinct units in long-term memory, and words that are known or are *potentially knowable* because they can be figured out through morphological analysis.

Thus, the research reported here was conducted to illuminate both quantitative and qualitative aspects of vocabulary development. With respect to quantitative aspects, an important aim of this investigation was to establish sound estimates of vocabulary size in children at different age and grade levels and from these to derive estimates of the rate of vocabulary development during different developmental periods. To accomplish this, children were tested on their knowledge of a sample of words drawn from *Webster's Third* that was larger than those used in previous related studies of children's vocabulary development and that was demonstrated to be representative of the words in the source dictionary, which had not been established for the samples used in previous studies. Moreover, children were tested on these words with a combination of methods and were credited for knowing them if they satisfied criteria that were designed to be neither too stringent nor too lax.

With respect to qualitative aspects of vocabulary development, this research focused on analyses of the kinds of morphologically defined types of words that make up children's recognition vocabulary at different age and grade levels and on whether children appeared to use morphological knowledge to construct the meanings of the complex words that they were credited with understanding. It is hoped that, besides being of interest in their own right, these qualitative analyses might elucidate the nature of the quantitative changes in vocabulary size during childhood revealed by this research. Thus, children's total vocabulary knowledge was partitioned into portions accounted for by different morphologically defined word types and by words characterized by different degrees of morphemic complexity. Such analyses make it possible to examine the growth functions for the different types of words and to discern any lags and spurts that might occur in children's growing understanding of words with respect to such categories. They also reveal the contributions that are made by knowledge of different word types to estimates of total vocabulary size at different age and grade levels and to estimates of the rate of vocabulary growth during different developmental periods.

The responses to complex words were examined to see whether the children appeared to use morphological knowledge to construct their meanings so as to illuminate the distinction between knowing words because they have been learned before and knowing words through morphological problem solving. On the basis of this analysis, estimates of total vocabulary knowledge and of rate of vocabulary development were partitioned into subestimates of words for which such evidence would have been found (had children been tested on all the words in the dictionary) and those for which it would not have been. The latter are offered as approximate estimates of *psychologically basic* or *actually learned* vocabulary and of the rate of *word learning*, the former as approximate estimates of vocabulary that is *potentially knowable* through morphological problem solving and of the rate of its growth. Finally, responses that suggested that complex words were figured out through morphological knowledge were scrutinized to see if they revealed any clues to the processes that children may have been using at different ages to construct the meanings of different word types, clues that might be useful to take into account in future, more specifically process-oriented research.

In the following chapters, the ideas and arguments presented briefly above are explained, refined, and elaborated further. The next chapter presents a critical review of previous attempts to estimate vocabulary size and rate of vocabulary development in children, with an emphasis on those investigations that have most directly influenced the present research. A limitation of previous studies that is stressed is the absence of a consideration of the morphological structure of known words and of the possibility that children's knowledge of morphology and word formation might enable them to figure out some complex word meanings. The morphological classification schemes adopted for this research are also presented, along with an explanation of their conceptual underpinnings and the considerations that motivated their use.

In Chapter III, previous research examining the development of morphological knowledge is reviewed, with an emphasis on studies that have focused on the acquisition of inflectional, compounding, and derivational rules that might enable children to figure out complex word meanings through morphological analysis in a test of vocabulary knowledge such as that used in the current research. Predictions suggested by previous research concerning the relation between vocabulary development and the growth of morphological knowledge are then offered.

In Chapter IV, the sample of words drawn from *Webster's Third* used in this study is described, and the classifications of these words according to morphological word type and degree of morphemic complexity are presented. Comparisons with other recent morphological analyses of English vocabulary and results from several tests of possible sample bias are also reported. Finally, the way in which the multiple-choice questions (one component of the vocabulary test) were constructed is specified.

Chapters V and VI present the study of vocabulary development in children from grades 1, 3, and 5. After the children and the method of testing them are described, many of the results from the study are reported in Chapter V. Estimates of vocabulary size at different age and grade levels are provided, followed by detailed analyses in which children's overall vocabulary knowledge is broken down into subcategories of words of different morphologically defined types and of different degrees of morphemic complexity. Estimates of overall rate of vocabulary development are also partitioned into specific rates for each of these subcategories.

The responses that children produced in the vocabulary test are then further analyzed in Chapter VI to illuminate the distinction between words that are known because they have been previously learned and words that are known because they are figured out through morphological problem solving. On the basis of these analyses, estimates of overall vocabulary knowledge and of rate of vocabulary development are partitioned into approximate subestimates for *psychologically basic vocabulary* and for *potentially knowable vocabulary*. Several examples of responses to different types of complex words suggesting the use of morphological problem solving are also presented as concrete illustrations, in the hope that they might provide clues to the processes that children may use to figure out such words at different age and grade levels.

Finally, in Chapter VII, the findings from this research are summarized, their theoretical implications for our understanding of vocabulary development are discussed, and some ideas for future research are suggested.

II. ESTIMATING CHILDREN'S VOCABULARY KNOWLEDGE

As noted in Chapter I, the basic method used in this study was to select a relatively large sample of words from a recent unabridged dictionary and to test children on their knowledge of these words. On the assumption (which I try to justify in Chap. IV) that this sample of words is reasonably representative of the entire vocabulary from which it was drawn, it is possible to extrapolate from children's knowledge of the sample to estimates of their approximate knowledge of all the words in the dictionary. This method was used to estimate both the size of recognition vocabularies and the composition of those vocabularies in terms of different morphologically defined types of words known by children at different age and grade levels.

PREVIOUS VOCABULARY ESTIMATION STUDIES

Previous studies using sampling-and-estimation methods have resulted in widely varying average estimates of children's vocabulary size (Anderson & Freebody, 1981; Beck & McKeown, in press; Graves, 1986; Lorge & Chall, 1963; McCarthy, 1954; Nagy & Anderson, 1984; Nagy & Herman, 1987; Seashore & Eckerson, 1940; Wysocki & Jenkins, 1987). For example, for children in grade 1, these have ranged from 2,562 words (M. E. Smith, 1926) to about 16,500 "basic" words (M. K. Smith, 1941) and 21,000–26,000 "total" words (Shibles, 1959; Smith, 1941). Average estimates for third-grade children have ranged from about 1,500 (Dupuy, 1974) to about 24,000 "basic" words (Smith, 1941) and about 38,000 "total" words (Smith, 1941). For seventh-grade children, they have varied from a low of about 4,500 (Dupuy, 1974) to about 34,000 "basic" words (Smith, 1941) and about 54,000 "total" words (Smith, 1941).

Factors Affecting Vocabulary Estimates

As has been noted by many authors (Anderson & Freebody, 1981; Beck & McKeown, in press; Graves, 1986; Lorge & Chall, 1963; Miller, 1977,

1991; Nagy & Anderson, 1984; Seashore & Eckerson, 1940), the variability in estimates is due to various factors, three of which are emphasized here. First, the estimates depend critically on the source from which the sample of words is selected. If drawn from a smaller dictionary, one with, say, 50,000 entries, the maximum estimate of vocabulary size would be 50,000 words, which would be achieved only if someone knew all the words in the sample. By contrast, if drawn from an unabridged dictionary with 250,000 entries, a person would have to know only 20% of the sample words to be credited with knowledge of 50,000 words. Virtually all the studies conducted prior to Seashore and Eckerson's (1940) investigation involved sampling from sources that underestimated the word stock in English; this has also been true of many of the more recent studies (for reviews, see Beck & McKeown, in press; Graves, 1986; and Nagy & Herman, 1987). As Miller (1977, 1991) has suggested, to avoid seriously underestimating vocabulary size, it is important to use an unabridged dictionary. *Webster's Third New International Dictionary of the English Language* (1981) was chosen as a source from which to sample words in the present study because, at the time of its inception, this was the most recent edition of what Landau (1984) described as "the only truly unabridged synchronic dictionary" of modern-day English and as "a masterpiece in the art of lexicography" (p. 352).

Second, vocabulary estimates depend substantially on the criteria used for determining that a word is known. Several types of criteria have been used in previous research (Anderson & Freebody, 1981; Beck & McKeown, in press; Graves, 1986; Seashore & Eckerson, 1940). These have included such relatively objective measures as requiring that the words be defined correctly, that they be used in sentences to indicate awareness of their meanings, and that a correct synonym or paraphrase of the word be selected on a multiple-choice test over incorrect alternatives. They have also included such relatively subjective measures as the "checking" or "yes/no" method in which subjects are simply asked to indicate whether they know the meanings of the words. Some of these criteria can lead to serious underestimation of an individual's knowledge of words, especially a young child's. For example, requiring the production of a dictionary-like definition of a word might be too stringent a criterion since the ability to produce such definitions is a metalinguistic skill that develops only gradually through the school years (e.g., Benelli, Arcuri, & Marchesini, 1988; Feifel & Lorge, 1950; Litowitz, 1977; McGhee-Bidlack, 1991; Snow, 1990; Vygotsky, 1986; Watson, 1985). Moreover, research with young children has shown that they often possess knowledge of words that is not revealed by their definitions (e.g., Anglin, 1985; Watson, 1985). On the other hand, such subjective measures as the checking method do not convincingly show that subjects really know the meanings of the words that they check and can lead to serious overestimation of the extent of vocabulary knowledge (cf. Chall & Dale, 1950; Drum

9

& Konopak, 1987; Graves, 1986). To assess vocabulary knowledge in a way that is neither too stringent nor too lenient, three relatively objective criteria were used in the current study: definition, sentence, and multiple-choice questions. Smith (1941) used these same multiple criteria of word knowledge, but it is unclear whether she corrected responses to multiple-choice questions for guessing (cf. Smith, 1941; Templin, 1957), a procedure necessary to avoid inflated estimates (Brown, 1983; Miller, 1977). In the present research, responses to multiple-choice questions were corrected for guessing, and considerable care has been taken in constructing the alternative choices, which is another important precaution to follow when such tests are used (Anderson & Freebody, 1981; Brown, 1983).

A third factor—the investigator's definition of what a word is—can influence estimates of vocabulary size and is especially important for the present research (Anderson & Freebody, 1981; Beck & McKeown, in press; Lorge & Chall, 1963; Miller, 1977, 1991; Nagy & Anderson, 1984; Seashore & Eckerson, 1940). A particular question arising in research on vocabulary size is how to treat morphologically complex words. For example, has the child who knows the root word *jump* as well as the inflected words *jumping*, *jumps*, and *jumped* learned one word or four different words? What about the child who knows the root word *happy* and also the derived words *unhappy*, *happiness*, and *unhappiness*? Should the child who knows *milk* and *cow* and also the compound word *milk cow* be credited with having learned three different words or just two? In the present study, it was assumed that a reasonable starting point is to define a word as a boldfaced entry in a dictionary. But then, as noted in Chapter I, an important objective of this research was to partition estimates of known vocabulary into different morphologically defined types (root words, inflected words, derived words, literal compounds, and idioms) as well as into linguistically unitary versus linguistically complex types. Ultimately, an attempt will also be made to shed some light on the distinction between psychologically or psycholinguistically basic words and those that are figured out through morphological problem solving, a distinction introduced briefly in Chapter I and expanded on below.

Rate of Vocabulary Growth

Although previous estimates of vocabulary size in children have varied greatly across different studies, there is little doubt that vocabulary knowledge develops at a remarkable rate. This conclusion seems strongly supported if previous studies that have made reasonable decisions about the three factors affecting estimates discussed above are emphasized (e.g., Templin, 1957) or when the results of other studies are reinterpreted or recalibrated in view of these factors (e.g., Nagy & Herman, 1987). There is a growing consensus that, during the school years, vocabulary is acquired at an average rate of thousands of words a year, or, to put it another way, of several words per day (e.g., Beck & McKeown, in press; Jones, Smith, & Landau, 1991; Miller, 1977, 1978a, 1981, 1986a, 1986b, 1988, 1991; Miller & Gildea, 1987; Marcus et al., 1992; Nagy & Anderson, 1984; Nagy & Herman, 1987; White, Power, & White, 1989; Wysocki & Jenkins, 1987). There is also evidence of considerable individual differences in rate of vocabulary growth (e.g., Beck & McKeown, in press; Graves, 1986; Miller & Gildea, 1987; Nagy & Herman, 1987; Smith, 1941; Templin, 1957), differences that may become increasingly pronounced during the school years (Miller, 1988; Stanovich, 1986).

What factors may be involved in promoting this growth (as well as individual differences in it) is a matter of debate. Three hypotheses that are currently receiving considerable attention relate the rapid development of vocabulary knowledge to (1) direct instruction of vocabulary in school (see Beck & McKeown, in press; Beck, Perfetti, & McKeown, 1982; McKeown, Beck, Omanson, & Perfetti, 1983); (2) learning words and their meanings from context, especially during reading activities (e.g., Miller, 1988, 1991; Miller & Gildea, 1987; Nagy & Anderson, 1984; Nagy, Anderson, & Herman, 1987; Nagy & Herman, 1987); and (3) a growing ability to infer the meanings of words through morphological knowledge (e.g., Derwing & Baker, 1979, 1986; Freyd & Baron, 1982; Gordon, 1989; Nagy & Anderson, 1984; Tyler & Nagy, 1989; White et al., 1989; Wysocki & Jenkins, 1987; see also Clark, 1981, 1983a; Clark & Berman, 1987; Clark, Gelman, & Lane, 1985; Clark & Hecht, 1982; Clark et al., 1986).

The Studies of Seashore and Eckerson, M. K. Smith, and Templin

Of the many studies that have used sampling methods to estimate vocabulary size, one line of research in this tradition has been particularly important in influencing the present investigation. Seashore and Eckerson (1940) developed the Seashore-Eckerson Recognition Vocabulary Test and used it to estimate the breadth of vocabulary knowledge in college undergraduates; M. K. Smith (1941) and Templin (1957) subsequently adapted this test for use in developmental studies of schoolchildren. These researchers were among the few to use a sample of words taken from an unabridged dictionary (Funk and Wagnalls's 1937 unabridged *New Standard Dictionary of the English Language*), which, as argued earlier, is essential to avoid seriously underestimating breadth of vocabulary knowledge. Moreover, the results of these studies are still being discussed in the recent research literature and have been especially influential in leading current researchers and theorists to conclude that vocabulary develops in children at a remarkable rate (e.g., Carey, 1978; Clark, 1983a, 1983b, 1987; Jones et al., 1991; Just & Carpenter, 1987; Keil, 1983; Marcus et al., 1992; Markman, 1987; Miller,

11

1977, 1978a, 1981, 1986a; Nagy & Anderson, 1984; Nagy & Herman, 1987; Waxman & Kosowski, 1990).[2] Although more recent reviews and discussions (see Anderson & Freebody, 1981; Beck & McKeown, in press; Graves, 1986; Nagy & Anderson, 1984; Nagy & Herman, 1987) have illuminated many of the important issues that must be considered in work of this type, only a few recent studies have provided new data and new estimates of vocabulary size and rate of vocabulary development. Moreover, while interesting in many ways, most of these studies have involved unrealistically low estimates of the word stock of English, either because samples were drawn from small populations of words (e.g., D'Anna et al., 1991; Graves, Brunetti, & Slater, 1982), or because "words" were defined in such a way as to exclude large numbers of what most observers, including lexicographers, would count as legitimate English words (e.g., Dupuy, 1974; Goulden et al., 1990). Because the present investigation represents the first in a series of studies in which my colleagues and I have tried to improve and expand the approach developed by Seashore and Eckerson, Smith, and Templin, their research is reviewed briefly, and then discussed critically, below.

Seashore and Eckerson (1940) sampled 331 main entries (boldfaced words flush to the left-hand margin) and 46 subentries (boldfaced words that occurred within the definitions for main entries) from Funk and Wagnalls's *New Standard Dictionary,* a large, unabridged, and, in its day, relatively good dictionary. Undergraduate students were then tested on these words. By multiplying the proportion of main entries known by the total number of main entries that they reckoned to be in the dictionary, Seashore and Eckerson estimated that the undergraduates tested had a mean main entry vocabulary, which they called a "basic" vocabulary, of a little less than 60,000 words. Similarly, they estimated their subjects to have a mean subentry

---

[2] Templin's study in particular and conclusions drawn from it by Carey (1978), Miller (1977), and others are also discussed in many recent leading textbooks in developmental psychology (e.g., Cole & Cole, 1993, p. 276; Collins & Kuczaj, 1991, p. 178; Harris & Liebert, 1991, p. 306; Hetherington & Parke, 1993, pp. 255, 268; Santrock & Yussen, 1992, p. 350; Shaffer, 1993, p. 383; Vasta, Haith, & Miller, 1992, p. 379), cognitive development (e.g., Flavell et al., 1993, pp. 294, 301), and language development (e.g., Owens, 1992, p. 343). Her study is important and deserves the attention that it has received. However, Templin's estimates are often presented as indicating the number of words that children have *learned,* or they are used to approximate the rate of *word learning* in the preschool or the postschool years. It will be argued that not all words that children are credited with knowing in recognition vocabulary tests, such as Templin's and the one presented here, have necessarily been learned by them before; rather, some of them may have been figured out through morphological analysis at the time of the test. Thus, it will be argued that, when considering estimates of recognition vocabulary knowledge and of the rate of vocabulary development derived from such studies, it is important to distinguish between words that are known because they have been learned before and words that have not been previously learned but are known or at least knowable in the sense that they could be figured out through morphological decoding.

vocabulary, which they called a "derivative" vocabulary, of about 95,000 words. By adding these two estimates together, they concluded that, on average, these undergraduates had a total vocabulary of about 155,000 words. These estimates were far larger than any reported earlier, but no previous researchers had sampled words from as large a dictionary.

Several investigators (e.g., Colvin, 1951; Schulman & Havighurst, 1947; Shibles, 1959) tested children at a single grade level using the Seashore-Eckerson Recognition Vocabulary Test, but only two (Smith, 1941; Templin, 1957) did so with children at more than one grade level. Smith tested children and adolescents from grades 1–12 on the same 331 main entries and 46 subentries used by Seashore and Eckerson. She estimated that children in grade 1 have a median main entry or "basic" vocabulary of about 16,500 words and a median total vocabulary of about 21,000 words. Her estimates were about 24,000 and 38,000 for third-grade children and about 28,000 and 43,000 for fifth-grade children for median "basic" and total vocabulary, respectively. By grade 12, she found that the median "basic" and total vocabularies had increased to about 45,000 and 80,000 words, respectively, and also that the percentage of subentries or "derivative" words in the total vocabulary increased with age and grade as well. Although Smith was able to adapt Seashore and Eckerson's test for use with children, and although she introduced some methodological improvements in the way the test was actually conducted, her study can be criticized on the grounds that it is not clear that multiple-choice questions were corrected for guessing and that she sometimes provided hints or "leading questions" (in such instances, a child who then showed an understanding of the words was given half credit).

Templin replicated Smith's study with 6-, 7-, and 8-year-olds in grades 1, 2, and 3. However, she did not use leading questions or hints, and she did correct responses to multiple-choice questions for guessing. She estimated that the median main entry or "basic" vocabulary increased from 7,800 to 17,600 words and the median total vocabulary from 13,000 to 28,300 words over this age range. Additionally, she examined sex and socioeconomic effects and found that, whereas the estimates for boys and girls did not differ significantly, children from upper socioeconomic strata knew significantly more words than those from lower socioeconomic levels in terms of both "basic" and total vocabulary.

Miller (1977, 1978a, 1981, 1986a) and Carey (1978) recently revived interest in Templin's study by converting her estimates into approximate rates of vocabulary development. By dividing the difference between Templin's median estimates for 6- and 8-year-old children by their average age difference (in days), Miller (1977) estimated that, taken at face value, Templin's data indicated that, between 6 and 8 years of age, the average child "learns" about 14.5 "basic" or "root" words, and about 21 words in all, per day. Miller (1978a, 1986a) suggested that the process of learning any given word is not likely to be completed in one day and that, in fact, a child will be gradually working out the meanings of a great number of words during the same developmental period (see also Carey, 1978). He also suggested that most cases of word learning during the early grade school years are probably based on the child's ability to infer the meanings of words from the contexts in which they are heard. In his more recent writings on the rate of vocabulary development during the later school years, Miller has continued to emphasize the importance of contextual learning, except that, in these later years, starting around the fourth grade, new words are often encountered in and eventually learned from written contexts during reading activities (Miller, 1988, 1991; Miller & Gildea, 1987; see also Nagy & Anderson, 1984; Nagy et al., 1987; Nagy & Herman, 1987).

Carey (1978) assumed that word learning is minimal prior to 18 months and, like Miller (1977), used Templin's estimates for recognition vocabulary in 6-year-olds to deduce that, between 1½ and 6 years of age, children "learn" about five "root" words a day (see also Waxman & Kosowski, 1990) and about nine new words per day in all (see also Clark, 1983a, 1983b, 1987; Keil, 1983; Markman, 1987). Carey proposed two steps in word learning by young children: a "fast mapping" process in which a new word is immediately assigned to a semantic category, followed by a much slower process in which the distinctions among words from the same semantic category are gradually learned (see also Miller, 1977, 1986a). Carey argued, as did Miller, that, in accordance with this second, slower process, the child is probably working out the meanings of a large number of words during a given interval. In an innovative study, Carey and Bartlett (Carey, 1978; Carey & Bartlett, 1978) introduced a nonsense word into natural conversations with nursery school children and illustrated some of the details of these two steps in word learning (see also Dockrell & Campbell, 1986).

This suggestion of the rapid rate of vocabulary growth during the preschool years has contributed to several recent attempts to illuminate the constraints, biases, predispositions, and strategies that might aid children in limiting their hypotheses about the meanings of new words and thereby to account for their apparently remarkable skill at word learning (e.g., Au & Glusman, 1990; Carey, 1988; Clark, 1987; Jones et al., 1991; Keil, 1983; Markman, 1987, 1989; Smith, Jones, & Landau, 1992; Waxman & Kosowski, 1990). The role played by such factors and the evidence offered to support them are currently being actively debated (e.g., Carey, 1983; Gathercole, 1987; Merriman & Bowman, 1989; Mervis, 1987; Nelson, 1988; Waxman & Hatch, 1992).

Although Carey's (1978) reanalysis of Templin's data does suggest remarkable vocabulary development during the preschool years, Miller's (1977) reanalysis of these same data suggests that the rate of vocabulary development is even more rapid in the early school years. Data from the current study (presented in Chaps. V and VI) also suggest considerable vocabulary growth during the preschool years and even more rapid growth in the early school years. However, a distinction not stressed by these other researchers will be emphasized here: the distinction between words that can be understood on the basis of morphological knowledge and words that have been previously learned. It will be suggested that the dramatic growth of recognition vocabulary knowledge observed by Templin (1957), Smith (1941), and others, as well as in the present study, may *in part* reflect children's increasing ability to engage in *morphological problem solving*. That is to say, it may be due in part to the fact that, increasingly with age, children can decipher the meanings of some previously unlearned morphologically complex words through morphological analysis (breaking complex words into and identifying the meanings of their morphological components) and composition (synthesizing the meanings of the component morphemes to figure out the meanings of the complex words).

Critique

As important as they are, the studies by Seashore and Eckerson, Smith, and Templin can be critiqued on various statistical, methodological, linguistic, and psychological grounds. The three lines of criticism that are especially important to the current research are discussed next.

The first centers on the sample of words used in these studies. Seashore and Eckerson selected the third boldfaced main entry on every eighth page of Funk and Wagnalls. Discarding nonwords such as abbreviations, prefixes, and suffixes left them with their sample of 331 "basic" words; selecting every tenth subentry associated with these main entries then resulted in their sample of 46 "derivative" words. The latter is rather too small to allow much confidence in previous estimates of "derivative" vocabulary (e.g., Conway, 1967) and therefore also renders those of total vocabulary (which is the sum of "basic" and "derivative" vocabularies) somewhat suspect. In the present study, we focused solely on main entry vocabulary, using a somewhat larger sample of 434 main entries selected by choosing every seventh boldfaced entry on every sixth page of *Webster's Third*.

Moreover, as Lorge and Chall (1963) have pointed out, in selecting their sample of words, Seashore and Eckerson counted homographs (e.g., $kill^1$, $kill^2$, $kill^3$, $kill^4$) as separate entries, but then they (as well as Smith, 1941, and Templin, 1957) accepted the word as known if a subject could recognize or express the meaning of any of the homographs.[3] Lorge and

---

[3] A homograph is one of two or more words that are spelled identically but that differ in meaning and derivation. For example, *fair* meaning "market" and *fair* meaning

Chall found that the sample of words used by these researchers was biased in favor of more frequently occurring words and concluded that the failure to adjust for homographs or multiple entries of the same word was probably responsible for this bias in the Seashore-Eckerson Recognition Vocabulary Test. Our own examination of Seashore and Eckerson's data and of Funk and Wagnalls's *New Standard Dictionary* confirms that these researchers had counted homographs as separate entries both in their sampling of words and in their estimation of the number of different main entries in the dictionary. In the present study, each set of homographs was treated only as a single main entry. Moreover, none of the several tests that we developed to assess whether our sample of words is biased with respect to either frequency of occurrence or distribution according to morphological type showed such to be the case (see Chap. IV).

The second line of criticism is that very little attention was paid to the quality (as opposed to the quantity) of children's (or adults') vocabulary knowledge in these studies. Apart from the distinction between main entry (or "basic") and subentry (or "derivative") vocabulary, virtually nothing was said about either the kinds of words known at different ages or the quality of knowledge of known words that subjects manifested. Symptomatic of this lack of concern with the quality of vocabulary knowledge was the almost complete absence in these studies of examples of the kinds of words known and of illustrations of what was said about known words. Although the present research focuses primarily on morphological aspects of word knowledge, both the kinds of words known and what is known about them are major concerns, and several specific examples of known words and of what children said about them are included.

The third line of criticism, which can be viewed as a particular instance of the preceding one and which is the most crucial for the present research, is that no attempt was made in these studies to analyze the linguistic, psycholinguistic, and, in particular, the morphological properties of the words sampled or known, nor was there any attempt to examine the quality of subjects' morphological knowledge of known words. For example, although these previous researchers called subentries "derivative" or "derived" words and distinguished these from what they called "basic" words (the main entries), many main entries in Funk and Wagnalls's *New Standard Dictionary*, as well as in other dictionaries, would be classified by linguists (e.g., Aronoff, 1976; Bauer, 1983; Marchand, 1969) as well as by psycholinguists and developmental psycholinguists (e.g., Clark, 1983b; Miller, 1991; Tyler & Nagy, 1989) as derived words or derivatives. Thus, in addition to the root word *rob*, the derived words *robber* and *robbery* are also listed as main entries in

---

"beautiful" are homographs. Dictionaries commonly list homographs as separate bold-faced main entries, with a numerical superscript to distinguish them.

Funk and Wagnalls; the same holds for the root word *short* and the derived words *shortage, shorten, shortish, shortly, shortness,* etc. Furthermore, many of the relatively easy "basic" words sampled by Seashore and Eckerson were in fact derived words such as *adhesive, cowardly, percolator, constructive, devotion, weighty, creation, falsehood, reposeful,* etc. Derived words are very common as main entries in Funk and Wagnalls and most other dictionaries of English.

Moreover, Funk and Wagnalls's *New Standard Dictionary, Webster's Third* (the dictionary used in the present research), and most other large dictionaries of English contain at least five different morphological types of main entries (as well as different subtypes). The five types include root words (e.g., *short, closet*), inflected words (e.g., *smoking, reports*), derived words (e.g, *shortish, treelet*), literal compounds (e.g., *sunburn, birthday*), and opaque, idiomatic compounds or lexical idioms, which will here be called simply "idioms" (e.g., *mouse tail,* "a plant of the crowfoot family"; *pink lady,* "a cocktail"). Thus, although previous researchers have called main entries "basic," not all of them are so from a morphological point of view.

Because these and related types of words are central to the morphological analyses reported here, they are defined, exemplified, and discussed in greater detail below. Arguments are also presented concerning why it is important to examine the morphological characteristics of words sampled and known in tests of recognition vocabulary and how it is hoped that, by studying different morphologically defined types of words and children's responses to them, the present investigation will elucidate the nature of vocabulary development in ways that were not possible in previous research such as that of Seashore and Eckerson, Smith, and Templin.

MORPHOLOGICAL CLASSIFICATIONS OF ENGLISH WORDS

The unit of analysis used in classifying words into morphological types is the morpheme. A morpheme is a minimal meaningful linguistic unit that contains no smaller meaningful parts; it can be a free form, such as *happy,* or a bound form, such as the *-ness* in *happiness.* The morpheme has been used as the minimal unit of grammatical analysis (e.g., Bauer, 1983; Brown, 1973; Lyons, 1968), but for research on the lexicon, as in the present study, it can also be employed as the minimal unit of semantic analysis. Although not all linguists accept the definition of morphemes as being the smallest individually meaningful elements of a language (e.g., Aronoff, 1976), many others do so (e.g., Adams, 1973; Bloomfield, 1933; Hockett, 1958); in the case of developmental psycholinguistic research on the growth of the mental lexicon such as that represented by the present study, this definition of morphemes serves its purposes especially well (cf. Brown, 1973; Derwing & Baker, 1979).

Two Morphological Classification Schemes

The five major types of morphologically defined words mentioned above, and used in the present research, can be characterized as follows:

1. *Root words* are monomorphemic lexical entries that consist of single, free morphemes. Examples from the sample of words selected for the present study are *closet, flop, hermit,* and *pep.*

2. *Inflected words* usually consist of one free morpheme and one inflectional suffix. Inflectional suffixes generally modulate a base grammatically for tense, aspect, person, number, gender, case, etc. They do not usually result in a change of part of speech, they almost always appear at the end of words in English, and they are thought to produce mere paradigmatic variants of the base as, for instance, when the suffix *-s* is added to *boy,* resulting in the plural form *boys.* In English, there are eight types of inflectional suffixes: the plural inflection (e.g., the *-s* in *cats*), the possessive inflection (e.g., the *-'s* in *mother's*), the third-person-singular verb inflection (e.g., the *-s* in *jumps*), the progressive inflection (e.g., the *-ing* in *soaking*), the past-tense inflection (e.g., the *-ed* in *jumped*), the past participle (e.g., the *-en* in *fallen*), the comparative inflection (e.g., the *-er* in *sourer*), and the superlative inflection (e.g., the *-est* in *fairest*). Examples of inflected words from the sample of words used in this study are *soaking, changed, sourer,* and *baits.*[4]

3. *Derived words* are lexical entries that consist of one root and one or more derivational affixes. This root is often a root word or a free morpheme, such as the *sad* in *sadness* or *sadly;* however, as discussed in Chapter III, it may sometimes be a bound morpheme, such as the *quant-* in *quantity* or *quantify,* particularly when the derived word has a nonneutral derivational affix in it (see Aronoff, 1976; Chomsky & Halle, 1968; Gordon, 1989; Kiparsky, 1982, 1983; Selkirk, 1982; Tyler & Nagy, 1989). Derivational affixes in English can be prefixes or suffixes, and derivational suffixes often result in a change in part of speech (compare the adjective *happy* and the noun *happiness*). Rather than producing a mere paradigmatic variation of a base, the addition of a derivational affix is thought to result in an entirely different, although semantically related, word, as when the agentive suffix *-er* is added to the verb *preach* to produce the derived noun *preacher.* Examples of derived words tested in this study are *treelet, mucky, stillness, incomparable,* and *talkativeness.*

4. *Literal compounds* are lexical entries that consist of two or more words (Bloomfield, 1933). The words making up a literal compound

---

[4] Some inflected words in English are irregular, such as the past of *go* (*went*), the plural of *man* (*men*), and the superlative of *good* (*best*). In the present psycholinguistic work, it makes most sense to treat such irregularly inflected words as monomorphemic (cf. Brown, 1973; Derwing & Baker, 1979); however, no such irregularly inflected words were sampled in the present study.

may be root words (e.g., *payday, milk cow*), but one or more of them may be derived or inflected words (e.g., *tax payer, bare-eyed cockatoo*). An additional criterion used in defining literal compounds in this study was that it be possible to determine the meaning of the literal compound from knowledge of its component morphemes (Makkai, 1972). Examples of literal compounds from our sample of words are *milk cow, live-born, seabound, bare-eyed cockatoo,* and *malarial fever.*

5. *Idioms* (*idiomatic compounds, opaque compounds,* or *lexical idioms*) are lexical entries that are like literal compounds in that they consist of two or more words (with or without derivational or inflectional affixes), but, unlike literal compounds, they are idiomatic in the sense that it is not possible to determine their meaning from knowledge of their component morphemes (Makkai, 1972). For example, one cannot deduce that the idiom *pink lady* refers to an alcoholic drink from knowledge of its constituent root words *pink* and *lady*. Examples of idioms from the sample of words used in this study are *strange woman* (a female prostitute), *carrying on* (misbehavior), *lady's slipper* (a type of orchid), *twenty questions* (a game), and *pony league* (a baseball league for juveniles).

In the current study, all words sampled were categorized in terms of this fivefold classification scheme. Such classifications enable examination of the growth functions associated with each of these qualitatively distinct kinds of words, which, as mentioned in Chapter I, is one of the objectives of this research.

We have also classified the words in our sample in a second, complementary way, according to the number of morphemes making up a given word; this permits a more direct examination of the portions of vocabulary knowledge accounted for by words of different levels of morphemic complexity at different times in development. There is evidence that, in the earliest period of language acquisition, the child does not engage in any morphological analysis when attempting to comprehend words, does not combine morphemes when producing words, and that all words are psychologically monomorphemic (e.g., Bowerman, 1982; Brown, 1973; Miller, 1991). It is not until somewhat later that the child's vocabulary begins to include words with more than one morpheme, such as nouns marked with the plural inflection, verbs marked with the progressive inflection (e.g., Brown, 1973), or two-term compounds (e.g., Clark, 1981). Moreover, there is evidence to suggest that lexical development at later ages is characterized by growth in morphemic complexity with increasingly complex forms being added to vocabulary knowledge as children grow older and learn more about language (e.g., Clark & Berman, 1987; Clark et al., 1986).

The fivefold classification scheme outlined above does not allow a direct analysis of this issue because some of its qualitatively distinct categories include words of different levels of morphemic complexity. For example, some derived words are bimorphemic (e.g., *happiness, comparable, institution*), whereas others are multimorphemic (e.g., *unhappiness, incomparable, reinstitutionalization*). Similarly, some literal compounds are bimorphemic (e.g., *whole wheat, payday, seabound*), whereas others are multimorphemic (e.g., *whole wheat flour, western saddle, northwest coast indian*). To enable an analysis of the morphemic complexity of the words known by children (i.e., of the number of morphemes making up known words), the following classification scheme was also used in this research:

1. *Monomorphemic words* consist of single free morphemes and are identical to *root words* as defined above.

2. *Bimorphemic words* are lexical entries consisting of two morphemes; examples from the sample of words used in this study are *soaking, sourer, treelet, stillness, milk cow,* and *firesafe.*

3. *Multimorphemic words* are lexical entries consisting of three or more morphemes; examples from our test words are *incomparable, talkativeness, readmission, hopelessness, bare-eyed cockatoo,* and *malarial fever.*

4. *Idioms* are defined as above.

Rationale for the Morphological Classification Schemes

Three major considerations led to the use of these classification schemes in this research. The first arose from extensive attempts to classify large samples of lexical entries from *Webster's Third* and also from less extensive attempts to classify smaller samples from Funk and Wagnalls's *New Standard Dictionary* and other dictionaries of English. The classification schemes emerged on the basis of this work as being the most suitable to use in view of the goals of the study presented in this *Monograph.*

Second, the writings of experts on word formation and morphology in the fields of linguistics, psycholinguistics, and developmental psycholinguistics (e.g., Adams, 1973; Aronoff, 1976; Bauer, 1983; Berko, 1958; Bloomfield, 1933; Brown, 1973; Chomsky, 1970; Clark, 1981, 1983a, 1983b; Clark et al., 1985; Clark & Hecht, 1982; Clark et al., 1986; Derwing & Baker, 1979, 1986; Fraser, 1970; Halle, 1973; Hockett, 1958; Jackendoff, 1975; Makkai, 1972; Marchand, 1969; Miller, 1978b; Miller & Johnson-Laird, 1976; Nagy & Anderson, 1984; Tyler & Nagy, 1989) were studied, and an attempt was made to respect linguistic distinctions that have been well worked out by such scholars. For example, linguists and psycholinguists have developed good reasons for distinguishing among root words, inflected words, derived words, and compounds, and it seemed important to acknowledge such distinctions in the present research. Indeed, it is hoped that this research will contribute to our understanding of the acquisition by children of such word types. Although to my knowledge no linguist or psycholinguist has explicitly used the exact fivefold and fourfold classification systems outlined above, these schemes are largely consistent with the work of the scholars cited above. Moreover, the vast majority of our classification decisions can be justified by referring to combinations of the writings of experts on word formation (e.g., Adams, 1973; Aronoff, 1976; Bauer, 1983; Bloomfield, 1933; Marchand, 1969; Miller, 1991) and on idioms (e.g., Makkai, 1972; see also Fraser, 1970; Hockett, 1958).

Third, as stated earlier, an important aim of the current research was to attempt to distinguish between *psychologically basic* or *actually learned* vocabulary and vocabulary that is *figured out* or *potentially knowable* on the basis of morphological problem solving. Hence, in classifying the words into morphological categories, we have endeavored to respect this fundamental distinction. Generally, in both classification schemes, it is the root or monomorphemic words and idioms that cannot be correctly construed through morphological analysis, whereas the remaining word types can (but may not always) be.

Any differences between the classifications used in this research and other linguistically but not necessarily psychologically oriented morphological classification systems are a consequence of our adherence to this fundamental distinction. For example, it is what led to the decision to define morphemes as the smallest *meaningful* elements of the language and not to accept as such the *fer* in *referendum,* the *con* in *convocate,* or the *ad* in *advisable,* for example, even though some linguists have treated such psycholinguistically meaningless particles as morphemes (while often acknowledging the debatable nature of such decisions). Doing so may be justifiable in a diachronic (i.e., historical) analysis, but it would be counterproductive in a synchronic (i.e., psycholinguistic) analysis such as the present investigation. Similarly, it is what led to our decision not to treat as morphemes such particles as, for example, the *im-* in *improve* and the *re-* in *retailing* even though in other words (e.g., *immobile, impossible, improper, redefine, reborn, recapture*) *im-* and *re-* would be classified as morphemes (specifically, derivational prefixes) using the present classification schemes. Whereas the meanings of these latter words (in which *im-* means "not" and *re-* means "again") could be figured out given knowledge of these prefixes and of the corresponding root words, such analysis would be misleading (e.g., White et al., 1989) if applied to words like *improve* or *retailing* and would result in incorrect semantic interpretations. Such decisions, however, should not be controversial since other developmental psycholinguists (e.g., Brown, 1973; Derwing & Baker, 1979, 1986; White et al., 1989) have made similar decisions for related reasons.

Perhaps the one aspect of the current classification systems that might be somewhat controversial is the treatment of idioms as a separate category and the distinction drawn here between literal compounds and idioms. Although other recent analyses of the contents of large dictionaries (e.g., Dupuy, 1974; Goulden et al., 1990) have distinguished morphologically basic or root words from derived and compound words, they have not further subclassified compound words, as we have, into literal compounds and idioms. Moreover, many authorities in morphology and word formation (e.g., Adams, 1973; Bauer, 1983; Bloomfield, 1933; Marchand, 1969; Miller, 1991) scarcely mention the term *idiom* at all and would treat many lexical entries classified here as idioms as types of compounds. Because our distinction between literal compounds and idioms may seem unorthodox to some, the following discussion attempts to show that it is not actually inconsistent with the writings of linguists on morphology and word formation and also to clarify further its importance in view of the objectives of the present research.

Although several authorities on word formation have not explicitly contrasted literal compounds and idioms, many have subcategorized compounds in ways that at least partially capture the distinction used here. For instance, some (e.g., Adams, 1973; Bauer, 1983; Bloomfield, 1933; Jackendoff, 1975; Miller, 1991) have distinguished between endocentric and exocentric compounds. Endocentric noun compounds (e.g., *beehive, birthday, milk cow, malarial fever*) are subtypes of the head noun, which in English is usually the last noun in the compound. Thus, a beehive is a type of hive, a birthday a type of day, a milk cow a type of cow, and malarial fever a type of fever. In exocentric noun compounds (e.g., *redhead, yellow jacket, greenback, lady's slipper, pickpocket*), however, the compound is not a subtype of the grammatical head: a redhead is not a head but a person, a yellow jacket not a jacket but a wasp, a greenback not a back but a bill, a lady's slipper not a slipper but a type of orchid, and a pickpocket not a pocket but a type of thief. We almost always classify compounds that are exocentric as idioms, and we classify many that are endocentric as literal compounds. However, we classify some endocentric compounds as idioms. For example, *strange woman* denotes a type of woman, but, because one could not infer from its component words that it means "female prostitute," it was classified as an idiom. *Pony league* is a type of league, but, because one could not surmise from its constituent words that it is a baseball league for juveniles, it was also classified as an idiom. Contrasts introduced by other linguists, such as Marchand's (1969) distinction between compounds and pseudocompounds, also bear some similarity to the literal compound/idiom distinction used here, and Bauer's (1983) contrast between transparent (e.g., *airmail*) and opaque (e.g., *blackmail*) compounds is virtually identical to it.

Some other linguists have used the term *idiom* explicitly in a way that is consistent with its usage here. Working within the framework of transformational grammar, Fraser (1970) and Katz and Postal (1963) focused on "phrasal idioms" (e.g., *to kick the bucket*), but they also recognized the exis-tence of "lexical idioms" (e.g., *knucklehead* and *turncoat*). Hockett (1958) viewed many linguistic constructions as idioms, including those lexical compounds the meanings of which are not transparent from their component words. Makkai (1972, 1975), a leading authority on idioms, distinguished several types, including (1) lexemic idioms, which (like Fraser's and Katz and Postal's lexical idioms) are often compound words (e.g., *hot dog, turn in,* or *acid head*); (2) "phraseological idioms" or "tournures" (e.g., *to kick the bucket* and *to fly off the handle*); and (3) proverbs and sayings (e.g., "Don't count your chickens before they are hatched"). Makkai contrasts lexemic idioms, the meaning of which cannot be determined from the meanings of their component words, with *literal compounds,* for which this is possible, in a way entirely consistent with the terminology used here.[5] Finally, it should be noted that lexicographers (e.g., Urdang & Abate, 1983) and authors of dictionaries of idioms also often recognize opaque compounds as idiomatic (see, e.g., *A Dictionary of American Idioms* [Makkai, 1975] or Vols. 1 and 2 of *The Oxford Dictionary of Current Idiomatic English* [Cowie & Mackin, 1975; Cowie, Mackin, & McCaig, 1983]).

It should be acknowledged that literal compounds and idioms actually lie along a continuum (from transparent to opaque); however, this is also true of the distinctions between inflected and derived words and between derived words and compounds (Bauer, 1983) as well as of many other conceptual distinctions (Rosch, 1973). It is also the case that literal compounds are not themselves totally transparent (Clark, 1983b), which is one reason I prefer the term *literal compounds* to *transparent compounds.* In addition to having to know the component words of a literal compound, one must also be able to infer the relation(s) between the words in order to construct the compound's meaning through morphological analysis and composition. For example, *milk cow* is not a cow that drinks milk, or one that is made of milk, but rather one that gives milk; *birthday* is not the day after birth, or the day before birth, but rather the day of birth; etc. However, for these and other words classified as literal compounds in our word sample (e.g., *live-born, outgrow, seabound, malarial fever,* etc.), it seemed to us that, with knowledge of the component words and a little common sense, it should often be possible to infer their meanings, which makes them very different from such idioms as *pink lady, strange woman, twenty questions,* and *lady's slipper,* for which this is not possible. Nagy and Anderson (1984, p. 310) classified many compounds of the type called "literal" here as among the most morphologically transparent words in English.

---

[5] It is worth mentioning that, in the Webster's dictionary used in the present research, the vast majority of idioms occurring as main entries are lexical or lexemic idioms; phrasal or phraseological idioms or tournures such as *to kick the bucket* are also sometimes listed, but almost always as subentries.

In spite of the above qualifications, the *literal compound/idiom* distinction used here seemed natural to make in view of the sample of lexical entries selected for this research as well as important to maintain on conceptual grounds. Given the objectives of this project, it was deemed critical to distinguish between words whose meanings could and could not be figured out from knowledge of their constituent morphemes. Indeed, from a psycholinguistic point of view, it seems more natural to align idioms with root words than with literal compounds since, like regular inflected and derived words, the latter are amenable to decoding through morphological analysis and composition whereas, generally, neither root words nor idioms are. Within a child's or an adult's mental lexicon—the representation of vocabulary knowledge in long-term memory—idioms that are known, like known root words, would typically be stored somehow as unitary wholes, whereas this would not necessarily be the case for the morphologically complex word types (regular inflected words, derived words, and literal compounds). It is interesting to note that both linguists (e.g., Jackendoff, 1975) and psycholinguists (e.g., Swinney & Cutler, 1979; see also Clark & Clark, 1977, p. 446; McNeill, 1987, p. 171) have concluded that, like root words, phrasal idioms such as *to kick the bucket* have to be stored in the lexicon as whole units since they cannot be decomposed into or composed from morphological parts in a semantically revealing way. The same is most often true for lexical idioms, and this is why we deemed it important to distinguish lexical entries that are idioms from those that are literal compounds.[6]

Psychologically Basic Vocabulary

Our analyses of the sample of words selected for this study as well as of other samples taken from *Webster's Third* showed that morphologically complex words occur very frequently as main entries. In terms of our first (fivefold) classification of words into morphological types, inflected words are relatively uncommon as main entries (although they are very common as subentries). However, derived words and literal compounds are very common as main entries, as are root words and idioms. Linguists (e.g., Adams, 1973; Bauer, 1983; Bloomfield, 1933; Marchand, 1969; Miller, 1991) have identified derivation and compounding as the two major pro-

---

[6] In addition to this theoretical justification for the *literal compound/idiom* distinction, there is empirical support for it in the study that is reported here. Specifically, interrater reliability for the morphological classifications in general, and for the *literal compound/idiom* distinction in particular, was quite high (see Chap. IV), and the performance of children at all age levels tested was very different (both in terms of number of words known and in terms of whether there was evidence of morphological analysis and composition for known words) for literal compounds and idioms (see Chaps. V and VI).

cesses of word formation, and derived words and compounds occur frequently as main entries in this and other dictionaries of English. Indeed, the sample of main entries selected for this study, and others that we have taken from *Webster's Third*, contain more derived words than root words or words of any other of the five types. In terms of our second (fourfold) classification of words according to level of morphemic complexity, the most common type by a considerable margin has been bimorphemic words, and, in the sample used in the present study, morphemically complex words (bimorphemic and multimorphemic words combined) are slightly more frequent than the linguistically nondecomposable words (root words and idioms combined).

Thus, although previous researchers (e.g., Seashore & Eckerson, 1940; Smith, 1941; Templin, 1957) have called main entries "basic," not all of them are basic from a linguistic point of view, and they may not be psychologically (or psycholinguistically) basic either. By *psychologically basic vocabulary* is meant here words for which there are distinct representations in long-term memory or, to use psycholinguistic terminology, words for which there are distinct entries in one's mental lexicon. As suggested above, it would seem that, to identify most root words or idioms correctly on a vocabulary test, one would have had to have learned them before and to have stored them somehow as individual units in long-term memory. However, for inflected words, derived words, and literal compounds, this is not necessarily the case; one could possibly work out their meanings through knowledge of their component morphemes and a tacit understanding of the inflectional, derivational, or compounding rules of English. For example, some adults and possibly some grade school children might be able to figure out the meaning of *treelet* if they know the meaning of the root word *tree* and of the affix *-let* ("little" or "baby"), even though they may never have learned or even encountered the word previously.

Some linguists and psycholinguists (e.g., Chomsky, 1970; Halle, 1973; Jackendoff, 1975; Miller, 1978b; Stanners, Neiser, Hernon, & Hall, 1979; see also Miller & Johnson-Laird, 1976) have raised the possibility that, whereas regularly inflected words, as well as gerundive nominals, may not have separate representations in the (adult mental) lexicon, derived and compound words probably often do, although they may be grouped with their constituent root words. This may often be the case for relatively common derived and compound words, although there may be exceptions (e.g., Aronoff, 1976; Chomsky, 1970; Miller & Johnson-Laird, 1976). Intuitively, however, it seems quite possible that some common regularly inflected words (e.g., *bored, soaking,* etc.) are heard, read, spoken, or written so often that they might be represented as distinct entries in the mental lexicon. On the other hand, it also seems quite likely that there might be numerous uncommon derived words and literal compounds that, because they have not been encountered before frequently or at all, would not be stored as such in long-term memory but that nonetheless could be figured out when read or heard or when taking a recognition vocabulary test of the type developed by Seashore and Eckerson (1940). For example, many adults might be able to figure out and get credit for knowing the derived words *treelet, unbribable, modernish,* and *unreluctant* and the literal compounds *sea-bound, overfulfill, underprize,* and *malarial fever,* which were sampled for the present study, even though they may not have encoded these exact forms in memory or even encountered them before. Similarly, some children might be able to figure out the meanings of certain inflected words (e.g., *reports, sourer, baits*), derived words (e.g., *mucky, treelet, stillness*), and literal compounds (e.g., *milk cow, live-born, outgrow*), even though they may not have learned them as whole words before, provided that they know the relevant root words, and provided that they have the requisite knowledge of the inflectional, derivational, and compounding rules of English.

In the study presented in this *Monograph,* words that were known by children in a recognition vocabulary test are broken down in terms of the morphological categories presented above, and the children's responses to complex word types (inflected words, derived words, and literal compounds) are analyzed in an attempt to illuminate the distinction between words that have been previously learned and words that are figured out through morphological analysis and composition. On the basis of this analysis, estimates of total recognition vocabulary are partitioned into subestimates that are intended to approximate *psychologically basic vocabulary* as opposed to vocabulary that has not been previously learned but rather is *potentially knowable* through morphological problem solving.

III. MORPHOLOGICAL DEVELOPMENT

Because knowledge of morphological rules is necessary for morphological problem solving, and because an important concern of this *Monograph* is the extent to which the growth of recognition vocabulary might be accounted for by such problem solving, I review below previous research that has examined the growth of morphological knowledge in children. I focus specifically on those studies of children's knowledge of inflectional morphology, compound formation, and derivational morphology that pertain to the issue of whether children at different age levels have acquired morphological rules that might enable them to decode inflected, compound, and derived words. The aim is to indicate the extent to which children in the early and middle elementary school years might use such knowledge to figure out complex word meanings in a recognition vocabulary test of the type used in the present investigation. A related purpose of this review is to generate predictions about developmental differences that might be expected in the growth functions associated with different types of morphologically complex words and with words at different levels of morphemic complexity.

CHILDREN'S KNOWLEDGE OF INFLECTIONAL MORPHOLOGY

It is well known that most children whose first language is English master many of the basic English inflections in the preschool years. In a detailed longitudinal study of three children, Brown (1973) observed that there was an early period in grammatical development in which inflections and other "modulators of meaning" were largely absent from the words that these children combined in their first attempts to construct sentences. However, after the children's mean length of utterance (MLU) assessed in morphemes exceeded a value of 2, nouns and verbs were increasingly inflected in contexts for which inflections are obligatory for adults. Brown found that the five English inflections that he studied were acquired by the children in a consistent order: the progressive inflection was learned first, followed by the plural, possessive, past regular, and third-person-singular regular inflections. Brown's criterion for acquisition was relatively stringent (90% correct applications in obligatory contexts in spontaneous speech), but he still found that all five regular inflections were mastered during the preschool years. More specifically, "Adam, Eve and Sarah all attained the 90 percent criterion of acquisition for the progressive, possessive, and plural inflections before their fourth birthdays (Eve by about her second birthday), and the regular past and third person inflections were not far behind" (Brown, 1973, p. 284).

Brown emphasized the idea that language development can be predicted by linguistic complexity, with more complex forms being acquired after less complex forms. Of particular relevance to the present *Monograph* is his finding that the words produced by children early in their language development are monomorphemic, that is, unmarked by inflections or other bound morphemes, but that subsequently those words become increasingly marked by inflectional suffixes when required by context. Thus, Brown's research is consistent with the proposition that the words used by children in the first years of language development become increasingly morphologically complex. Many of Brown's findings have been confirmed by Cazden (1968), who used the same data base, and by de Villiers and de Villiers (1973) and Anglin (1980), who conducted cross-sectional studies involving larger numbers of preschool children.

Brown, Cazden, and de Villiers and de Villiers noted that, even prior to attaining their criterion of acquisition, the preschool children whom they studied were often observed to overregularize or overgeneralize inflections, producing forms such as *goed, doed, mans, mouses,* etc. (see also Kuczaj, 1977). For this and other reasons, these investigators concluded that these preschool children had acquired the inflections not just by rote but rather as productive rules.[7] Marcus et al. (1992) have recently presented a very thorough analysis of overregularization of the past tense inflection *-ed* (which

---

[7] When applied to inflectional or derivational affixes, the term *productive* is used by psycholinguists to mean that those affixes are used constructively to *produce new words*. Children's overregularizations provide especially convincing evidence that affixes are being used productively to create words since such forms (e.g., *goed, mans*) are unlikely to have been heard by children in the speech of others. Hence, they suggest the knowledge and use of an underlying rule that enables such novel coinages. When discussing affixes, linguists also use the term *productive* in a quite related sense. An affix is productive to the extent that it is used to *produce new words* in a language. For example, the derivational agentive affix *-er* (as in *preacher*) is more productive in English than other derivational agentive affixes, such as *-ist* (as in *typist*) and *-ian* (as in *musician*), because the former is used much more often in the creation of new English words than the latter (see, e.g., Clark & Cohen, 1984).

results in such forms as *comed, goed,* and *eated*) in the spontaneous speech of 83 (predominantly preschool-aged) children. Although overregularization errors were found to be rarer overall than has commonly been assumed, the evidence of these researchers supports the notion that preschoolers do indeed acquire a productive affixation rule (i.e., add *-ed* to a root verb to indicate past tense) that they apply to irregular root verbs when rote memory retrieval of the conventional irregular past form fails. Such developmental analyses, as well as other findings pertaining to language use and breakdown in adults and children, suggest the need to distinguish between knowledge of *morphological rules,* which enable the production and comprehension of many regularly inflected words, and an *associative memory,* in which irregulars are presumably stored by rote along with root words and other unanalyzed forms (Pinker, 1991). Such a distinction is obviously related to the one that I emphasize in this *Monograph* between words that can be figured out through knowledge of morphological rules and words that have been actually learned and stored in long-term memory.

In a classic study, Berko (1958) devised a task involving the use of nonsense words that required inflections (and derivational affixes) to be used productively. For example, she showed children a picture of an imaginary creature, saying, "This is a wug." Then she showed them a picture of two of these imaginary creatures, saying, "Now there is another one. There are two of them. There are two ———." If the children could append the plural inflection to the nonsense word stem and say "wugs," it would imply that they had learned to do so in a productive sense (i.e., by rule) rather than by rote since it is clear that *wugs* would not have been heard by them before. Berko developed similar tests for seven of the eight regular English inflections (all but the past participle, which for regular verbs is usually identical in form to the past tense inflection). As Brown (1973) noted, this laboratory task is somewhat more difficult than using the morphemes correctly in spontaneous speech, and Berko required that children use the correct allomorph (/-z/, /-s/, or /-əz/ for the plural, possessive, and third person singular; /-d/, /-t/ or /-əd/ for the past tense) in cases where the inflection has different phonological realizations, a requirement not made by Brown. Nonetheless, Berko found that, with the exception of the least common allomorph of the plural morpheme /-əz/ and the least common allomorph of the past tense inflection /-əd/, a majority of children aged 4–5 years supplied the correct suffix for all her other tests of the plural, past, possessive, third-person-singular, and present progressive inflections. On the other hand, neither preschool nor first-grade children were adept at supplying the comparative (*-er*) or the superlative (*-est*) inflections in Berko's test. These results have been essentially confirmed by others (e.g., Derwing & Baker, 1979; Selby, 1972).

Thus, with respect to the acquisition of regular inflections, it is clear that, with the possible exceptions of the comparative and the superlative (see, however, Layton & Stick, 1979), most of them have been mastered as productive rules by many children by the end of the preschool period. Indeed, there have been two recent reports of a few children acquiring certain common English inflections (such as the plural and possessive morphemes) productively during the latter half of the second year of life and before the onset of syntax (Mervis & Johnson, 1991; Munson & Ingram, 1985). Therefore, even the youngest children in grade 1 interviewed in the present study should be able to interpret the meanings of many regularly inflected words through morphological analysis, provided that they know the meanings of the corresponding root words.

CHILDREN'S KNOWLEDGE OF COMPOUND FORMATION

It also appears that even preschoolers have some, and perhaps considerable, knowledge of the compounding rules of English. Berko (1958) developed three tests using nonsense words to examine children's ability to produce derived words and found that children from 4 to 7 years of age "use almost exclusively a compounding pattern" (p. 168), appropriately stressing the first word in the compound as adults do. For example, when asked what they would call a very tiny wug, none of the children produced a diminutive suffix, but 52% of them used compounds like *baby wug* or *little wug*, correctly stressing the first word (e.g., *baby* or *little*) in them. A majority of adults produced derived words such as *wuglet* or *wugling* for this item. Although in an additional test these children did not generally give etymological explanations for why compounds like *blackboard* were so called, their performance on the tests with nonsense syllable stems suggested that they had some tacit appreciation of how to produce compounds and that they tended to produce compounds on items for which adults produced derived words (cf. Clark & Hecht, 1982). In a Berko-type task assessing the psychological productivity of five derivational rules and one compounding rule (the latter being tested with questions like "What do you call a house for zabes? It's a ———"; for details, see Derwing, 1976), Derwing and Baker (1979, 1986) also found that only one, the noun compound, was productively used by a substantial proportion (47%) of the preschool children tested.

In an important series of studies, Eve Clark and her colleagues have investigated word-formation processes in young children and have studied compounding extensively (e.g., Clark, 1981, 1983a, 1983b; Clark & Berman, 1987; Clark et al., 1985; Clark & Hecht, 1982; Clark et al., 1986). Although these authors analyzed and commented on the occurrence of well-established compounds in preschool children (which are relatively numerous and often take the form of noun + noun compounds), their focus was on the innovative compounds that children as young as 3 and even 2 years of age often coin to fill lexical gaps, that is, to express ideas for which they have no established words in their lexicons (Clark, 1981, 1983a; Clark & Hecht, 1982). Such innovative compounds show an appreciation of the word-formation processes involved in constructing them more clearly than do well-established compounds, which might simply have been learned by rote. Clark and her colleagues found that even 2-year-olds often coin compound words like *car-smoke* (exhaust), *house-smoke* (smoke from a chimney), *fix-man* (car mechanic), and *plant-man* (gardener) in their spontaneous speech (Clark, 1981, 1983a) and that these are almost always produced with the correct primary stress on the first word of the compound (cf. Berko, 1958). In spontaneous speech, noun + noun innovative compounds are especially common, just as they are in the case of well-established compounds. Similarly, these researchers found that, in experimental studies, compounds such as *build-man* (for a man who builds things), *pumpkin-house* (for a house made out of a pumpkin), and *horse-truck* (for a truck with a horse in it) can be elicited from children as young as 3 years of age (Clark et al., 1985; Clark & Hecht, 1982) and that these compounds are almost always produced with the correct primary stress on the first word. As Berko (1958) found with somewhat older children, Clark and Hecht (1982) observed a tendency in some, but not all, of their youngest 3-year-olds to coin compounds (like *build-man, sweep-man, smile-person,* or *hider-man*) in an elicitation task calling for agent nominals, whereas most older children and adults coined derived words (like *builder, sweeper, smiler,* and *hider*). Clark et al. (1985) found that, in an elicitation task, young preschoolers, like adults, coined more compounds when presented with pairs of pictures contrasting exemplars of the same category (e.g., a horse in a truck and a bicycle in a truck) than when presented with pictures of exemplars from unrelated categories (a bicycle in a truck and a man riding a horse). Also, like adults, Clark et al.'s subjects produced more compounds for objects with different intrinsic properties (e.g., a house made of a pumpkin vs. a house made of a tree) than for objects with different accidental properties in momentary juxtaposition (e.g., a chair with spiders on it vs. a chair with books on it).

Although Clark et al. (1985) found that young preschoolers (from the age of 3 years on) could coin such simple noun + noun compounds as *pumpkin-house* and *horse-truck* appropriately, Clark et al. (1986) reported that preschoolers had more difficulty coining complex compounds, specifically, noun compounds with a derived verbal base (e.g., *paper-ripper, ball-kicker,* and *wall-builder*). It was only after 5 years of age that children could produce acceptable complex noun compounds such as these in a majority of cases. Similarly, in a study of Hebrew-speaking children, Clark and Berman (1987) found that it was only after 5 years of age that, in a majority of cases, children could correctly produce correct compounds when the head noun required a change in morphological form. Generally, the fewer the morphological changes required by the head noun, the more likely were the children to produce a well-formed compound. These findings in production are consistent with the principle of simplicity of form: "As children get older and learn more about a language, they should add progressively more complex forms to their repertoires" (Clark & Berman, 1987, p. 559). In other words, morphologically simpler forms should be acquired earlier and morphologically more complex forms later in development.

With respect to the comprehension of compounds, Clark and Berman (1987) found that, from the age of 4 years, children did very well on a task involving interpreting or paraphrasing both simple and complex compounds and that morphological form had little effect, except on the performance of 3-year-olds. Thus, comprehension of compounds in this study was found to be in advance of production. In the study reported in Clark et al. (1985), most preschoolers aged 3 years and older were also able to demonstrate important knowledge about the structure of (endocentric) compounds in a comprehension task. For example, when asked to show the experimenter the *apple-knife*, these children consistently chose a picture of a knife as opposed to a picture of an apple or pictures of other distractors, suggesting that they knew that such compounds (endocentric noun + noun compounds) usually have a head noun in the second, right-most position that picks out the category being denoted. In a related task, these children also indicated that they understood that such compounds also usually have a modifier noun in the first, left position that qualifies or subcategorizes the head noun.

Clark and her colleagues interpret their findings on the development of compounding and on other aspects of word formation as supporting several theoretical principles. These include the general principles of contrast (e.g., a child will coin a novel compound like *car-smoke* to contrast with her names for other instances of a category such as *house-smoke*) and of conventionality (e.g., a child who initially coins an innovative compound such as *fix-man* will eventually give it up in favor of a conventional term such as *mechanic*). They also include the specific principles of semantic transparency (e.g., children will initially prefer a relatively transparent two-word compound like *plant-man* over what, for them, is a less transparent, more semantically opaque form like *gardener*), productivity (e.g., children will initially learn to coin more productive word forms such as noun + noun compounds as opposed to less productive types), regularization (e.g., once the child adopts a device such as adding *-man* to a verb to indicate agency, he or she will apply that device generally, sometimes resulting in overregularization), and simplicity of form (e.g., morphologically simpler forms such as the compound *rip-man* should be produced before more complex forms such as *paper-ripper*).

The results obtained by Clark and her colleagues, as well as those reported in Berko (1958) and Derwing and Baker (1979, 1986), suggest that, although knowledge of compounding increases after the child has gone to school, even relatively young preschool children have considerable knowledge of the rules of compound formation, which they manifest in both production and comprehension, particularly with respect to relatively simple endocentric compounds. Therefore, even the youngest children in grade 1 interviewed in the current study should be able to construct the meanings of at least some literal compounds on the basis of what I have called "morphological problem solving," provided that they know the constituent words in those compounds.

CHILDREN'S KNOWLEDGE OF DERIVATIONAL MORPHOLOGY

Research by developmental psycholinguists suggests that, in general, appreciation of derivational morphology (with the possible exception of conversion or "zero derivation" without the use of any overt morphological marker, as when the noun *walk* is derived from the verb *walk* [Clark, 1982]) begins somewhat later than appreciation of inflectional morphology and compound formation and is associated with a quite gradual development extending throughout the school years (e.g., Berko, 1958; Derwing, 1976; Derwing & Baker, 1979, 1986; Freyd & Baron, 1982; Selby, 1972; Tyler & Nagy, 1989; White et al., 1989; Wysocki & Jenkins, 1987; but see also Bowerman, 1982; Clark & Cohen, 1984; Clark & Hecht, 1982; Gordon, 1989). As noted above, in her pioneering study, Berko (1958) tested preschoolers and first-grade children on their ability to produce a few derived words (e.g., "A dog covered with quirks is a ——— dog"; answer: *quirky*). In general, these children were not able to produce derived words but tended to form compounds (e.g., *quirk dog*) instead. Derwing (1976) and Derwing and Baker (1979, 1986) extended Berko's method to test more derivational rules and a greater age range of subjects. They found that none of the derivational rules that they examined were productively mastered by preschoolers and that each was associated with a developmental trend from lower to higher performance from the early school years to adulthood (see also Selby, 1972). They also found that some derivational affixes (e.g., the agentive *-er*) were associated with better performance at earlier, as well as at later, ages than were others (e.g., the adverbial *-ly*).

Derwing (1976) and Derwing and Baker (1979, 1986) also looked at children's and college students' recognition of derivational morphological relations by asking them, for several word pairs, if they thought that one member of the pair (often a derived form) "came from" the other member of the pair (usually an underived form). Some of the word pairs were phonetically similar but not semantically related (e.g., *bash/bashful*), whereas others shared a semantic relation but little phonetic similarity (e.g., *cat/kitten*). Finally, the members of other word pairs were clearly morphologically related, being similar on both dimensions (e.g., *teach/teacher*). Derwing and Baker's results suggested a strong developmental trend of increasing awareness of morphological relations from elementary school through college. Generally, adults tended to consider both semantic and phonetic similarity as being necessary in their judgments of morphological relatedness, whereas young elementary school children often required only either a high degree of semantic similarity (e.g., *cat/kitten*) or a high degree of phonetic similarity (e.g., *bash/bashful*) to judge one member of a pair of words as "coming from" the other.

Wysocki and Jenkins (1987) studied elementary school children's ability to derive words through morphological generalization. In their investigation, children in grades 4, 6, and 8 were taught infrequent stimulus words (e.g., *sapient, stipulate, melancholic*) and then tested 2 weeks later on the meanings of derivationally related transfer words that they were asked to define (e.g., *sapience, stipulation, melancholia*). Morphological generalization involved generalizing from a root word to a suffixed derivative, from a suffixed derivative to another suffixed derivative, or from a suffixed derivative to a root word. Words were presented in both weak contexts (e.g., "Her *melancholia* lasted for several days") and strong contexts (e.g., "After Jack's puppy died, his *melancholia* was so bad he didn't want to play with his friends"). Two different scoring criteria were used: strict (both part of speech and meaning had to be correct) and lenient (only meaning had to be correct). The extent of morphological generalization was assessed by comparing the subjects' performance on transfer words with their performance on control words for which they had not received prior training. The results indicated far better performance on the transfer words when the lenient scoring criterion was used as many subjects responded by simply providing a definition for the taught stimulus word without adjusting the part of speech. For example, when presented with the transfer word *sapience*, they often responded with the word *wise*, the definition of the stimulus word *sapient*, rather than its appropriate noun form, *wisdom*. When the lenient scoring system was used, Wysocki and Jenkins found that children at all grade levels performed considerably better on transfer words than on control words regardless of whether they were tested in strong or weak contexts. When the strict scoring system was used, these differences were considerably attenuated, but there was still a highly significant word-type effect, with performance on transfer words being superior to performance on control words.

Thus, there was evidence of morphological generalization using either scoring criterion. When the strict scoring system was used in the weak context condition (perhaps the purest and most stringent test of morphological generalization), children from the sixth and the eighth grades showed more evidence of morphological generalization than did children in the fourth grade. Wysocki and Jenkins concluded that morphological generalization with derivational affixes may partially account for the large growth in vocabulary that occurs during the elementary school years.

In another study, Freyd and Baron (1982) examined differences in knowledge of derived words between superior word learners in grade 5 and average word learners in grade 8. Using a vocabulary test, they found that the superiority of the fifth-grade students was greater for derived words (e.g., *tubular, oceanic*) than it was for morphologically simple words (e.g., *benign, bachelor*). In another part of their study, Freyd and Baron also gave these same students a paired associates task that tested their ability to learn the "meanings" of pseudowords; they found that the fifth graders performed better when the word pairs were derivationally related (e.g., *skaf* = steal, *skaffist* = thief) than when they were not but that the average word learners in grade 8 showed no such advantage. The authors concluded that superior word learners are particularly skilled at analyzing derived words into morphological components and that they are especially good at using derivational knowledge to learn new words.

The studies reviewed so far suggest that the acquisition of derivational morphology is quite gradual and occurs relatively late. For example, Freyd and Baron (1982) found that, even as late as grade 8, average students did not make use of derivational relations to aid them in their paired associates task. Wysocki and Jenkins (1987) found that, when their strict scoring criterion was used (which one could argue to be the only criterion that clearly showed knowledge of derivational morphology), evidence of morphological generalization increased from grade 4 to grade 8 but that, even by grade 8, students appeared to have generalized to only 2.4 words (out of a possible 6) on which they were tested. However, other studies (Gordon, 1989; Tyler & Nagy, 1989) have suggested a greater degree of knowledge of derivational morphology among children in the earlier school grades, and still others (e.g., Bowerman, 1982; Clark & Cohen, 1984; Clark & Hecht, 1982) have suggested some appreciation of a few (usually highly productive) derivational affixes in preschoolers. As Tyler and Nagy (1989) have pointed out, certain task demands of the tests devised by Freyd and Baron (1982) and Wysocki and Jenkins (1987), such as the use of unfamiliar and only recently and perhaps superficially learned stems (e.g., *skaff* or *sapient*) and the requirement of producing correct definitions, may have made their tests especially difficult.

Tyler and Nagy (1989) distinguished three aspects of knowledge of derivational morphology: relational, or the ability to see morphological relations between two words (e.g., *celebrate, celebratory*) that share a common base morpheme; syntactic, or the knowledge that derivational suffixes usually mark words for part of speech (e.g., words ending in *-ize* such as *regularize* or *concretize* are usually verbs); and distributional, or the realization that derivational affixes are generally constrained in terms of the stems to which they attach (e.g., *-ness* attaches to adjectives like *quiet* but not to verbs like *play*). They also distinguished between two types of derivational suffixes: neutral and nonneutral (cf. Aronoff, 1976; Chomsky & Halle, 1968; Kiparsky, 1982, 1983; Selkirk, 1982). Neutral suffixes, sometimes called Level 2 suffixes (e.g., *-ness, -er, -ize, -able*), are usually added to independent words (e.g., the *-er* in *teacher* or the *-ness* in *sadness*), whereas nonneutral or Level 1 suffixes (e.g., *-ity, -ion, -ify,* or *-ive*) often attach to bound morphemes (e.g., the *-ion* in *deception* or the *-ify* in *quantify*). Neutral suffixes do not usually cause changes in stress or vowel quality or other phonological changes in the word or stem to which they are added (e.g., *teacher, happiness*), whereas nonneutral suffixes often do (e.g., *profanity, reception*). Usually, although not always, the meaning of a word formed with neutral suffixes is transparently related to the meaning of the stem (e.g., *happiness*), whereas this tends to be somewhat less true for nonneutral suffixes (e.g., *nativity*). Neutral suffixes generally have a wider range of application than do nonneutral suffixes and tend to be associated with fewer idiosyncratic exceptions. Another interesting linguistic phenomenon observed by Gordon (1989), Kiparsky (1982, 1983), Selkirk (1982), and others is that, when both neutral and nonneutral suffixes occur in the same word, the nonneutral suffix is applied before the neutral suffix, as in *repetitiveness* and *quantifier*. Many of these differences might lead one to hypothesize that, in general, and other things being equal, neutral suffixes would be mastered earlier than nonneutral suffixes (cf. Gordon, 1989; Tyler & Nagy, 1989).

Tyler and Nagy (1989) developed tests in which they attempted to reduce extraneous task demands for each of the three kinds of knowledge for derived words with both neutral and nonneutral suffixes. They administered these tests to children in grades 4, 6, and 8 and found evidence of considerable relational knowledge at all grade levels for both types of suffixes. They also found evidence of syntactic knowledge at all grade levels for both types of suffixes, but this type of knowledge more clearly increased with grade level. Similarly, they found evidence of distributional knowledge at all grade levels, and this kind of knowledge also increased with grade level, but only in this instance did the performance of the children differ on words with neutral as opposed to nonneutral suffixes. The sixth-grade children, in particular, made overgeneralization errors when dealing with neutral suffixes but not nonneutral suffixes, which led Tyler and Nagy to hypothesize that children formulate general combinatory rules for neutral suffixes but narrow rules of phonological analogy for nonneutral suffixes (cf. MacWhinney, 1978). The authors also make the point that, in a *comprehension* or *recognition* task (such as is used in the present study), relational knowledge and syntactic knowledge are required but that distributional knowledge is not; the production of novel derivatives does, however, require distributional knowledge. Their study indicates that, even by grade 4, children may have the former kinds of knowledge for at least some words with both neutral and nonneutral derivational affixes.

Gordon (1989) conducted a study that suggests some knowledge of derivational morphology at even earlier ages. He tested 5-, 7-, and 9-year-old children in an auditory lexical decision task involving low-frequency (and therefore presumably unfamiliar) derived words formed with high-frequency stems and either neutral (Level 2) or nonneutral (Level 1) suffixes. He found that the derived words formed with neutral suffixes were associated with higher recognition rates than those formed with nonneutral suffixes at all ages. However, he also found that both types of words were recognized as words at considerably higher rates than would be predicted on the basis of individual frequency, again at all ages.

Finally, some studies have reported knowledge of a few derivational affixes in preschool children 3 years of age and older (Bowerman, 1982; Clark & Cohen, 1984; Clark & Hecht, 1982). Bowerman (1982) presented evidence from a naturalistic study of her two daughters, Christy and Eva, indicating that, during the preschool years, they developed productive knowledge of the reversative morpheme *un-*, which, when prefixed to verbs, conveys the idea of undoing the action denoted by the verb (as in *untie, undress,* and *uncover*). Initially, both children had acquired a number of verbs prefixed with *un-* (e.g., *uncover, unfasten*) but showed no evidence of appreciating their morphological structure. However, starting in their fourth year of life, both girls spontaneously produced unconventional novel coinages such as *unstraighting* (= bending), *unburied* (= disinterred), and *uncapture* (= set free). Like the overregularization of inflections, such unconventional novel coinages suggest that the children had analyzed morphologically at least some previously unanalyzed reversative verbs in their repertoires and had developed a productive rule for this prefix. Bowerman further reported that it took Christy much longer than Eva to limit the application of this prefix to verbs that have a covering, enclosing, or surface-attaching meaning, which is a conventional restriction respected by adult speakers of English. How typical Bowerman's results would be for preschool children generally is currently unknown, but they do indicate that at least some children are capable of analyzing the reversative derivational prefix *un-* during the later preschool years.

Eve Clark and her colleagues (e.g., Clark & Cohen, 1984; Clark & Hecht, 1982) found evidence of knowledge of certain highly productive derivational suffixes (the agentive *-er* and the instrumental *-er*) in greater numbers of children in the later preschool years. For example, Clark and Hecht (1982) tested 3-, 4-, and 5-year-old children on their ability to comprehend and produce agentive and instrumental word forms. In the test of comprehension, the children were posed problems of the kind, "I've got a picture of a person/thing called a burner. What does a burner do?/What is a burner used for? A burner is someone who/something that ———." In the test of production, they might be asked, for example, "I've got a picture here of someone who/something that hides things. What could we call someone who/something that hides things? Someone who/something that hides things is a ———." The verbs chosen for these tests were likely to be in the children's vocabularies, but none of the base + *-er* forms were likely to be in their vocabularies with the relevant agent and instrument meanings. Their results indicated that the majority of children at all ages understood both the agentive *-er* and instrumental *-er*, although they appeared to understand the former somewhat better than the latter. There were clear developmental trends in production, with agents (e.g., *hider, burner*) being coined 55% of the time by the youngest 3-year-olds (mean age 3-4) and 91% of the time by the oldest 5-year-olds (mean age 5-8), and with instruments (e.g., *hider, burner*) being coined 42% of the time by the youngest and 72% of the time by the oldest children in the study.

The impressive ability of these young children to produce (and comprehend) the agentive suffix *-er* and the instrumental suffix *-er* contrasts with the results of Derwing and Baker (1979, 1986; see also Berko, 1958), who found that preschoolers were generally unable to produce either suffix when given Berko's wug tests. Many differences in method might account for these divergent results, including the fact that Clark and Hecht (1982) used stems familiar to the children (e.g., *burn, clean*) whereas Derwing and Baker (1979, 1986) used unfamiliar nonsense stems (cf. Tyler & Nagy, 1989). Also, Clark and Hecht began each block of both production and comprehension questions with "one sample instance where the experimenter provided an appropriate answer" (p. 8), which might have helped guide the children toward correct responses.

In another study, Clark and Cohen (1984) included a shortened version of Clark and Hecht's elicitation task for producing the agentive *-er*. (The authors do not mention whether they gave the children a sample instance with an appropriate answer.) The nursery school children in this investigation did not do as well as the children studied by Clark and Hecht—18% of the responses of the 4-year-olds (mean age 4-1) and 46% of the responses of the 5-year-olds (mean age 5-2) contained the agentive suffix *-er* appended to a stem (p. 616). Still, these and other results presented by Clark and Cohen suggest that a significant number of children do learn the agentive suffix *-er* prior to going to elementary school (i.e., grade 1). Clark and

Cohen also demonstrated that children acquire the agentive *-er* before the less productive and less frequently occurring suffixes *-ist* and *-ian*, which are also used to form agent nouns in English, supporting their contention that children learn the most productive word-formation devices first.

Conclusion

The picture that emerges from the literature on the acquisition of morphological knowledge suggests that children often master many of the basic English inflections in the preschool years (e.g., Berko, 1958; Brown, 1973; Cazden, 1968; Derwing & Baker, 1979; de Villiers & de Villiers, 1973; Kuczaj, 1977; Marcus et al., 1992; Mervis & Johnson, 1991; Munson & Ingram, 1985). Preschoolers also appear to have considerable knowledge of compounding (at least with respect to simple endocentric compounds), which they manifest in both production (e.g., Berko, 1958; Clark, 1981, 1983a; Clark et al., 1985; Clark & Hecht, 1982; Derwing & Baker, 1979) and comprehension (e.g., Clark, 1981; Clark et al., 1985). Therefore, even the youngest children in grade 1 interviewed in the present study might be able to figure out the meanings of certain inflected words and literal compounds through what I have called morphological problem solving. Appreciation of derivational morphology appears, in general, to be a later and quite gradual development (Berko, 1958; Derwing, 1976; Derwing & Baker, 1979, 1986; Freyd & Baron, 1982; Tyler & Nagy, 1989; Wysocki & Jenkins, 1987), with the exception of conversion or "zero derivation," which seems to be an early acquisition (Clark, 1981, 1982). However, children in kindergarten and the early grade school years appear to have some knowledge of derivational affixes (Gordon, 1989), and by grade 4 this can be shown to be considerable (Tyler & Nagy, 1989). Even many preschool children appear to have knowledge of certain highly productive derivational affixes such as the agentive *-er* in *teacher, preacher, walker, runner*, etc. (Clark, 1981; Clark & Cohen, 1984; Clark & Hecht, 1982). Thus, even the youngest children in the present study may be able to figure out the meanings of certain derived words; nonetheless, with development, children should become more and more adept at using knowledge of derivational morphology to figure out word meanings since the evidence indicates that children do gradually but increasingly learn the rules of derivational morphology throughout the school years (e.g., Derwing & Baker, 1979, 1986; Freyd & Baron, 1982; Tyler & Nagy, 1989; Wysocki & Jenkins, 1987).

RESEARCH GOALS, QUESTIONS, AND PREDICTIONS

A basic but important goal of the present study was to provide estimates of recognition vocabulary size for children in the elementary school grades (specifically grades 1, 3, and 5) based on their knowledge of a relatively large sample of main entry words taken from a recent unabridged dictionary, *Webster's Third*. The method used in this study is similar in some respects to that used by Smith (1941) and Templin (1957), who tested schoolchildren on the Seashore-Eckerson Recognition Vocabulary Test (see the discussion in Chap. II). However, in the present study, an attempt has been made to improve on such previous work by using a sample of main entries that is larger than those used in earlier studies, that is taken from a more recent unabridged dictionary, and that is not biased in terms of frequently occurring words or words of different morphological types and by using criteria for knowledge of the words that are relatively objective and neither too stringent nor too lax. The intent was to provide answers to such basic questions as, What are reasonable estimates of vocabulary size in the early and middle grade school years? Are children's recognition vocabularies and the corresponding estimated rates of vocabulary development really as large as some previous studies have suggested?

A second goal was to partition children's main entry recognition vocabulary knowledge into different morphologically defined types of words: into root words, inflected words, derived words, literal compounds, and idioms; and into monomorphemic words, bimorphemic words, multimorphemic words, and idioms. To what extent are children's recognition vocabularies made up of these different types, and how does each type contribute to total known main entry vocabulary in children at different age and grade levels? Are there developmental changes with age and grade in the relative contributions of these different kinds of words to vocabulary knowledge? How do estimated rates of vocabulary development break down in terms of specific estimated rates for the different word types?

The final goal was to make an initial attempt to examine children's expressed knowledge of morphologically complex word types to see whether there is evidence that children use morphological decoding to figure out the meanings of such words. To what degree is there evidence of morphological problem solving at different age and grade levels? Does this evidence suggest that the extent of morphological analysis and composition increases as a function of age and grade? What portions of children's estimated recognition vocabulary knowledge and of the rate of growth of recognition vocabulary might be accounted for by the development of morphological problem-solving ability as opposed to actual word learning? Do the ways in which children express their knowledge of morphologically complex words provide any clues about the processes underlying morphological problem solving at different age levels and for different word types?

In addition to seeking answers to the questions posed above, the study was also intended to allow an examination of the veracity of three basic predictions suggested by the review of previous research presented in this chapter. The first of these concerns the extent to which children's vocabularies at different age and grade levels are made up of the different morphologically complex word types—inflected words, derived words, and literal compounds. Although some derived words have been observed in preschoolers' vocabularies (e.g., Bowerman, 1982; Clark, 1981; Clark & Cohen, 1984), they are apparently considerably less numerous and less frequently used than either inflected words (e.g., Brown, 1973) or endocentric compounds (e.g., Clark, 1981; Clark et al., 1985). And, although some preschoolers appear to have learned a small number of certain highly productive derivational rules (e.g., Clark & Cohen, 1984; Clark & Hecht, 1982), their understanding of derivational morphology has generally been found to lag behind their understanding of inflectional morphology and compounding (e.g., Berko, 1958; Derwing & Baker, 1979). Several investigations have suggested that most of the derivational rules that are eventually learned are acquired only gradually during the school years and beyond (Berko, 1958; Derwing, 1976; Derwing & Baker, 1979, 1986; Freyd & Baron, 1982; Wysocki & Jenkins, 1987), although at least one important recent study has suggested that, by grade 4, children's knowledge of derivational morphology is substantial (Tyler & Nagy, 1989). Thus, we predicted that comprehension of derived words would manifest particular growth in children from grade 1 to grade 5, being generally not well known in grade 1 (at least relative to inflected words and literal compounds) and becoming better known by grade 5.

A second basic prediction pertains to our second system of classification (according to morphemic complexity). Bimorphemic words, including regularly inflected words (e.g., Brown, 1973) and simple two-term compounds (e.g., Clark, 1981; Clark et al., 1985), have been commonly found in the speech of preschool children. Although they are apparently not as common, some bimorphemic derived words with relatively productive affixes have also been observed (e.g., Clark, 1981; Clark & Cohen, 1984; see also Bowerman, 1982). However, multimorphemic words consisting of three or more morphemes are rarely reported in preschool children's speech. Children's language development has often been characterized as increasing in complexity in general and morphological complexity in particular (e.g., Brown, 1973; Clark, 1983b; Slobin, 1973; Wells, 1984), and Clark and her colleagues (e.g., Clark & Berman, 1987; Clark et al., 1986) have found developmental evidence consistent with the principle of simplicity of form (i.e., as children get older and learn more about a language, they go beyond morphologically simple forms and increasingly add morphologically more complex forms to their lexical knowledge). Thus, we predicted that multimorphemic words would manifest particular growth between grade 1 and grade 5, being not well understood in grade 1 and becoming better understood by grade 5.

The third basic prediction pertains to the extent to which evidence of morphological problem solving would be found with respect to known morphologically complex words. Some studies have suggested that, even prior to the beginning of formal education, young children should have the requisite knowledge to enable them to figure out the meanings of some inflected words (e.g., Berko, 1958; Brown, 1973; Marcus et al., 1992), some compound words (e.g., Clark et al., 1985; Derwing & Baker, 1979), and even some derived words (e.g., Bowerman, 1982; Clark & Hecht, 1982). Other studies, however, indicate that skill at morphological analysis increases gradually throughout the elementary school years (e.g., Derwing, 1976; Derwing & Baker, 1979, 1986; Tyler & Nagy, 1989; White et al., 1989; Wysocki & Jenkins, 1987; see also Freyd & Baron, 1982). Thus, we predicted that we would find evidence of some morphological problem solving in children at each grade level tested but that the extent of morphological problem solving would increase with age and grade. If this prediction is confirmed, it may account in part for the dramatic growth in vocabulary knowledge that has been reported to occur during the elementary school years.

IV. CONSTRUCTING A BASIS
FOR ESTIMATING VOCABULARY KNOWLEDGE

To prepare for the study of vocabulary development in children, a set of words from *Webster's Third New International Dictionary of the English Language* was sampled, classified into morphological categories, and analyzed in several ways. The details of this work are presented in this chapter as well as the manner in which we composed the multiple-choice questions that were used as one component of our test of children's vocabulary knowledge.

THE SAMPLE OF WORDS

Preliminary Work

To begin, we selected every seventh boldfaced main entry (flush to the left-hand margin) from every second page in the 1981 edition of *Webster's Third*, including the addenda section (pp. 55a–102a), which contains words that have entered the language since the main dictionary (pp. 1–2,662) was first compiled in 1961.[8] This resulted in a master list of 1,355 main entries (1,331 from the main dictionary and 24 from the addenda section). We then divided this master list into three separate samples of 452, 452, and 451 entries by including the 1st, 4th, 7th, . . . , 1,354th entries in Sample 1, the 2d, 5th, 8th, . . . , 1,355th entries in Sample 2, and the 3d, 6th, 9th, . . . , 1,353d entries in Sample 3. Subsequent elimination of all nonwords (abbreviations, prefixes, suffixes, and combining forms) left 434, 433, and 440 main entry words, respectively, in the three samples. These procedures follow Seashore and Eckerson's (1940) methods, but with two important improvements. First, in selecting the seventh boldfaced entry on every second page, sets of homographs (e.g., ^1flop, ^2flop, ^3flop) were counted as one main entry only. As described in Chapter II, Seashore and Eckerson

[8] See also n. 1 above.

counted each homograph as a separate main entry, which may have biased their sample to include a disproportionate number of common words (Lorge & Chall, 1963). (We also developed tests, presented below, to determine whether our list was biased in favor of commonly occurring words.) Second, dividing our master list into three samples resulted in larger samples (433–440 words) than those obtained by Seashore and Eckerson (329–331 words), who divided their master list into four. The use of somewhat larger samples of words permits a reasonable degree of confidence in our estimates (see, e.g., Barnett, 1974; Conway, 1967).

The first of the three samples, containing 434 main entry words, was used in the present study. These words were ranked according to their relative difficulty by 10 adult judges. Pilot testing of 20 children was then conducted on the words ordered in terms of increasing difficulty according to the average adult rankings to determine a final ordering of the words from simplest to most difficult.

Additional preliminary work involved the estimation of the number of main entries in the dictionary and, more important for this study, of the number of *different main entry words* (i.e., the number of main entries excluding homographs and nonwords such as abbreviations, prefixes, suffixes, and combining forms). We estimated the number of main entries by systematically sampling (which can be shown to be unbiased; cf. Barnett, 1974) every twentieth page in the dictionary starting with the first full page (p. 2), counting the number of main entries on each of these pages, computing the average number of main entries per page (108.51), and multiplying this average by the total number of full pages (2,709) in the dictionary. *Webster's Third* actually contains 2,710 pages, but the first and last pages of the main body and of the addenda section are closer to three full pages rather than four; because we deliberately avoided these beginning and end pages in our sampling, we used the figure of 2,709 full pages in deriving our estimates. This resulted in an estimate of 293,954 main entries, which is reasonably consistent with Merriam-Webster's advertisement for *Webster's Third* stating that it contains over 460,000 entries, of which 65%, or over 299,000, are main entries (Miller, 1986b).

To estimate the number of different main entry words, we counted all the main entries that were different words (excluding homographs, abbreviations, suffixes, prefixes, and combining forms) on every twentieth page, computed their average number per page (95.46), and multiplied this average by the total number of full pages in the dictionary. This resulted in an estimate of 258,601 different main entry words, a value that falls between two other estimates of the number of different main entry words in *Webster's Third*. One of these estimates can be obtained by subtracting our estimate of the number of main entries that are homographs, abbreviations, prefixes, suffixes, and combining forms (35,353) from 299,000 (the approximate number of main entries advertised by Merriam-Webster), which yields an estimate of 263,647 different main entry words. The second can be attained by adding Dupuy's (1974) estimate of 240,000 different main entry words in the 1961 edition of *Webster's Third* to the roughly 5,000 additional different main entry words contained in the addenda section (which was added to the 1961 ed. to form the 1981 ed.), yielding an estimate of about 245,000. These values indicate that our estimate of 258,601 is of the right order of magnitude; because it was calculated in most detail, and also because it falls between the others, that estimate is used in this research.

Morphological Classifications of the Sample Words

We classified the 434 words in the sample into morphological types— root words (R), inflected words (IW), derived words (D), literal compounds (C), and idioms (I). As noted in Chapter II, we also decided to categorize the words according to morphemic complexity into monomorphemic words, bimorphemic words, multimorphemic words, and idioms. Given the way in which we classified the words into morphological types, both literal compounds and derived words could be either bimorphemic (consisting of two morphemes) or multimorphemic (consisting of three or more morphemes). To generate a complete morphological classification of the words, and to allow for analyses in terms of morphemic complexity, all literal compounds and all derived words were classified according to both type and subtype. For example, *milk cow* was coded as C (a literal compound made of two root words), *block and tackle* as CC (a literal compound made of three root words), *malarial fever* as C_D (a literal compound made of one root word and one derived word with a derivational affix), *talkativeness* as DD (a derived word with two derivational affixes), etc. Thus, our final classification of the words revealed not only the type of word but also, for the morphologically complex words, the number and types of constituent morphemes. (A complete explanation of our morphological classifications is given in the Appendix.)

To obtain a measure of the reliability of the classifications, a graduate student with some background in linguistics was trained on the coding scheme and then independently classified the words from the sample according to type and subtype. For the full set of 434 words, there was 94% agreement with respect to the five major categories and 91% agreement when both type and subtype were considered. For the first 196 words on which children were actually tested (see below), the corresponding levels of agreement were 96% and 95%, respectively. With respect to the literal compound/idiom distinction discussed in Chapter II, the level of agreement was 90% for the entire list and 91% for the first 196 words. All cases of disagreements were resolved through further reflection, study, and discussion. The Appendix lists the 196 words on which children were tested in this study, ordered from simplest to most difficult, along with the morphological classification for each word.

The number and percentage of each of the five morphologically defined word types in the sample are shown in Table 1. Interestingly, according to our classifications, derived words were the most common type, accounting for 32.26% of all main entries; root words were next most common (28.57%), followed by idioms (18.89%), literal compounds (15.67%), and, finally, inflected words (4.61%).

The distribution of main entry words when classified according to the number of morphemes in them (i.e., according to morphemic complexity) is shown in Table 2. Bimorphemic words constituted 37.1% and multimorphemic words 15.44% of the total sample. The percentage for monomorphemic words is the same as for root words shown in Table 1, and the percentage of idioms, of course, remains unchanged.

Tables 1 and 2 indicate clearly that the main entries in *Webster's Third* are not all root or linguistically "basic" words and that, in this sample at least, over half (52.54%) are morphologically complex words whose meanings might be determined through knowledge of their component morphemes.

Comparison with the Morphological Classifications of English Vocabulary by Others

It may seem surprising that root words were not found to be the most frequent type of main entry in the sample and that they accounted for fewer than one-third of all the words in it. Nonetheless, classifications of other samples of words taken from *Webster's Third* made by me and my students (see, e.g., below) and by other researchers (e.g., Dupuy, 1974; Goulden et al., 1990) are consistent with the present analyses. Previous researchers have not categorized such samples according to morphemic complexity; however, they have used classification schemes that are somewhat similar to the fivefold classification scheme (see Table 1) used here. Both Dupuy and Goulden et al. found, as we did, that derived words are more common in *Webster's Third* than morphologically basic or root words, and Goulden et al. note that this is consistent with other analyses of English vocabulary such as those presented by Nagy and Anderson (1984) and Seashore and Eckerson (1940).

If one adjusts for differences between our classification scheme and those used by Dupuy (1974) and by Goulden et al. (1990), the overall distributions of morphologically defined word types obtained in their studies and in this one correspond to one another reasonably well. A comparison of our data with that reported by Goulden et al. is of particular interest because these investigators presented a detailed analysis of main entries from essen-

TABLE 1

The Number and Percentage of Morphologically
Defined Word Types in the Sample of 434 Main Entries

Word Type	Number	Percentage
Root words	124	28.57
Inflected words	20	4.61
Derived words	140	32.26
Literal compounds	68	15.67
Idioms	82	18.89
Total	434	100.00

TABLE 2

The Number and Percentage of Each Type of Word
Classified According to Morphemic Complexity
in the Sample of 434 Main Entries

Word Type	Number	Percentage
Monomorphemic words	124	28.57
Bimorphemic words	161	37.10
Multimorphemic words	67	15.44
Idioms	82	18.89
Total	434	100.00

tially the same dictionary as was used in the present research. Goulden et al. chose *Webster's Third* for the same reason we did—because it is the largest nonhistorical dictionary of present-day English. They analyzed samples of words drawn from the 1961 edition as well as from a recent addition to it, comparable to our inclusion of the addenda section in the 1981 edition, and classified words as either base words (a classification similar to our root words), derived words, proper words, compound words, and "others."[9]

On the basis of analyses of three large samples of words from the 1961 edition of *Webster's Third*, Goulden et al. (1990, table 1, p. 347) report that 23.9% were base words, 28.1% derived words, 8.5% proper words (words indicated as usually, often, or sometimes capitalized), 29.6% compound words, and 9.9% "others" (including symbols, prefixes and suffixes, letters, abbreviations, alternative spellings, archaic words, and dialect words). In

[9] The recent addition to the 1961 ed. of *Webster's Third* analyzed by Goulden et al. was a separate list of words published by Merriam-Webster (1983) that includes the new words in the addenda section of the 1981 ed. of *Webster's Third* as well as some others. For details, see Merriam-Webster (1983) and Goulden et al. (1990).

the present analysis, the set of what Goulden et al. called "proper words" was classified in terms of the morphological categories described above. Thus, in this study, *Rembrantish* was classified as a derived word, *northwest coast indian* as a literal compound, *doubting Thomas* as an idiom, and so on. With respect to the category that they called "others," we had excluded some such main entries (prefixes, suffixes, and abbreviations) on the grounds that they are not words and had categorized the remaining ones according to the scheme presented above. It should also be noted that we distinguished literal compounds from idioms, whereas Goulden et al. did not.

If one excludes from their analyses words classified as "proper words" and as "others," one finds that the proportions of the remaining words that Goulden et al. sampled from the 1961 edition of *Webster's Third* that were classified as base, derived, and compound words are 28.98% (492/1,698), 34.39% (584/1,698), and 36.63% (622/1,698), respectively. If the words from the sample from the recent addition to the 1961 edition are included, the corresponding proportions are 29.40% (521/1,772), 33.80% (599/1,772), and 36.79% (652/1,772), respectively (see Goulden et al., 1990, tables 1, 5). If one combines literal and idiomatic compounds under the single heading "compounds" as Goulden et al. did, the comparable percentages for this study are 28.57%, 32.26%, and 34.56%, respectively (see Table 1 above). If one treats inflected words as derived words (Goulden et al. state that they treated irregularly inflected words as derived words), the comparable percentages are 28.57%, 36.87%, and 34.56%, respectively. Thus, these comparisons reveal considerable consistency across the two studies.

It should be acknowledged that, beyond the fact that Goulden et al. did not distinguish between literal compounds and idioms as we did, their criteria for derived and compound words were also slightly different from ours. However, except for the fact that they treated "proper words" and "others" separately, their criteria for base words and ours for root words are very similar, which allows a relatively straightforward comparison of the proportion of main entries accounted for by morphologically simple words in the two studies. As indicated above, excluding "proper words" and "others," 28.98% of their samples from the 1961 edition of *Webster's Third*, and 29.40% when words from the recent addition to it were included, were classified as base words. These values are very close to the 28.57% of the present sample that we classified as root words. Thus, when one adjusts Goulden et al.'s analysis to allow more direct comparison with ours, both sets of data suggest that approximately 29% of the different main entry words in *Webster's Third* are morphologically basic or root words and that approximately 71% are not.

It is also of interest to compare the distribution of words according to morphological types obtained in the current research with that presented by Nagy and Anderson (1984), who analyzed in detail the types of words found in a random sample of 7,260 words taken from the 86,741 words contained in Carroll, Davies, and Richman's *Word Frequency Book* (1971). Of these, Nagy and Anderson classified 3,015 into categories (shown in the top two panels of their table 4, p. 313) that were judged to be included in most definitions of *word* or to be likely to have their own separate entries in most dictionaries. Eliminating the 12 abbreviations from this set as we did (on the grounds that abbreviations are not words) leaves 3,003 words. Of these, 846 (28.17%) were classified as morphologically basic, 955 (31.80%) as words with derivational suffixes or prefixes, 1,038 (34.57%) as compounds and contractions, and 60 (2.00%) as inflected words (irregular inflections, irregular comparatives and superlatives, semantically irregular plurals, and "scientific plurals"). The corresponding percentages in the present analysis of the sample from the 1981 edition of *Webster's Third* were 28.57% for root words, 32.26% for derived words, 34.56% for literal and idiomatic compounds,[10] and 4.61% for inflected words. It is evident that the corresponding percentages from the two studies are in very close agreement except that the percentage of inflected words in the sample of main entries from *Webster's Third* is somewhat higher. Nagy and Anderson (1984) quite logically assumed that only irregularly inflected words would occur as separate entries in a dictionary; however, although regularly inflected words are usually included as subentries in *Webster's Third,* on some occasions they are included as main entries (e.g., *reports, changed, sourer, baits*). This may in part account for the slight discrepancy between the two studies. Otherwise, given that different kinds of books were used as sources, the studies are in surprisingly close agreement.

Nagy and Anderson (1984) also used their findings to estimate—in terms of different word types—the composition of the total vocabulary of printed school English (for grades 3–9) from which the *Word Frequency Book,* and hence their sample, was drawn. They argued plausibly (in a note on pp. 329–330) that, to do so, it is necessary to assign to each word a weight that is an inverse function of its frequency since frequent words were more likely to be included in the *Word Frequency Book* than infrequent words. When they computed these estimates (shown in their table 4), they found that, of the 232,283 words (excluding abbreviations) from the total population of over 600,000, 45,453 (19.57%) were estimated to be morphologically basic, 70,888 (30.52%) to be words with derivational suffixes or prefixes, 105,044 (45.22%) to be compounds and contractions, and 1,822 (0.78%) to be inflected words likely to have their own separate entries in most dictionar-

---

[10] Nagy and Anderson did not distinguish literal compounds from idioms as we did, although they dealt with this distinction in their own way when, later in their paper, they classified words in terms of semantic transparency.

ies. These estimated percentages are not as consistent with the correspond-ing percentages from the present sample (28.57% for root words, 32.26% for derived words, 34.56% for literal and idiomatic compounds, and 4.61% for inflected words) as were their sample percentages discussed previously, although the percentages for derived words are quite close again. If Nagy and Anderson's estimates of the proportions of different word types in printed school English are approximately correct, one important possible reason for the greater proportion of compounds and the corresponding lower proportion of root words in their study might be that many semanti-cally transparent compound words that are coined for particular purposes or contexts in specific materials in printed school English are not likely to be found in any dictionary, even one as large as *Webster's Third*. For example, the compound words *essayist-poet, European-owned,* and *everlengthening* that occurred in their sample are not listed in *Webster's* (see Nagy & Anderson, 1984, p. 318).

Some degree of disagreement between the proportions of main entries accounted for by different word types in the sample used in this study and the comparable estimated proportions for printed school English should not be surprising given that the populations of words from which the sam-ples are drawn differ. Nevertheless, the analyses presented in this *Mono-graph* are consistent with those presented in Goulden et al. (1990) and Nagy and Anderson (1984) in suggesting that both derived and compound words (including literal compounds and idioms) are more frequent than root words, whether the vocabulary of English is operationally defined as main entries in *Webster's Third,* as words found in Carroll et al.'s *Word Frequency Book* (1971), or as words occurring in printed school English. And the exis-tence of large numbers of derived words and transparent compounds in each of these sources confirms the possibly important role (suggested by Nagy & Anderson, 1984) that knowledge of morphology and of word-formation processes plays in children's comprehension of English vocab-ulary.

While comparisons with the work of others are of interest, a more direct way of establishing that the distribution of the main entries in the sample used in this research in terms of our morphological classifications is consistent with what obtains in general for the main entry words in *Webster's Third* is to compare this distribution with that of another large sample of words taken from the same dictionary and classified according to the same criteria. If the two distributions prove to be similar, this would support the contention that the present sample is not biased in terms of our morphologi-cal classifications and is reasonably representative of the different main entry words in *Webster's Third*. Such a comparison is described below, follow-ing the presentation of some other tests for sample bias.

Tests for Sample Bias

Tests for Sample Bias with Respect to Word Frequency

As noted previously, Lorge and Chall (1963) reported that the list used by Seashore and Eckerson (1940) was biased in favor of frequently occurring or common words. Lorge and Chall reasoned that, if a sample of words were unbiased, the percentage of words in the sample that would be in Thorndike and Lorge's (1944) list of the most frequently occurring words in the language should be approximated by the ratio of the words in Thorndike and Lorge divided by the total number of words in the dictionary. Applying this logic to our sample (drawn from an estimated 258,601 main entries), one would expect that approximately 30,000/258,601 or 11.6% of the 434 words in the sample or about 50.3 words would be listed among the 30,000 words in Thorndike and Lorge and that about 383.7 words would not. An empirical count showed these two values to be in fact 53 (12.2%) and 381 words, respectively; a test of the difference between expected and observed frequencies proved not to be significant, $\chi^2(1, N = 434) = .16$, N.S. Similar tests for the first 20,000 most frequently occurring words in Thorndike and Lorge and for the 14,571 words most frequently occurring in children's speech and writing listed by Rinsland (1945) also yielded nonsignificant results, $\chi^2(1, N = 434) = 1.82$, N.S., and $\chi^2(1, N = 434) = .27$, N.S., respectively. A more detailed test comparing observed and expected frequencies for the first 10,000, the next 10,000, and the least frequent 10,000 words in Thorndike and Lorge and the remaining 228,601 words also showed that these differences were not significant, $\chi^2(3, N = 434) = 3.11$, N.S.

In performing these tests, we noticed that some words listed in Thorndike and Lorge (usually proper nouns) as well as in Rinsland (usually inflected words) were not included as main entries in *Webster's Third*. To take this into account, we reconducted all the tests outlined above with reduced expected values; furthermore, we performed similar revised Lorge and Chall tests using two more recent frequency books. In no instance was the difference between expected and observed frequencies significant. For interested readers, details of these tests of sample bias are given below:

We selected 24 pages at random from Thorndike and Lorge (1944)—20 from the pages for the first 20,000 words and four from the denser pages for the next 10,000 words. The 3,046 words on these pages were then looked up in *Webster's Third,* where we found that 91.2% were listed as main entries and that 8.8% were not. Thus, of the 30,000 words in Thorndike and Lorge, we estimated that 91.2% (27,360) were actually in *Webster's Third* as main entries. Using this estimate, one would therefore expect that, if the sample were unbiased, about 45.92 (27,360/258,601 = 10.6%) of the 434 words in it would be listed in Thorndike and Lorge and that about 388.08 would not. Of our sample words, 53 were listed in Thorndike and Lorge, and 381 were not, differences that proved not to be significant, $\chi^2(1, N = 434)$ = 1.22, N.S. All other revised tests involving Thorndike and Lorge, comparable to those described above but with reduced expected values, yielded nonsignificant results.

We then selected 60 pages at random from Rinsland (1945). This gave us 1,429 words, each of which we looked up in *Webster's Third*, where we found that 76.9% were listed as main entries and that 23.1% were not. Thus, of the 14,571 words in Rinsland, we estimated that 76.9% (about 11,205) are actually in *Webster's Third* as main entries. Using this estimate, one would therefore expect that, if the sample were unbiased, about 18.8 (11,205/258,601 = 4.33%) of the 434 words in it would be listed in Rinsland and that about 415.2 would not. Counts showed these numbers to be 22 and 412, respectively, and the differences proved not to be significant, $\chi^2(1, N = 434) = .56$, N.S.

The two more recent frequency books to which we applied the revised Lorge and Chall tests were Kucera and Francis (1967) and Carroll et al. (1971). It was especially important to use the revised tests with these books since each of them includes in their frequency lists both inflected words and proper names, which are not commonly listed as main entries in *Webster's Third*. For Kucera and Francis (1967), we selected 30 pages at random and looked up each of the 2,842 words contained therein in *Webster's Third* to see whether they were listed as main entries there, finding that 1,489 (52.39%) were and that 1,353 were not. Thus, of the 50,406 words listed in Kucera and Francis, we estimated that 52.39% (26,408) are main entries in *Webster's Third*. Using this estimate, one would therefore expect that, if the sample were unbiased, about 44.32 (26,408/258,601 = 10.21%) of the 434 words in it would be listed in Kucera and Francis and that about 389.68 would not. In fact, 47 were found listed in Kucera and Francis, and 387 were not, differences that are not significant, $\chi^2(1, N = 434) = .18$, N.S.

For Carroll et al. (1971), we selected 20 pages at random and looked up each of the 3,072 words contained therein in *Webster's Third*, where 1,229 (40.01%) were main entries and 1,843 were not. Thus, of the 86,741 words listed in Carroll et al., we estimated that 40.01% (34,705) are main entries in *Webster's Third*. Using this estimate, one would therefore expect that, if the sample were unbiased, about 58.24 (34,705/258,601 = 13.42%) of the 434 words in it would be in Carroll et al. and that about 375.76 would not. In fact, 60 were found in Carroll et al., and 374 were not, differences that are not significant, $\chi^2(1, N = 434) = .061$, N.S.

Thus, with respect to the commonness of the words in the sample, none of the tests outlined above indicate that our sample was significantly biased.

Tests for Sample Bias with Respect to the Morphological Classifications

We also wanted to develop tests to see whether the distributions of our sample words according to morphological type and morphemic complexity might be biased. Toward this end, we created another sample of words based on sampling procedures shown by statisticians (e.g., Barnett, 1974) to be unbiased, classified the words in it according to morphological type and morphemic complexity, and compared the resulting distributions with the distributions shown in Tables 1 and 2 above.

Two sampling methods known to be unbiased are *random sampling,* in which elements are chosen at random from the entire population, and *systematic sampling,* in which every nth element from the population is sampled (Barnett, 1974). It would not be practical to use either of these methods alone when sampling from over a quarter of a million words. However, a combination of the two is more practical, and, because each method by itself is unbiased, the resulting sample should be unbiased as well. Thus, our approach to creating an unbiased sample was first to sample *at random* a set of 52 pages from the dictionary and then to sample *systematically* every tenth word on each of these randomly chosen pages. This process resulted in a sample of 435 main entries, which we classified according to morphological type. A second judge trained in our classification methods categorized these words, and there was 96% agreement with respect to the five major morphological word types and 95% agreement in terms of both type and subtype. Instances of disagreements were resolved through further reflection, study, and discussion.

The resultant classifications of this random-systematic sample of 435 words showed it to contain 114 root words, 20 inflected words, 120 derived words, 90 literal compounds, and 91 idioms; as shown in Table 1, our sample contained, respectively, 124, 20, 140, 68, and 82 of each of these word types. Although the distributions are not identical, the rank orders of the frequencies for the five word types are the same, and the two distributions are not significantly different from one another, $\chi^2(4, N = 869) = 5.14$, N.S.

With respect to morphemic complexity, the random-systematic sample contained 114 monomorphemic words, 168 bimorphemic words, 62 multimorphemic words, and 91 idioms; as shown in Table 2, our sample contained 124, 161, 67, and 82 of these types of words, respectively. The rank orders of the frequencies are the same in both cases, and the two distributions are not significantly different from one another, $\chi^2(3, N = 869) =$

1.10, N.S. Consequently, we can conclude that the distribution of words in our sample was not biased in terms of morphological type or morphemic complexity.

Further Tests for Sample Bias with Respect to Word Frequency

The creation of this list of 435 words based on random and systematic sampling procedures allowed for a type of test of bias for frequency or commonness of words in the test sample that differs from those described above. Each of the 435 words in this sample was looked up in Thorndike and Lorge (1944), in Rinsland (1945), in Kucera and Francis (1967), and in Carroll et al. (1971). A series of χ^2 tests was performed comparing the number of frequently occurring words in our test sample against the number in the random-systematic sample, and none of the differences were found to be significant. For interested readers, details are given below:

> Of the random-systematic sample words, 42 were found among the 30,000 words listed in Thorndike and Lorge (1944), and 393 were not. In our test sample, the corresponding numbers were 53 and 381, respectively, differences that were not found to be significant, $\chi^2(1, N = 869) = 1.46$, N.S. Similarly, 24 of the words in the random-systematic sample were found in Rinsland, and 411 were not. In our test sample, the corresponding numbers were 22 and 412, respectively, again differences that were not significant, $\chi^2(1, N = 869) = .08$, N.S. Of the words in the random-systematic sample, 47 were found in Kucera and Francis (1967), and 388 were not. In our test sample, the corresponding numbers were 47 and 387, differences that were not significant, $\chi^2(1, N = 869) = .0001$, N.S. Likewise, 55 words from the random-systematic list were found in Carroll et al. (1971), and 380 were not. In our test sample, the corresponding numbers were 60 and 374, differences that were not significant, $\chi^2(1, N = 869) = .27$, N.S. When we examined only the more frequent words in Carroll et al.—those with a frequency (F value) greater than 1—we found that 48 of the random-systematic sample words were in this set and that 387 were not. In our test sample, the corresponding numbers were 46 and 388, respectively, differences that were not significant, $\chi^2(1, N = 869) = .042$, N.S.

Thus, none of the tests that we developed indicated evidence of bias with respect to frequency, morphological type, or morphemic complexity of the words included in our sample. These results also suggest that Lorge and Chall (1963) were correct in emphasizing that counting homographs as different main entries was the likely source of bias in the sample of words studied by Seashore and Eckerson (1940).

DEVELOPING MULTIPLE-CHOICE QUESTIONS

Of the 434 words in the test sample, there were only 157 that pilot testing showed children to know or that adult judges thought 10-year-olds would have a chance of knowing. Multiple-choice questions, with one correct answer and three incorrect alternatives each, were developed for these words for use in instances when the child could not express knowledge of their meanings in definition or sentence tests. (An additional 39 words were used in testing fifth-grade children, but, since we judged it extremely unlikely that these would be known by even our oldest subjects, only definition and sentence questions were asked about them.)

In constructing the multiple-choice questions, we followed a set of nine guidelines:

1. All alternatives should be expressed simply and clearly.

2. There should be only one correct answer; the remaining alternatives should be clearly incorrect in view of all possible meanings for the word.

3. Although clearly incorrect, the wrong alternatives (distractors) should be plausible. They should be of the same part of speech as the right answer and of roughly the same length and complexity. In general, avoid irrelevant clues to the correct choice and avoid farfetched alternatives. For example, for the word *elastic*, the correct choice might be "a rubber band" and the incorrect ones "a long string," "a round ball," and "a narrow river," each alternative a noun phrase of similar construction. For *flop*, the correct choice might be "to drop in a heavy way" and the incorrect ones "to walk in a slow way," "to jump in a quick way," and "to mix in a gentle way"; here, each alternative is a verb phrase of similar construction.

4. The correct choice should be a simple paraphrase, or in some cases a synonym, of the most common meaning. (The most common meaning was selected by two judges independently from the meanings listed in *Webster's Third*. In cases of disagreement, the author made the final decision.)

5. Choices should be phrased in words that occur more frequently than the test word. Frequency of occurrence norms should be consulted for this purpose—Rinsland (1945) first, then Thorndike and Lorge (1944), then Kucera and Francis (1967).

6. Never use a test word, or a component morpheme of the test word, in the alternatives.

7. Do not use "none of the above," "all of the above," or "some of the above" as choices.

8. The correct alternative for inflected words, derived words, and literal compounds should capture the entire meaning of the word. In constructing the distractors as well as the right answer for such words,

each component part of the word should therefore be varied. For example, for the word *sourer,* both the meaning of *sour* and the meaning of the comparative inflection *-er* should be varied systematically. Thus, the correct choice for *sourer* might be "that something tastes more like a lemon than something else does," with the words "tastes . . . like a lemon" capturing the meaning of *sour* and the words "more . . . than" capturing the meaning of *-er.* Distractors should systematically manipulate these meanings so that incorrect choices might be "that something tastes less like a lemon than something else does," "that something tastes more like salt than something else does," and "that something tastes less like salt than something else does." For words with three or more morphemes, follow the same procedure of systematically varying the meaning of each of the components. For example, for the word *quarrelsomeness,* each of the three component morphemes—*quarrel, -some,* and *-ness*—should be varied systematically. Here, the correct alternative might be "the quality of being inclined to argue," with the word "argue" capturing the meaning of *quarrel,* the words "being inclined to" capturing the meaning of *-some,* and the words "the quality of" capturing the meaning of *-ness.* Since in this example there are three different meanings to vary, the result will be 2^3 or eight alternatives, one correct and the others wrong. Hence, incorrect alternatives initially generated for *quarrelsomeness* might be "the quality of being inclined to quit," "the quality of not wanting to quit," "the quality of not wanting to argue," "the reason for being inclined to argue," "the reason for being inclined to quit," "the reason for not wanting to argue," and "the reason for not wanting to quit." For use in the test, choose three of the distractors at random from the entire set.

9. The final set of four choices should be randomly assigned to the first, second, third, and fourth position, with the restriction that the correct answer never occurs in the same position for more than two consecutive test words.

V. A STUDY OF VOCABULARY DEVELOPMENT IN ELEMENTARY SCHOOL CHILDREN

Using the sample of words and the multiple-choice questions described in Chapter IV, we conducted a study of children's vocabulary knowledge in view of our research goals and questions presented earlier. The details of how the study was conducted and some of its findings are reported in this chapter.

METHOD

Subjects

A total of 96 children from two elementary schools participated in this study. Specifically, there were 32 children in each of grades 1, 3, and 5; within each grade, there were equal numbers of boys and girls who, in turn, were equally divided according to upper or lower socioeconomic status (SES). The children were predominantly Caucasian, and all were in the regular English program. After the study had been approved by the Office of Human Research at the University of Waterloo, the Waterloo County Board of Education, and the participating schools, consent from parents was obtained by sending them a letter describing the study, a consent form, and a questionnaire. Only children whose parents returned a signed consent form and who themselves agreed to participate were interviewed. Also, in order to be included in the study children had to have English as their first language, have no speech impediments or language disabilities (as reported by their parents and teachers), and be between 6 and 7 years of age in grade 1, 8 and 9 years of age in grade 3, and 10 and 11 years of age in grade 5 at the time they began participating in the study. The average age was 6 years, 7 months, and 28 days for the first-grade children, 8 years, 8 months, and 10 days for the third-grade children, and 10 years, 8 months, and 15 days for the fifth-grade children. To determine SES level, Blishen and McRoberts's (1976) revised socioeconomic index was used in conjunction with questionnaire information on parents' occupations provided by the parents prior to the beginning of the study. Each child's SES rating was based on the scale value for the parent whose occupation yielded the highest score; scores of 50 or over were classified as reflecting upper socioeconomic status (USES) and those below 50 as lower socioeconomic status (LSES) (see Blishen & McRoberts, 1976). Across all three grade levels, the average SES rating was 62.88 for the USES group and 35.81 for the LSES group. In grades 1, 3, and 5, the means were 62.33, 61.07, and 65.23, respectively, for the USES groups and 34.69, 37.81, and 34.92, respectively, for the LSES groups.

Procedure

Interviews with the children took place during the academic year (between January and June) in a relatively quiet, unused room in their school, one equipped with a table or desk and two chairs. All were recorded using either Bell and Howell or Sony cassette tape recorders. The interviewer, a paid full-time research assistant who as an undergraduate was an honors psychology major and who had previous experience interviewing children, referred to a written list of 196 words (see the Appendix) and to a booklet containing multiple-choice questions for the first 157 words on the list. Each child was tested individually. Questions were asked by the interviewer and responses given by the children orally. Although the interviewer referred to the list of words and to the booklet containing multiple-choice questions, the children did not see the words or questions in print.

The nature of the study was explained to the children at the outset, and they were told that their performance would remain confidential and would in no way affect their school grades. They were also told that the words would get harder as the interview proceeded and not to feel badly if they did not know a word; they were encouraged not to guess. They were then given a practice session with simple words until they understood the task clearly. At this point, they were tested on the words on the list, moving from simplest to most difficult, with definition, sentence, and multiple-choice questions.

For each word, a child was asked, "What does the word ——— mean?" After he or she responded, the interviewer would often pose a second definitional question, such as, "Can you tell me anything more about what the word ——— means?" if it was felt that this might clarify the child's comprehension of the word's meaning. Further optional general probe questions were sometimes also used, but care was taken not to ask leading questions or to provide hints. The procedure for a given word was terminated if the child expressed sufficient knowledge of the word during the definitional phase to be given credit for knowing it (the criteria used to determine this are described in the "Coding" section below). If not, the sentence phase of the test was initiated, and the child was asked, "Can you use the word ——— in a sentence to show me you know what it means?" After the children had attempted a sentence, the interviewer had the option of following up with a general probe to clarify what they meant by asking a question such as, "What does the word ——— mean in that sentence?" The procedure was terminated if the children expressed adequate knowledge of the word during this phase. If they did not, they were given the opportunity to try the multiple-choice test, which the interviewer explained in detail and then administered, asking the children to choose the alternative that they thought was the most correct. Each alternative was introduced by "The word ——— means. . . ." A child could answer "yes," "no," or "maybe" to each of the four statements. If he or she answered "yes" or "maybe" to more than one alternative, the interviewer proceeded to reread these until the child felt comfortable choosing one of them. Children who remained unsure were encouraged not to guess but simply to say that they did not know.

This procedure, called Method 1, continued until the child had failed to express knowledge of seven consecutive words on the list and, of these seven, had not succeeded in choosing the correct answer in the multiple-choice phase more than twice. (Pilot testing had indicated that, if children could not express knowledge of seven words in a row, they were unlikely to show knowledge of many remaining words.) At this point, the Method 2 procedure began. Each consecutive word from the list was read to the child, who was to indicate whether he or she might know what the word means. If the child did not know, the interviewer continued on to the next word on the list. If the child indicated he or she did, or might, know the word's meaning, the standard definitional, sentence, and multiple-choice questions were asked as in Method 1. The entire procedure terminated at word 103 for the 6-year-olds, at word 160 for the 8-year-olds, and at word 196 for the 10-year-olds. These termination points were chosen on the basis of pilot testing, which had indicated that children of these ages never knew words beyond them.

The average time taken to complete the interview was about 1 hour, 15 min, for first-grade children (usually split into one fairly long session and one shorter one), about 1 hour, 45 min, for third-grade children (usually split into two sessions), and about 3 hours for fifth-grade children (usually divided into three or four sessions). When more than two sessions were required, the experimenter usually did not interview the subject more than twice in the same week, and no subject was interviewed more than once on the same day.

Coding

The taped interviews were transcribed and then coded to indicate whether the child received credit for each word and, if credit was given, whether it was attained in the definition, sentence, or multiple-choice phase of the procedure. When credit was not given for a word, it was coded "X" if the child had not attempted the multiple-choice question and "I" if he or she had but had answered it incorrectly.

In assigning credit for knowledge of a word, we tried to be neither too strict nor too lenient. In the definition and sentence parts of the procedure, children did not have to produce an exact dictionary definition, but they did have to paraphrase the meaning of the word and/or use it in a sentence so as clearly to indicate knowledge of it. This knowledge had to be expressed in words and morphemes other than those making up the test word. For example, if a child defined *milk cow* as "a cow that gives milk," she would be asked further, "What does *cow* mean?" and "What does *milk* mean?" and credit would be given only if she could express knowledge of the component words. An adequate paraphrase or expression of knowledge of any meaning of the word or a homograph of it (i.e., a word with an identical spelling) found in *Webster's Third* was given credit. For example, credit for *flop* would be given for both the idea of "dropping heavily" and the idea of "failing completely" since each of these meanings is listed in *Webster's*. However, knowledge of a homophone (i.e., a word with the same pronunciation but a different spelling) was not credited. For example, knowing the meaning of *seen* when the test word was *scene* was insufficient. (In such instances, the interviewer would ask the child if she knew a different word that sounded the same as the one for which she had expressed knowledge.) For morphologically complex words, the child had to express knowledge of the whole word. For example, while "to make something different" is a good definition of *change,* it would not by itself be given credit as a definition of *changed;* also necessary was an indication of knowledge of the meaning of the inflection *-ed,* which could be expressed in general terms (e.g., "It happened in the past") or, more typically, in terms of a specific sentence (e.g., "I changed my clothes yesterday"). Finally, with respect to idioms, the child had to express knowledge of their idiomatic meanings. Thus, credit would not be given if a child treated the idiom *moneybags* as a literal compound (e.g., "bags full of money") but only if she expressed its idiomatic meaning as it is listed in *Webster's* (e.g., "a rich person").

Coding reliability was established by having a second person, a fourth-year honors undergraduate majoring in developmental psychology, code 25% of the transcripts, which were randomly selected with the restriction that they be balanced according to grade, sex, and SES. Intercoder agreement—computed as

$$\frac{(\text{no. of agreements})}{(\text{no. of agreements}) + (\text{no. of disagreements})}$$

—on whether to give credit was 99%; agreement on whether credit should be given in the definition, sentence, or multiple-choice phase of the procedure was 96%.

For purposes of subsequent morphological analyses, each child was assigned five scores—reflecting the number of words of a given type (root words, inflected words, derived words, literal compounds, idioms) for which he was credited in the definition and sentence parts of the procedure—plus a corrected score for his multiple-choice answers. We used the standard correction (see Brown, 1983; see also Dupuy, 1974; Seashore & Eckerson, 1940; Templin, 1957) of subtracting one-third of the wrong choices from the number of right answers on multiple-choice questions for words of a given type. A "zero minimum rule" was invoked (but only very infrequently) in the scoring of the multiple-choice questions, which meant that a child's score on them was never less than zero for any given word type.

RESULTS

Vocabulary Size

The mean number of all sampled words that were known by the children and the estimated mean number of known main entries listed in the dictionary are shown in Table 3.[11] Estimates were derived by multiplying raw scores by 595.85 since the sample of 434 words on which children were tested represented approximately 434/258,601 or 1/595.85 of all the main entries in the dictionary (see Chap. IV).

A 3 (grade) × 2 (sex) × 2 (SES) ANOVA conducted on the raw scores revealed a significant effect of grade, $F(2, 84) = 130.20$, $p < .001$, and of SES, $F(1, 84) = 6.28$, $p < .014$. Across grades and sex, upper-SES children knew an average of 42.28 words, and lower-SES children knew an average of 35.82 words. Table 3 reveals that not only the mean raw scores and

---

[11] The values shown in Table 3 as "sample words known" are the average numbers of words for which children received credit for knowing in the vocabulary test. The values shown as "estimated main entries known" are our estimates of the total number of main entries in the dictionary of which the children could have shown knowledge had they been tested on them. It will be argued later in this chapter that some of the words included in the estimates were known in the sense that they had been previously learned and could have been remembered whereas others were known (or knowable) in the sense that the children could have understood them and shown knowledge of them by constructing their meanings through morphological analysis and composition.

TABLE 3

<small>MEANS AND STANDARD DEVIATIONS FOR NUMBER OF SAMPLE WORDS KNOWN
AND FOR THE ESTIMATED TOTAL NUMBER OF MAIN ENTRIES IN THE DICTIONARY
KNOWN AT EACH GRADE</small>

	SAMPLE WORDS KNOWN		ESTIMATED MAIN ENTRIES KNOWN	
	M	SD	M	SD
Grade 1	17.45	4.97	10,398	2,961
Grade 3	32.58	5.19	19,412	3,092
Grade 5	67.12	21.21	39,994	12,638

estimates but also their standard deviations increase as a function of grade level, especially between grade 3 and grade 5 (cf. Miller, 1988; Stanovich, 1986). As a statistical precaution, square roots of the raw scores were computed, and the ANOVA was reconducted on the transformed scores (see Howell, 1987; Winer, 1971). As for the untransformed scores, the results indicated significant effects of grade, $F(2, 84) = 182.95$, $p < .001$, and SES, $F(1, 84) = 8.29$, $p < .01$. (For similar precautionary reasons, all ANOVAs and MANOVAs performed on raw scores reported in this *Monograph* were repeated on their square root transformations; all significant effects found for raw scores were also significant in analyses of the square root transformations.)

A trend analysis of the number of main entries known as a function of grade revealed a significant linear, $F(1, 93) = 235.99$, $p < .0001$, and a significant quadratic, $F(1, 93) = 12.02$, $p < .001$, component. Children knew more words with increasing age and grade, but the increase in their vocabulary between grades 3 and 5 was greater than that between grades 1 and 3. In terms of the estimates shown in Table 3, the average increase between grades 3 and 5 was slightly greater than 20,000 words, whereas from grade 1 to grade 3 it was slightly greater than 9,000 words.[12]

---

[12] These analyses were repeated, making the conservative assumption that all children eliminated two incorrect choices on multiple-choice questions for unknown inflected words, derived words, and literal compounds before guessing. The result of that assumption was a stringent correction factor for such words of -1 (as opposed to $-\frac{1}{3}$ in the standard correction for guessing) for each incorrectly answered multiple-choice question. Raw scores and estimates were reduced only slightly as a result, and, with one exception, all statistically significant results reported above, including the significant quadratic effect, $F(1, 93) = 11.29$, $p < .0011$, were found again. (The exception was that the SES effect was not found to be significant.) The stringent correction for guessing is based on several conservative assumptions that may not often be valid, and, since a goal of this research is to produce estimates that are neither too lax nor too conservative, all other analyses reported in this *Monograph* are based on scores that have been corrected in the standard way. Previous researchers (e.g., Templin, 1957) who have corrected multiple-choice questions for guessing in related studies have also always used the standard correction factor.

Proportion of Credit Achieved in Each Phase of the Vocabulary Test

The proportion of the total number of words known for which each child received credit in each of the three phases of the interview—definition, sentence, and multiple choice—was examined to see whether these proportions changed as a function of grade. In grades 1, 3, and 5, respectively, 53%, 49%, and 55% of credit was accounted for by responses in the definition phase; 14%, 14%, and 12% by responses in the sentence phase; and 33%, 37%, and 33% by multiple-choice responses.

Three univariate ANOVAs with grade as the independent variable and these proportions as the dependent measures revealed no significant effect for grade, and this finding was replicated when the proportional data were subjected to the logit transformation (Cohen & Cohen, 1975). (As a statistical precaution, all ANOVAs and MANOVAs reported in this *Monograph* in which the dependent measures are proportions were repeated with this transformation; any instance of a discrepancy between the results for the two analyses is noted.) Across all grades, children received a little more than half (52.33%) of their credit in the definition phase, a little more than one-third (34.33%) in the multiple-choice phase, and the remainder (13.33%) in the sentence phase. Thus, at each grade level, approximately two-thirds of total credit for knowing words was obtained by *expressing* knowledge in definitions and/or sentences and approximately one-third by *recognizing* the correct answers in multiple-choice tests.

Vocabulary Development in Terms of Morphologically Defined Word Types

The child's knowledge of morphologically defined word types and the contribution of different types at different ages to total vocabulary knowledge were examined through several analyses.

Raw Scores and Estimates for Morphologically Defined Word Types

The mean number of sampled words known and the estimated mean number of main entry words known in the dictionary for each morphologically defined word type are shown in Table 4 for each grade level.[13] The

---

[13] In Table 4 and the other tables reporting data on morphologically defined word types, findings for idioms are presented immediately below those for literal compounds so that researchers interested in results for all compounds (literal and idiomatic combined) can readily perceive them. For example, the estimated average number of all compounds known by the children in grades 1, 3, and 5 is the sum of the estimates in the fourth and fifth rows of Table 4 for literal compounds and idioms: 2,759, 5,118, and 10,779 compounds, respectively. In other parts of the *Monograph* (e.g., Figs. 2 and 4 below) when

TABLE 4

THE MEAN NUMBER OF WORDS KNOWN IN THE SAMPLE AND THE ESTIMATED MEAN
NUMBER OF MAIN ENTRY WORDS KNOWN IN THE DICTIONARY FOR EACH
MORPHOLOGICALLY DEFINED WORD TYPE AT EACH GRADE

	GRADE 1		GRADE 3		GRADE 5	
WORD TYPE	No. of Words	Estimate	No. of Words	Estimate	No. of Words	Estimate
Root words	5.19	3,092	7.69	4,582	12.64	7,532
Inflected words	4.62	2,753	6.94	4,135	9.39	5,595
Derived words	3.01	1,794	9.36	5,577	27.00	16,088
Literal compounds ..	4.38	2,610	7.47	4,451	13.95	8,312
Idioms	.25	149	1.12	667	4.14	2,467
Total	17.45	10,398	32.58	19,412	67.12	39,994

data for the estimates are also depicted in Figure 1. It is evident that knowledge of each word type increased with age but that performance varied considerably depending on the particular morphological type. Idioms, for example, were associated with the lowest raw scores and estimates at each grade level. Relative performance on different word types also changed with grade; for example, derived words were associated with the second lowest score and estimate in grade 1, but with the highest in grade 3, and with by far the highest in grade 5.

A multivariate analysis of variance (MANOVA) was conducted with grade, sex, and SES level as the independent variables and the five scores for the different word types as the dependent measures. The multivariate F for grade was significant, $F(10, 160) = 22.06, p < .001$. Univariate F tests for grade on each of the five scores were also significant, values ranging from $F(2, 84) = 24.48$ to $F(2, 84) = 135.71, p < .001$. Thus, performance on each word type improved significantly with age. Newman-Keuls tests revealed that the differences between mean scores at consecutive grades were all significant ($p < .001$ in all cases), with one exception—the mean raw score on idioms for first-grade children (0.25) did not differ significantly from that for third-grade children (1.12).

Trend analyses for the number of each word type known as a function of grade (collapsed across SES level and sex) revealed significant linear components for all word types, $F(1, 93) = 121.55–241.53, p < .001$. Inflected words were the only type that did not also show a significant qua-

---

the distinction between words that can and words that cannot be decoded by means of morphological analysis is being emphasized, idioms are aligned with root words because, as argued in Chap. II, these words are least likely to be figured out through such analysis and most likely to be "psychologically basic."

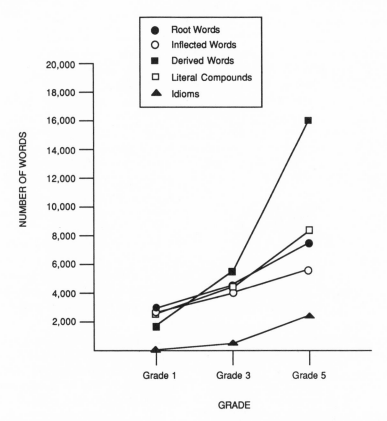

FIG. 1.—Mean estimated number of words known for each morphologically defined word type as a function of grade.

dratic component, $F(1, 93) = .03$, N.S. The quadratic components for root words, $F(1, 93) = 7.01$, $p < .01$, for literal compounds, $F(1, 93) = 5.07$, $p < .05$, and for idioms, $F(1, 93) = 4.60$, $p < .05$, were significant, and inspection of Table 4 and Figure 1 reveals that, in each case, the increase between grades 3 and 5 was greater than the corresponding increase from grade 1 to grade 3. The quadratic component for derived words was also significant, $F(1, 93) = 17.74$, $p < .001$, and, as Table 4 and Figure 1 show, performance on this type of word increased most sharply as a function of grade, particularly between grades 3 and 5.

The only other significant multivariate F was obtained for SES, $F(5, 80) = 3.68$, $p < .01$. Univariate F tests revealed significant SES effects in favor of the upper-SES children for root words, $F(1, 84) = 17.29$, $p < .001$, inflected words, $F(1, 84) = 4.05$, $p < .047$, and derived words, $F(1, 84) = 4.26$, $p < .042$. Newman-Keuls tests showed no specific significant differences between the two SES groups in grade 1 for any word type. In grade 3, upper-SES children had a significantly higher mean score on root words (8.33) than the lower-SES children (7.04); in grade 5, the upper-SES children had significantly higher mean scores on root words (14.00 vs. 11.27) and on derived words (30.47 vs. 23.52, $p < .05$ in each case).

A repeated-measures ANOVA (with grade, sex, and SES level as the between factors and word type as the within factor) was also conducted on the raw scores. There were significant effects of grade, $F(2, 84) = 130.20$, $p < .001$, and SES, $F(1, 84) = 6.28$, $p < .014$, but of greater interest were the significant word-type effect, $F(4, 336) = 217.46$, $p < .001$, and especially the significant grade × word type interaction, $F(8, 336) = 80.44$, $p < .001$. The word-type effect and the grade × word type interaction were also significant when the degrees of freedom were adjusted according to the conservative procedure suggested by Greenhouse and Geisser (1959) and Winer (1971), $F(1, 84) = 217.46$, $p < .001$, and $F(2, 84) = 80.44$, $p < .001$, respectively.[14]

The word-type effect reflects the fact that, collapsing across grade, sex, and SES level, the children's performance varied according to word type. The average number of idioms known (1.84) was the lowest, followed by the average number of inflected words (6.98), root words (8.51), literal compounds (8.60), and derived words (13.12). The average for idioms was significantly lower than those of the other word types at each grade (Newman-Keuls, $p < .05$ in each case).[15] However, as indicated by the significant

---

[14] All significant main effects for word type and interactions involving word type reported in this *Monograph* remained significant when the degrees of freedom for the *F* tests were reduced according to this conservative procedure. It should also be noted that several considerations led to the decision to treat word type as the sole repeated measure for mixed-model ANOVAs in this research. Thus, in the analysis reported here, each subject was assigned five scores, one for each word type, after correction for guessing based on his or her overall performance on that word type. Given the large sample of words tested, which was shown in Chap. IV to be representative of all the words in *Webster's Third* in terms of both frequency of occurrence and distribution according to morphological categories, and given the highly significant *F* values obtained for word-type effects and for grade × word type interactions in this research, one can hypothesize with some confidence that these effects would be replicated if different samples of words were tested in further studies. Indeed, the long-range approach adopted in this research program with respect to this issue of generalizability is to replicate the findings of the present study in further similar studies, but with different samples of words. At this time, two such further studies, one conducted with Teresa Alexander and one with Nancy Malloy, have been completed with samples of 433 and 435 main entries, respectively, and all significant word-type effects and grade × word type interactions reported in the present *Monograph* have been found to be highly significant in each of these studies as well.

[15] Significant effects for these and all subsequent Newman-Keuls tests that were performed to illuminate interactions and main effects involving word type and are reported here were also obtained when the degrees of freedom were adjusted according to the conservative procedure suggested by Greenhouse and Geisser (1959) and Winer (1971).

grade × word type interaction, the relations among the remaining word types varied as a function of grade. Newman-Keuls tests revealed that, in grade 1, the number of known root words, inflected words, and literal compounds was each significantly greater than that of derived words ($p <$ .05 in each case). However, in grades 3 and 5, the opposite was true: the number of known derived words was significantly greater than that of root words, inflected words, and literal compounds ($p < .05$ in each case). Thus, the grade × word type interaction can be at least partly understood in terms of the older children's relatively superior performance on derived words (see Table 4 and Figure 1).[16] Additional results from the Newman-Keuls tests indicated that, in grades 1 and 3, there were no significant differences in the numbers of root words, literal compounds, and inflected words known; however, in grade 5, the number of known root words and that of literal compounds were both significantly greater than that of known inflected words ($p < .05$ in each case).

Cumulative vocabulary growth functions.—The estimates displayed in Table 4 and Figure 1 are shown in Figure 2 in a more theoretically motivated way by plotting cumulative functions for known root words; root words + idioms; root words + idioms + derived words; root words + idioms + derived words + literal compounds; and, finally, root words + idioms + derived words + literal compounds + inflected words (i.e., total main entries known). These cumulative functions add, at each step, the next least likely word type to have been figured out by the children through morphological problem solving in view of previous research on morphological development (see Chap. III). The middle function in Figure 2 reveals that it is when derived words are added to root words and idioms that the cumulative vocabulary growth curves increase in a steeper and more strikingly positively accelerated fashion.

As argued in Chapter II, it would seem that, to get credit for knowing most root words or idioms, children would have had to have learned them before and to have encoded them somehow in long-term memory. How-

---

[16] A significant grade × word type interaction was also found when only bimorphemic inflected, derived, and literal compound words were analyzed, $F(4, 168) = 75.33$, $p <$ .001. Consistent with the overall analysis described above, first-grade children knew fewer bimorphemic derived words than bimorphemic inflected words and literal compounds; however, third- and fifth-grade children knew more bimorphemic derived words than bimorphemic inflected words or literal compounds. Similarly, when only multimorphemic derived words and literal compounds were analyzed, a significant grade × word type interaction was again found, $F(2, 84) = 40.16$, $p < .001$. In grade 1, children knew more multimorphemic literal compounds than derived words, whereas, in grades 3 and 5, children knew more multimorphemic derived words than literal compounds. These analyses show that the grade × word type interaction and the rapid rise in relative knowledge of derived words are independent of level of morphemic complexity; they obtain for both bimorphemic words and multimorphemic words considered alone.

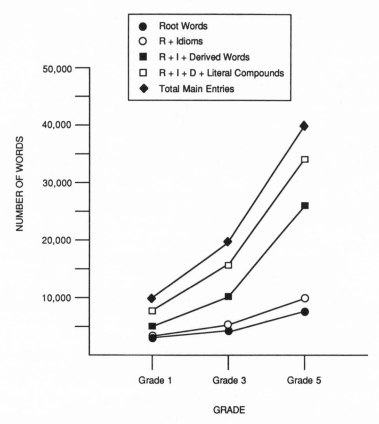

Fig. 2.—Cumulative functions showing mean estimated number of words known at each grade for root words; root words + idioms; root words + idioms + derived words; root words + idioms + derived words + literal compounds; and total main entries.

ever, some, but not necessarily all, of the other words might have been figured out through morphological analysis and composition. Thus, learned or "psychologically basic" vocabulary—the words for which there are distinct entries in the mental lexicon—would likely show a growth curve somewhere between the curve for root words + idioms and that for total main entries known. This idea will be pursued further later in Chapter VI, where an initial attempt will be made to approximate the growth curve for "psychologically basic" vocabulary on the basis of the findings from this study.

Proportional Analyses for Morphologically Defined Word Types

Proportion$_1$: The proportion of vocabulary knowledge accounted for by each morphologically defined word type.—By dividing each child's score for each word type by his or her total score for main entries known, we calculated the proportion (called "proportion₁") of vocabulary knowledge accounted for by each word type for every child. On the assumption that our sample of words is representative of all the main entries in the dictionary, each proportion₁ score provides an estimate of the proportion of all main entries in the dictionary known by a given child that are accounted for by each type of word. By showing what fractions of total vocabulary knowledge are accounted for by different word types, proportion₁ scores reveal more simply and clearly than raw scores or estimates the exact portions of such knowledge contributed by each word type. Moreover, an examination of how proportion₁ scores change with development illuminates which word types decrease, which increase, and which remain roughly constant in terms of their *relative* contribution to total vocabulary knowledge as children get older more clearly than do raw scores and estimates, which increase for all word types as a function of age.

Mean proportion₁ scores at the three grades for each word type are shown in Table 5. The proportion of children's vocabulary knowledge accounted for by root words declined from .31 to .20 between grades 1 and 5; that accounted for by inflected words also declined, from .27 to .15, over this same period; and the proportion accounted for by literal compounds declined slightly, from .25 to .21. By contrast, the proportion accounted for by derived words increased from .16 to .39 between grades 1 and 5, and, although the proportion accounted for by idioms was relatively low at all grades, it increased over this period from .01 to .05.

A MANOVA with grade, sex, and SES level as independent variables was conducted on the five proportion₁ scores after they had been subjected to the logit transformation (Cohen & Cohen, 1975). The analysis revealed a significant multivariate effect for grade, $F(10, 160) = 21.50$, $p < .001$; subsequent univariate F tests revealed that the transformed proportions changed significantly for four of the word types: root words, $F(2, 84) = 33.91$, $p < .001$; inflected words, $F(2, 84) = 48.33$, $p < .001$; derived words, $F(2, 84) = 81.42$, $p < .001$; and idioms, $F(2, 84) = 23.90$, $p < .001$. The effect for literal compounds was not significant. Univariate F tests on the raw proportion scores, with the alpha level set at .01, confirmed that the proportions for root words, $F(2, 84) = 36.45$, $p < .001$, and for inflected words, $F(2, 84) = 38.51$, $p < .001$, decreased significantly as a function of grade whereas the proportions for derived words, $F(2, 84) = 96.18$, $p < .001$, and for idioms, $F(2, 84) = 15.00$, $p < .001$, increased significantly. The effect for literal compounds again was not significant.

Proportion₂: The proportion of sample words known for each morphologically defined word type.—A second proportional measure (called "proportion₂") was obtained by dividing each child's score for each word type by the total number of words of that type in the entire sample of 434 words (see Table

TABLE 5

PROPORTION₁: THE MEAN PROPORTION OF CHILDREN'S MAIN
ENTRY VOCABULARY KNOWLEDGE ACCOUNTED FOR BY EACH
MORPHOLOGICALLY DEFINED WORD TYPE AT EACH GRADE

Word Type	Grade 1	Grade 3	Grade 5
Root words	.31	.24	.20
Inflected words	.27	.22	.15
Derived words	.16	.28	.39
Literal compounds	.25	.23	.21
Idioms	.01	.03	.05

1 above). On the assumption that our sample is representative of all the main entries in the dictionary, proportion₂ scores can be taken as estimates of the proportions of all main entries of each type listed in *Webster's Third* known by the children. The information provided by proportion₂ scores is somewhat different from that provided by proportion₁ and the raw scores presented above because, in calculating these proportions, known words of a given type are divided by all such words in the sample. The results for inflected words show this difference especially clearly. At each grade, the mean proportion₂ score was highest for inflected words, whereas this was never the case in the preceding analyses. This is because there were only 20 inflected words in the sample of 434 and because proportion₂ scores were obtained by dividing the number of known words of a given type by the number of such words in the sample. Although children did not know as many inflected words as they did words from some of the other morphological categories in absolute terms, the proportion of such words in the sample that they knew was higher than the corresponding proportions for the other word types.

This is shown in Table 6, which presents mean proportion₂ scores at each grade for each word type. The mean percentage of sampled words known by the children increased between grades 1 and 5 from 23.10% to 46.95% for inflected words, from 4.18% to 10.19% for root words, from 2.15% to 19.29% for derived words, from 6.43% to 20.51% for literal compounds, and from 0.30% to 5.04% for idioms.

A repeated-measures ANOVA on the proportion₂ data with grade, sex, and SES level as the between factors and word type as the within factor showed significant effects for grade, $F(2, 84) = 113.01$, $p < .001$, SES (in favor of upper-SES children), $F(1, 84) = 5.79$, $p < .025$, and word type, $F(4, 336) = 960.08$, $p < .001$, as well as a significant grade × word type interaction, $F(8, 336) = 32.67$, $p < .001$. Across all grades, the mean proportion₂ score was highest for inflected words (34.91%), followed by literal compounds (12.64%), derived words (9.38%), root words (6.86%), and idi-

TABLE 6

PROPORTION$_2$: THE MEAN PERCENTAGE OF ALL WORDS IN THE
SAMPLE FOR EACH MORPHOLOGICALLY DEFINED WORD TYPE
KNOWN BY CHILDREN AT EACH GRADE

Word Type	Grade 1	Grade 3	Grade 5
Root words	4.18	6.20	10.19
Inflected words	23.10	34.69	46.95
Derived words	2.15	6.69	19.29
Literal compounds	6.43	10.98	20.51
Idioms	.30	1.36	5.04

oms (2.23%), which accounts for the main effect of word type. To illuminate the grade × word type interaction, Newman-Keuls tests were used to reveal which word types were associated with higher proportion$_2$ scores at each grade level. All pairwise differences between the proportions listed in the columns of Table 6 were significant ($p < .05$ in each case), except for those between derived words and idioms at grade 1, between derived words and root words at grade 3, and between literal compounds and derived words at grade 5. Thus, the significant grade × word type interaction can be understood at least partly in terms of the sharply increasing proportion of derived words in the sample that were known as a function of grade. For example, whereas first-grade children knew a significantly greater proportion of root words (4.18%) than of derived words (2.15%) in the sample, fifth-grade children knew a significantly greater proportion of derived words (19.29%) than of root words (10.19%).[17]

Estimated Rates of Vocabulary Growth in Words per Day for Morphologically Defined Word Types

Estimates of rates of vocabulary growth can be obtained by methods similar to those used by other authors (see Chap. II) from the estimates of vocabulary size generated by this study. For example, the data shown in Table 4 above indicate that the fifth-grade children were estimated to know on average 29,596 more words in all than the first-grade children (i.e., $39,994 - 10,398$). The average difference between the ages of these children (assuming 365.25 days per year) was 1,478 days, yielding an estimated

---

[17] A MANOVA with grade, sex, and SES as the independent variables and the five proportion$_2$ scores as dependent measures was also conducted. The exact same results for this and all follow-up tests were found as for the raw scores reported in the text, including the significant grade effects for each proportion$_2$ score. This would be expected since the raw scores for each word type were simply divided by a constant.

average total rate of vocabulary development of 20.02 words per day (29,596/1,478) between grade 1 and grade 5. By the same logic, rate estimates can be computed for each morphologically defined word type. For example, on the basis of the estimates for numbers of root words known (see Table 4), fifth-grade children were estimated to know 4,440 more such words (7,532 − 3,092) than first-grade children, yielding an estimated average rate of 3.00 new root words per day (4,440/1,478) between grade 1 and grade 5.

Estimates of vocabulary growth rates for each word type and for total main entries during different developmental periods computed by this method are shown in Table 7. In column 2 of Table 7, Carey's (1978) assumption that vocabulary development is minimal before 1½ years of age was adopted to permit comparison with her estimated rate of vocabulary growth during the preschool years. Our estimate that, between age 1-6.0 and age 6-7.28 (the average age of the first-grade children in this study), vocabulary develops at a rate of 5.52 main entries per day is fairly consistent with Carey's estimate of about 5 per day. Similarly, our estimated rate of about 12.13 main entries per day between grade 1 and grade 3 compares fairly well with Miller's (1977) estimate of about 14.5 per day during this period. And, consistent with the estimated rates of these researchers, those of the present study suggest that, while the rate of vocabulary development is substantial in the preschool years, it is even more rapid in the early and middle elementary school years. However, Table 7 also makes it clear that "root words," at least as these are defined in the present study, are only one of several morphologically defined word types that contribute to the estimated rates for main entry vocabulary development.

In addition to the indication that rate of vocabulary development becomes increasingly rapid from the preschool through the early and middle elementary school years, Table 7 is also of interest because of the different patterns of estimated rates for the various word types during different developmental periods that the data suggest. For example, during the period from 1½ years of age to grade 1, Table 7 entries indicate that root words are associated with the highest estimated rate (1.64 words per day), followed by inflected words (1.46 words per day) and literal compounds (1.39 words per day); derived words are associated with the second lowest estimated rate (0.95 words per day) during this time, higher only than that for idioms (0.08 words per day). By contrast, at later ages, derived words are associated with the highest rate of growth, followed by literal compounds. For example, Table 7 indicates that, between grade 1 and grade 5, derived words are associated with an estimated rate of 9.67 words per day, followed by literal compounds (3.86 words per day), root words (3.00 words per day), inflected words (1.92 words per day), and idioms (1.57 words per day).

TABLE 7

Estimated Rates of Vocabulary Growth in Words per Day
(Morphological Word-Type Analysis)

Word Type	Grade 1– Grade 5	1.5 Years– Grade 1	Grade 1– Grade 3	Grade 3– Grade 5
Root words	3.00	1.64	2.00	4.01
Inflected words	1.92	1.46	1.86	1.98
Derived words	9.67	.95	5.09	14.28
Literal compounds	3.86	1.39	2.48	5.24
Idioms	1.57	.08	.70	2.45
Total	20.02	5.52	12.13	27.96

Vocabulary Development and Morphemic Complexity

Children's knowledge of words classified according to level of morphemic complexity and the contribution of words of different complexity levels at different ages to total vocabulary knowledge were also investigated through several analyses that parallel those conducted for morphologically defined word types. The reasons for conducting these analyses and the definitions of the levels of morphemic complexity examined were presented in Chapter II.

Raw Scores and Estimates for Words at Different Levels of Morphemic Complexity

The mean number of known words in the sample and the estimated number of main entries known at each level of morphemic complexity are shown in Table 8;[18] Figure 3 shows graphically how the estimates for each of the four word types change as a function of grade. (Estimates were again obtained by multiplying the mean number of each word type by 595.85 since the sample of 434 words on which children were tested represented 1/595.85 of all the main entries in the dictionary.) As indicated in Figure 3 and Table 8, children at all grades knew more bimorphemic words than words of any other type, and the growth of knowledge of bimorphemic

[18] The totals shown in Table 8 are slightly different from those shown in Tables 3 and 4 above; these differences are due to the effect of the zero minimum rule whereby a child could not achieve a score of less than zero on the multiple-choice questions for a given word type. Because inflected words, derived words, and literal compounds were collapsed in the present analysis into the two categories of bimorphemic and multimorphemic words, the zero minimum rule was invoked in slightly fewer cases, accounting for the small discrepancy in the totals.

TABLE 8

THE MEAN NUMBER OF WORDS KNOWN IN THE SAMPLE AND THE MEAN ESTIMATED
NUMBER OF MAIN ENTRY WORDS KNOWN IN THE DICTIONARY AT EACH GRADE FOR
WORDS OF DIFFERENT LEVELS OF MORPHEMIC COMPLEXITY

	GRADE 1		GRADE 3		GRADE 5	
WORD TYPE	No. of Words	Estimate	No. of Words	Estimate	No. of Words	Estimate
Monomorphemic words ..	5.19	3,092	7.69	4,582	12.64	7,532
Bimorphemic words	10.15	6,048	19.66	11,714	37.50	22,344
Multimorphemic words ..	1.48	882	4.09	2,347	12.74	7,591
Idioms	.25	149	1.12	667	4.14	2,467
Total	17.07	10,171	32.56	19,310	67.02	39,934

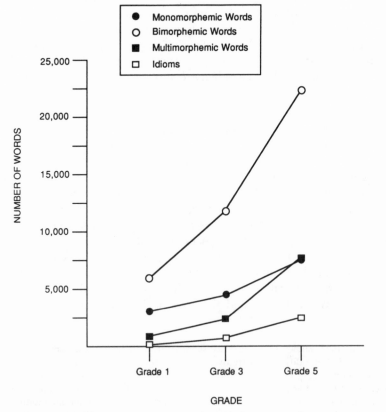

FIG. 3.—Mean estimated number of words known for each word type classified according to morphemic complexity as a function of grade.

words was relatively rapid. At all grades, they knew fewer idioms than any other type of word. In grades 1 and 3, children knew more monomorphemic than multimorphemic words; however, knowledge of multimorphemic words was associated with more rapid growth than that of monomorphemic words between grades 3 and 5, with the result that, by grade 5, children knew approximately equal numbers of these two word types.

A MANOVA with grade, sex, and SES as the independent variables and the raw scores for the four word types as the dependent variables showed a significant multivariate grade effect, $F(8, 162) = 27.08, p < .001$, and univariate F tests revealed significant grade effects for each word type. Newman-Keuls tests comparing performance on each word type at consecutive grade levels showed that all differences between mean scores for bimorphemic as well as multimorphemic words were significant, $t(1, 93) = 2.86–10.52, p < .05$ (at least) in all cases. The results for idioms, of course, were the same as in the previous analyses, and those for monomorphemic words were identical to the results reported for root words.

Trend analyses for each word type as a function of grade (collapsed across SES and sex) were also conducted. In addition to being associated with a significant linear component ($p < .001$ in each case), each word type was also associated with a significant quadratic component—for monomorphemic words, $F(1, 93) = 7.01, p < .01$; for bimorphemic words, $F(1, 93) = 8.07, p < .01$; for multimorphemic words, $F(1, 93) = 14.45, p < .001$; and for idioms, $F(1, 93) = 4.60, p < .05$. Inspection of Table 8 and Figure 3 reveals that, for each word type, the increase in known words is greater between grade 3 and grade 5 than between grade 1 and grade 3 and also that the positive acceleration in the growth curve for multimorphemic words is especially pronounced.[19]

The only other significant multivariate effect resulting from the MANOVA was for SES, $F(4, 81) = 4.39, p < .003$. Univariate F tests revealed significant effects, in favor of upper-SES children, for monomorphe-

---

[19] Trend analyses were also conducted on each type of multimorphemic word separately, specifically on multimorphemic derived words and multimorphemic literal compounds. It was found that, in addition to being associated with a significant linear component, each type of multimorphemic word was also associated with a significant quadratic component: $F(1, 93) = 13.80, p < .001$, for multimorphemic derived words; $F(1, 93) = 4.59, p < .035$, for multimorphemic literal compounds. For each word type, the increase between grade 3 and grade 5 was greater than that between grade 1 and grade 3. Thus, the growth of knowledge of multimorphemic words was found to be significantly positively accelerated for both word types (although the positive acceleration in the growth functions was most pronounced for multimorphemic derived words). Therefore, the rapid growth of knowledge of multimorphemic words, especially between grade 3 and grade 5, was not solely dependent on one word type or another but was found for both derived words and literal compounds.

mic words, $F(1, 84) = 17.30$, $p < .001$, and for multimorphemic words, $F(1, 84) = 3.96$, $p < .05$.

A repeated-measures ANOVA (with grade, sex, and SES level as the between variables and word type as the within variable) replicated the significant grade, $F(2, 84) = 131.19$, $p < .001$, and SES, $F(1, 84) = 6.51$, $p < .013$, effects; of greater interest were the significant word-type effect, $F(3, 252) = 827.33$, $p < .001$, and the significant grade × word type interaction, $F(6, 252) = 95.52$, $p < .001$. To help illuminate these latter effects, the Student Newman-Keuls procedure was used to compare pairwise differences between word types at each grade level. All such differences were significant ($p < .05$ in each case), except the difference between multimorphemic words and idioms in grade 1 and that between multimorphemic and monomorphemic words in grade 5. The word-type effect reflects the finding that, collapsing across grades, knowledge of bimorphemic words ($\bar{x} = 22.44$) exceeded that of monomorphemic words ($\bar{x} = 8.51$), which, in turn, was greater than that of multimorphemic words ($\bar{x} = 6.10$); idioms were the least well known type of word ($\bar{x} = 1.84$). The grade × word type interaction can be understood at least partly in terms of the relatively rapid rise across grade in the number of multimorphemic words known (see Fig. 3). The first-grade children knew significantly more monomorphemic than multimorphemic words, and the number of known multimorphemic words was not significantly greater than the number of known idioms; in contrast, by grade 5, children knew as many multimorphemic as monomorphemic words and significantly more such words than idioms. Other developmental trends, such as the relatively rapid rise in bimorphemic words compared to the more gradual increases in monomorphemic words and idioms known (see Fig. 3), no doubt also contribute to the significant grade × word type interaction.

Proportional Analyses for Words
at Different Levels of Morphemic Complexity

Proportion$_1$: The proportion of vocabulary knowledge accounted for by each type of word classified according to morphemic complexity.—The proportion of all the words that each child knew that was accounted for by each of the four word types defined in terms of complexity (called "proportion$_1$") was calculated. As before, on the assumption that the sample of words is representative of all the main entries in the dictionary, a child's proportion$_1$ score for each word type can be taken as an estimate of the proportion of the child's total knowledge of main entry words in the dictionary that was accounted for by words of that type. Mean proportion$_1$ scores at the three grades for each word type are shown in Table 9.

TABLE 9

Proportion₁: The Mean Proportion of Children's Main
Entry Vocabulary Knowledge Accounted for by Each
Type of Word Classified According to Morphemic
Complexity at Each Grade

Word Type	Grade 1	Grade 3	Grade 5
Monomorphemic words	.31	.24	.20
Bimorphemic words	.60	.61	.56
Multimorphemic words	.08	.12	.19
Idioms	.01	.03	.05

A MANOVA with grade, sex, and SES level as independent variables conducted on the four proportion₁ scores after they had been subjected to the logit transformation (Cohen & Cohen, 1975) showed a highly significant multivariate effect for grade, $F(8, 162) = 13.93$, $p < .001$. Subsequent univariate F tests revealed that the transformed proportions changed significantly for each type of word: monomorphemic words, $F(2, 84) = 33.91$, $p < .001$; bimorphemic words, $F(2, 84) = 4.07$, $p < .03$; multimorphemic words, $F(2, 84) = 20.40$, $p < .001$; and idioms, $F(2, 84) = 23.90$, $p < .001$. Univariate F tests on the raw proportion scores, with the alpha level set at .0125, confirmed that the proportions for monomorphemic words decreased significantly as a function of grade, $F(2, 84) = 36.45$, $p < .001$, whereas the proportions for multimorphemic words, $F(2, 84) = 31.08$, $p < .001$, and for idioms, $F(2, 84) = 15.00$, $p < .001$, increased significantly (see Table 9); given the preset alpha level, the change in the raw proportions for bimorphemic words was not significant, $F(2, 84) = 4.05$, $p < .03$.

Proportion₂: The proportion of sample words known for each type of word classified according to morphemic complexity.—Proportion₂ scores were obtained by dividing each child's score for each word type by the total number of words of that type in the entire sample of 434 words (see Table 2 above). Again, on the assumption of representativeness of our sample, proportion₂ scores provide estimates of the proportions of all words of each type listed as main entries in *Webster's Third* known by the children. Mean proportion₂ scores for each word type at each grade are shown in Table 10.

A repeated-measures ANOVA (with grade, sex, and SES level as the between variables and with word type as the within variable) revealed significant effects of grade, $F(2, 84) = 118.26$, $p < .001$, and SES, $F(2, 84) = 6.29$, $p < .014$, but of greater interest were the significant effects for word type, $F(3, 252) = 334.02$, $p < .001$, and for the grade × word type interaction, $F(6, 252) = 56.36$, $p < .001$. To help interpret these latter effects, Student Newman-Keuls tests were conducted on all pairwise differences at each grade level, shown in the columns of Table 10. All these differences

TABLE 10

PROPORTION$_2$: THE MEAN PERCENTAGE OF ALL WORDS IN THE SAMPLE
FOR EACH TYPE OF WORD CLASSIFIED ACCORDING TO MORPHEMIC
COMPLEXITY KNOWN BY CHILDREN AT EACH GRADE

Word Type	Grade 1	Grade 3	Grade 5
Monomorphemic words	4.18	6.20	10.19
Bimorphemic words	6.31	12.21	23.29
Multimorphemic words	2.21	6.11	19.01
Idioms	.30	1.36	5.04

were significant ($p < .05$ in each case), except that between monomorphemic words and multimorphemic words at grade 3.

The pattern across all grades—the mean proportion$_2$ score is highest for bimorphemic words (13.94%), followed by multimorphemic (9.11%) and monomorphemic (6.86%) words, and lowest for idioms (2.23%)—accounts for the main effect for word type revealed by the ANOVA. The grade × word type interaction can be understood partly in terms of the relatively rapid rise with age in the proportions for multimorphemic words: whereas the proportion for monomorphemic words was significantly higher than that for multimorphemic words in grade 1, this difference was not significant in grade 3, and by grade 5 the proportion for multimorphemic words was significantly higher than that for monomorphemic words (see Table 10). Other changes with grade, such as the relatively rapid increase in the proportion of bimorphemic words known in comparison to the more gradual increases in the proportions for monomorphemic words and idioms, likely contribute to the significant grade × word type interaction as well.[20]

Estimated Rates of Vocabulary Growth in Words per Day for Words at Different Levels of Morphemic Complexity

Rates of vocabulary growth were estimated for words at different levels of morphemic complexity, as they had been earlier for morphologically defined word types. Estimated rates of vocabulary development during four

[20] A MANOVA with grade, sex, and SES level as the independent variables and the four proportion$_2$ scores as dependent measures was also conducted. The exact same results were found for this and all follow-up tests as for the raw scores reported in the text, including the significant univariate effects for grade for each proportion$_2$ score; this again would be expected since, for each word type, the raw scores were simply divided by a constant. When the logit transformation was applied to the proportion$_2$ scores, all the same effects were found, except that the univariate effect for SES on the multimorphemic words was not significant.

TABLE 11

ESTIMATED RATES OF VOCABULARY GROWTH IN WORDS PER DAY
(Morphemic Complexity Analysis)

Word Type	Grade 1– Grade 5	1.5 Years– Grade 1	Grade 1– Grade 3	Grade 3– Grade 5
Monomorphemic words	3.00	1.64	2.00	4.01
Bimorphemic words	11.03	3.21	7.63	14.44
Multimorphemic words	4.54	.47	1.97	7.12
Idioms	1.57	.08	.70	2.45
Total	20.14	5.40	12.30	28.02

different age ranges for each word type and for total main entries are shown in Table 11.[21]

Table 11 indicates not only that rate of vocabulary development increases for each word type as children get older but that the relative rapidity of rate of growth associated with certain word types changes with age also. Although bimorphemic words are associated with the highest and idioms with the lowest rates during each developmental period shown in Table 11, a shifting pattern can be observed for the two remaining word types. Specifically, during the period from 1½ years to grade 1, monomorphemic words are associated with a much higher rate (1.64 words per day) than multimorphemic words (0.47 words per day). From grade 1 to grade 3, the estimated rates for these word types are almost equal (1.97 words per day for multimorphemic words; 2.00 words per day for monomorphemic words), and, from grade 3 to grade 5, the estimated rate for multimorphemic words (7.12 words per day) is higher than that for monomorphemic words (4.01 words per day). The overall estimated rate for multimorphemic words from grade 1 to grade 5 (4.54 words per day) is also higher than the corresponding rate for monomorphemic words (3.00 words per day).

[21] Although the rates for monomorphemic words and idioms shown in Table 11 are identical to those shown for root words and idioms in Table 7 above, the rates for total main entries are slightly different in the two tables because of the operation of the zero minimum rule in correcting multiple-choice questions for guessing, as discussed earlier.

VI. DISTINGUISHING POTENTIALLY KNOWABLE WORDS FROM PSYCHOLOGICALLY BASIC VOCABULARY

Further analyses were undertaken, examining how children expressed their knowledge of words, particularly the morphologically complex ones. The goal was to illuminate, to the extent possible, the distinction between words known through morphological decoding and words known because they have been previously learned. The results of these analyses constitute the focus of this chapter.

APPARENT EXTENT OF MORPHOLOGICAL PROBLEM SOLVING

While studying the transcripts, my colleagues and I noticed that, for some morphologically complex words, children appeared to use what I have called "morphological problem solving" to figure out their meanings. That is, they would deal with one or more component morphemes in the word first, before eventually coming up with the meaning of the whole word. For example, having been asked about the word *treelet,* a 10-year-old girl said that she had never heard it before but that she knew *tree,* which she proceeded to define correctly. Then she said, "Well, a piglet is a small pig, so a treelet could be a small tree." When asked what the word *advisable* meant, a fifth-grade boy said, "I'm not sure. I really haven't heard it. *Advise* means to give advice to someone; it means to give them help with what they're doing. And *advisable* means the same thing except for it will be advisable to go to someone else."

In contrast with these relatively clear cases of "morphological problem solving," there were cases in which the child showed no evidence of breaking a complex word into its morphological components to deduce its meaning. For example, when asked about the word *enjoyable,* one young child said, "If it's enjoyable, it's a lot of fun." We took this to indicate that she knew the word, but her response revealed no evidence of breaking the word into its component morphemes. Another young child who said, "It's all wet," for *soaking* (again scored as correct) similarly showed no evidence of breaking the word into the root verb *soak* and the participial or progressive inflection *-ing*.

Having noticed such cases, we set out to code for evidence of this kind of problem solving on the basis of what each child said for each credited morphologically complex word. Complex main entries were coded as "PS" (evidence of problem solving) when there was evidence that the child had broken the word into its component morphemes in arriving at its meaning—specifically, when any of the following criteria was met:

1. The child mentioned and defined each component morpheme of the word separately in deriving the meaning of the whole word (e.g., if for *firesafe* the child defined *fire* as "flames" and *safe* as "protected" and then deduced that *firesafe* means "protected from flames").

2. The child mentioned and defined first a morphological component of a word, then two parts together, then three parts together, etc., until he or she had come up with the meaning of the whole word (e.g., if for *waspishly* the child defined *wasp* as a "flying insect that looks like a bee and can sting," then *waspish* as "like a wasp," then *waspishly* as "in a waspish way").

3. The child used a morphemic component of the word by itself before or during the phase of the interview in which credit for knowing the word was given (e.g., if for *soaking* the child mentioned *soak* by itself before or during the phase of the interview in which credit was given).

4. The child defined a morphological component by itself en route to getting credit for knowing the word (e.g., if the child said, "When you wish for something a lot," which was her definition of *hope,* and later got credit for *hopelessness*).

5. The child produced a different inflected or derived form of the word en route to getting credit for the word (e.g., *soaked* or *soaks* for *soaking, forgot* for *forgotten, hopeful* for *hopelessness,* etc.).

6. If the child defined or used one part of a literal compound separately from the others (see 3 and 4 above) or reordered the words in the literal compound in attempting to define it, it was coded as PS (e.g., if for *firesafe* the child said "safe from fire," or if for *milk cow* the child said "a cow that gives milk," etc.).

7. If the child used or defined a component of a word with more than two morphemes that was itself made up of more than one morpheme en route to getting credit for the whole word, it was coded as PS (e.g., if for *hopelessness* the child used or defined *hopeless* and then got credit for *hopelessness*).

When none of these seven criteria was met, the response was coded as "NE" (no evidence of problem solving). In doing this coding, the transcripts were examined only up to the phase in the procedure where the child received credit for knowing the word. For example, if a child received credit for knowing a word in the definition phase, only the responses made during the definition phase were examined for evidence of problem solving.

Although problem solving seemed possible mainly for morphologically complex words, we decided to examine root words and idioms as well. When there was evidence that the child was figuring out the meaning of such words through knowledge of other words (or morphemes), then they were also coded as PS. Although such cases were rare (seen in an average of 0.45 root words and an average of 0.49 idioms per subject across the 96 children), they did seem to occur occasionally. For example, one child received credit for knowing the root word *clark* when he noted that it sounded like *clerk* and appeared to guess that it might have the same meaning. Another who got credit for knowing the root word *pyro* appeared to figure out its meaning as a kind of back formation from *pyromaniac*. Yet another appeared to use a morphological problem-solving approach for the idiom *softheaded*, first speculating that it might mean "having a soft head," but then apparently guessing correctly that it might mean "not very smart."[22]

One-quarter of the transcripts were coded by a second judge; interrater reliability—calculated as

$$\frac{(\text{no. of agreements})}{(\text{no. of agreements}) + (\text{no. of disagreements})}$$

—was 90.34%. (So as not to inflate this statistic unduly, only cases in which at least one of the two raters had coded root words and idioms as PS were

---

[22] The rare cases of root words and idioms that were coded as PS were likely figured out through cognitive processes somewhat different from or additional to those involved for morphologically complex words coded as PS. For example, guessing correctly that *clark* might mean *clerk* presumably is based on a recognition that the test word sounds similar to another word stored in long-term memory and would clearly not be based on breaking the word into meaningful parts. Guessing correctly that *softheaded* might mean "not very smart," after first speculating that it might mean "having a soft head," may have involved metaphoric reasoning following the treatment of the idiom as a literal compound. However, since it seemed unlikely that in such cases the root words or idioms had been learned as whole units before, and since they were apparently figured out through knowledge of other known words and morphemes (e.g., *clerk* in the case of *clark; soft, head,* and *-ed* in the case of *softheaded*), they were coded as PS in the present analysis. The evidence suggested that these were exceptional cases of root words and idioms for which children received credit, not because they were "psychologically basic" (i.e., previously learned), but because they were figured out through knowledge of other words and morphemes at the time of the test. Because the ultimate goal of this analysis was to attempt to distinguish psychologically basic words with distinct entries in the mental lexicon from words figured out at the time of the test, these exceptional cases were coded as PS in spite of probable differences between the cognitive processes underlying how they were figured out and those underlying the decoding of morphologically complex words.

included in the calculation.) Instances of disagreement were resolved through further analysis and discussion.

Each child's PS and NE scores for each word type were corrected for guessing so that their sum would be the same as the corrected score that that child had received for each morphologically defined word type in the first morphological analysis presented above. This was accomplished by partitioning the total correction factor for a given word type for a given subject—CF(total)—into two correction factors in proportion to how many times words of a given type (for which the child originally received credit in the multiple-choice phase of the procedure) were coded as PS (PS_{MC}) and how many times as NE (NE_{MC}). These correction factors—CF(PS) and CF(NE)—were applied to the PS and NE scores, respectively, for that word type. Thus,[23]

$$CF(PS) = \left[\frac{PS_{MC}}{(PS_{MC} + NE_{MC})} \right] \times CF(total),$$

$$CF(NE) = \left[\frac{NE_{MC}}{(PS_{MC} + NE_{MC})} \right] \times CF(total).$$

The mean proportions of all known main entries that were coded as PS for each grade are shown in column 1 of Table 12. A grade × sex × SES ANOVA with the proportion of total known main entries coded as PS for each subject as the dependent measure showed a significant main effect for grade, $F(2, 84) = 8.99$, $p < .001$, indicating that the proportion of words for which there was evidence of problem solving increased reliably as a function of grade level. The only other significant effect was a grade × sex interaction, $F(2, 84) = 4.54$, $p < .013$: the mean proportion of words coded as PS was .46 for girls and .35 for boys in grade 1, .41 for girls and .45 for boys in grade 3, and .52 for girls and .50 for boys in grade 5.

The mean proportions of all known complex main entries (inflected words + derived words + literal compounds) coded as PS are shown in column 2 of Table 12. A grade × sex × SES ANOVA with the proportion of known complex main entries coded as PS as the dependent variable likewise revealed a significant main effect for grade, $F(2, 84) = 3.63$, $p < .031$, indicating that the proportion of complex words for which there was evidence of morphological problem solving also increased reliably as a function of grade level.[24]

---

[23] As an illustration, if the original correction factor for a particular child for derived words had been 3.00, and if one-third of her correct multiple-choice responses had been coded as PS and two-thirds as NE, the correction factor for derived words coded as PS would have been 1.00 and that for derived words coded as NE 2.00.

[24] The only other significant effect from this analysis was again the grade × sex

TABLE 12

Mean Proportion of Known Words Coded as Showing Evidence of Morphological Problem Solving (PS) for Each Grade

	Total Main Entries (All Words)	Complex Main Entries (Inflected Words, Derived Words, and Literal Compounds)
Grade 1	.40	.56
Grade 3	.43	.57
Grade 5	.51	.65

The data on complex words were further analyzed by means of a repeated-measures ANOVA with grade, sex, and SES level as between factors and word type (inflected words, derived words, literal compounds) as the within factor. In addition to replicating the grade effect, $F(2, 84) = 3.47$, $p < .035$, this analysis also showed a significant word-type effect, $F(2, 168) = 10.32$, $p < .001$, with the mean proportion score for literal compounds (.67) being higher than that for inflected (.57) or derived (.54) words. Neither the grade × word type interaction nor the grade × sex effect reached significance. Newman-Keuls tests performed to help illuminate the significant word-type effect showed that the mean proportion score for literal compounds was significantly higher than those for inflected and derived words ($p < .05$ in each case) but that the latter two were not significantly different.

EXAMPLES AND IMPRESSIONS OF RESPONSES CODED AS INDICATING MORPHOLOGICAL PROBLEM SOLVING

In this section, I present a number of examples of interviews in which children's responses to complex words were coded as manifesting evidence of morphological problem solving. Because one way in which the present investigation of vocabulary development differs from many previous studies is in its emphasis on the possible role played by morphological problem solving in contributing to total recognition vocabulary, it is worth illustrating children's responses that were coded in this way with some concrete examples. Moreover, it is hoped that they might provide some clues to the pro-

---

interaction, $F(2, 84) = 3.25$, $p < .044$, with girls receiving on average a coding of PS for .64, .55, and .67 of all known complex words in grades 1, 3, and 5, respectively, and boys receiving a coding of PS for .49, .58, and .63 of all known complex words in these three grades, respectively. This interaction was not quite significant when the proportion scores were subjected to the logit transformation before the ANOVA was conducted, $F(2, 84) = 2.97$, $p < .06$.

cesses that these children might have been using in working out the meanings of complex words.

"Figuring out" complex words through morphological analysis and composition can involve several different routes, as is suggested by the multiple criteria that we used to code the responses. The current study is not ideal for illuminating underlying processes in detail because it is primarily an investigation of the breadth of vocabulary knowledge that children possess at different grade levels, based on their understanding of a relatively large sample of words representative of a recent unabridged dictionary; ideally, investigation of the processes used in morphological problem solving would rely on more experimental and detailed studies involving smaller samples of words. Also, the data consist of what children said, and it is probable that what children express is an imperfect reflection of underlying mental processes (for further discussion of this point, see below). Even so, however, it is possible that considering concrete examples that illustrate my impressions of typical differences and developmental trends in what the children said about various types of words that indicated that they may have been using morphological problem solving can provide some clues about such processes, clues that could guide future, more specifically process-oriented research programs.

Teresa Alexander, Janet Gysbers, and I had originally read through all the transcripts in order to develop our coding criteria for morphological problem solving and to classify the words in terms of these criteria. On the basis of this and further work done with Tracy Cocivera, I developed some impressions of the typical response patterns manifested by children at different grade levels for words coded as PS. Subsequently, I selected at random several transcripts for children at each of the three grade levels and examined thoroughly every response that had been so coded. I also studied incorrect responses to idioms to see if these children appeared to analyze idioms morphologically as well. The examples presented below are drawn primarily from these transcripts, but I believe that they are reasonably representative of the data set as a whole and that they illustrate typical patterns.

Many of the interesting patterns can be characterized in terms of whether a response manifested either a "part to whole" pattern, in which the child dealt explicitly with just one morphological component before getting credit for knowing the whole word, or a "parts to whole" pattern, in which he or she dealt explicitly with more than one morphological component en route to getting credit. As well as being scrutinized for these two (and related) patterns, the responses were also inspected to see whether a child seemed explicitly to use analogy to another word of similar morphological form (as in the case of the child who seemed to work out the meaning of *treelet* by analogy to *piglet*, described above). Some researchers have suggested that most novel morphologically complex words are understood by analogy to known words of similar morphological construction (e.g., Derwing & Skousen, in press); others have proposed generative or rule-based models of morphological analysis and composition that involve breaking a complex word into morphological components, assigning meanings to each of those components, and synthesizing these meanings to construct the meaning of the complex word (e.g., White et al., 1989). Moreover, several researchers have suggested that some complex words might be analyzed in a generative or rule-based fashion whereas others might be comprehended by analogy (e.g., MacWhinney, 1978; Marcus et al., 1992; Pinker, 1991; Tyler & Nagy, 1989; see also Bauer, 1983). Given current interest in the possible role played by analogy in composing the meanings of complex words, the transcripts were studied for explicit instances of the apparent use of analogy as well as the explicit analysis of complex words into morphological parts.

The results of this detailed review of the randomly selected transcripts confirmed the impression that I had gained from reading the full corpus that, when there was evidence of morphological problem solving, inflected and derived words tended to be treated differently from literal compounds. Across all grades, inflected and derived words most often manifested a "part to whole" pattern, with just the constituent root word and not the affix usually being explicitly discussed, described, or defined by itself prior to the child's achieving credit for knowing the whole word. Final credit for such words was often ultimately achieved when children used them in illustrative sentences in a grammatically appropriate fashion. On the other hand, literal compounds most often manifested a "parts to whole" pattern because, across all grades, children tended to discuss, describe, or define two (or more) component words making up the compound en route to getting credit. Final credit for literal compounds was often ultimately achieved when children defined them, often in a general way, by putting the meanings of the constituent words together in a reasonable fashion.

Within each word type, there was also evidence of a developmental trend toward greater explicitness in treating more than one morphological component in defining a word. In the case of inflected and derived words, it was only the fifth-grade children who, in addition to discussing the corresponding root word, ever explicitly discussed the affix by itself, although explicit mention of disembedded bound morphemes was relatively infrequent even in the oldest group. In the case of literal compounds, the tendency to discuss more than one of the component words increased with age and grade, although even the youngest children did this fairly frequently. Instances of the explicit use of analogy to words of similar morphological form were found to be infrequent and, when they did occur, were usually observed in the transcripts of fifth graders.

Inflected Words

The most common approach that children of all grades took for inflected words was to begin by discussing the corresponding root words. Credit for knowing the entire inflected word was ultimately achieved most often when they cast the inflected word into an illustrative sentence in a grammatically correct way and sometimes when they answered the multiple-choice question correctly. Children rarely defined the entire inflected word in a general way. The vast majority of children's PS responses for inflected words manifested a "part to whole" pattern because they usually discussed only the root word by itself explicitly, not the inflectional suffix, prior to getting credit for knowing the word.

In the first two examples of first graders' responses to inflected words, it can be seen that these children discussed and defined mainly the root words (*report* and *sour*) and that it was not until they answered the multiple-choice questions that they were given credit for knowing these words:

First-Grade Child: reports
Interviewer. OK. The next word is *reports.* What does the word *reports* mean?
Child. Reports?
I. Mmm.
C. Um. Like if you're at school, and somebody said something bad about you, you report them to the principal.
I. And what does it mean if you report them to the principal, M.?
C. Like you take them up to the principal, and they give them heck, or something like that.
I. OK. Is there anything else you can tell me about the word *reports?*
C. Like if you're writing something and give it to your boss or something.
I. Could you use the word *reports* in a sentence to show me you know what it means?
C. Mmm. Like if somebody called you a name. You take them up to the principal. And that's reports.
I. OK. Is there anything else you can tell me about *reports,* M.?
C. No.
[*Multiple-choice question answered correctly.*]

First-Grade Child: sourer
I. OK. The next word is *sourer.* Can you tell me what the word *sourer* means?
C. Say something has . . . sour cream and . . . sour lemon. And

sometimes there's sour grapefruit if you don't put any salt on or something, it's pretty sour. And . . . no, no, I can't think of anything else.

I. OK. When you say "a sour lemon," what do you mean by the word *sour?*

C. Sour, something's sour. It doesn't taste so sweet.

I. What you've told me is about the word *sour*, J. Is there anything you can tell me about the word *sourer?*

C. Can I tell it in a sentence? . . . *Sourer*'s something like a lemon, and you taste it, and it's sour, and you have, sometimes you have to get a drink of water.

[*Multiple-choice question answered correctly.*]

In the next example, another first grader also began by discussing the root word *sour*. However, with probing, she attempted to illustrate the meaning of the whole word and to use it in a sentence. Although what she said was not sufficient to give her credit (she had to answer the multiple-choice question correctly first), her attempt to illustrate the meaning of *sourer* was on the right track and seemed to represent an advance over the attempt of the child in the previous example, who could articulate knowledge only of the root word *sour:*

First-Grade Child: *sourer*

I. Our next word is *sourer*. Can you tell me what the word *sourer* means?

C. Sour?

I. Sour-er. What does the word *sourer* mean?

C. Um, let me see. Something's, like something's sour. And you don't like it. Um, it's too sour.

I. OK. And what does it mean if it's sour, M.?

C. It means that, sour is too sour for you. Like if you had a, like if you had a hum, lemon.

I. Can you tell me what the word *sour-er* means?

C. [*Whispers* sour-er.] Like if something was just sour, you'd make it sourer if you wanted it sourer. . . . That's all I can think of.

I. OK. Can you try to use the word *sourer* in a sentence to show me you know what it means?

C. Like, if there was this watermelon in front of you, and you wanted it sour, you put it sour [*whispers* sourer] to make it sour. . . .

[*Multiple-choice question answered correctly.*]

In the next example, the child first illustrated what *sour* means with a good example and then received credit for expressing knowledge of *sourer* by casting it into a good illustrative sentence:

First-Grade Child: *sourer*

 I. Our next word is *sourer*. What does the word *sourer* mean?

 C. Um, a lemon's sour.

 I. Mmm.

 C. And more than um an orange.

 I. And when you say that a lemon is sour, what do you mean by the word *sour*?

 C. Well, I mean when I taste it um, you don't hardly like it. . . .

 I. Could you use the word *sourer* in a sentence to show me you know what it means?

 C. A lemon is s-, sourer than an orange. . . .

In the next examples, two first-grade children got credit for knowing *changed* and *soaking* by first discussing the root words *change* and *soak* and then by eventually using the inflected words appropriately when asked for an illustrative sentence:

First-Grade Child: *changed*

 I. What does the word *changed* mean?

 C. Like when you change clothes.

 I. Mmm.

 C. And change sports.

 I. J., if you change your clothes, what does that mean?

 C. You're putting on something different.

 I. And if you change sports, what does that mean?

 C. Like you go from one sport to another.

 I. OK . . . those things are about what the word *change* means. Can you tell me what the word *changed* means?

 C. I don't know.

 I. OK. Maybe you could use the word *changed* in a sentence to show me you know what it means?

 C. You can changed . . . nets. Like if you play in one end and change the ends . . . you change positions.

 I. Mmm. J., you are using the word *change* in your sentence. Could you try to use the word *changed* in your sentence?

 C. Yesterday, I changed numbers.

 I. You changed numbers. Very good.

First-Grade Child: *soaking*

 I. The next word is *soaking*. What does the word *soaking* mean?

 C. Um. When you throw snow in a bucket, the snow melts into slush.

 I. Is there anything else you can tell me about the word *soaking*?

 C. Um. You can soak your hands in some water to make 'em clean. . . . Um. I don't know anything else.

I. Could you use the word *soaking* in a sentence, B., to show me you know what it means?

C. Yesterday, my sister soaked her hands in the, in some water.

I. That's a sentence using the word *soaked,* B., but could you try to use the word *soaking* in a sentence?

C. Yesterday, my sister was soaking her hands in some water.

Like the first-grade children, when the older children seemed to use morphological knowledge to construct the meaning of an inflected word, they usually began by focusing on its corresponding root word. However, they were frequently able to express their knowledge of the inflected word without having to resort to the multiple-choice question. Like some younger children, they often did so by using it appropriately in a sentence. In the first two examples presented below, final credit for knowledge of the inflected words *soaking* and *changed* was given after the child responded to a request for a sentence. In the third example, credit for knowledge of the inflected word *sourer* was given during the definition phase, when the child illustrated its comparative meaning rather well:

Fifth-Grade Child: soaking

I. What does the word *soaking* mean?

C. If you put a pot with something hard in it, and you let it soak for a while, you put it in water, and it makes the food or whatever is in it soft.

I. Can you tell me anything more about the word *soaking?*

C. Some people soak in the bath.

I. OK. Could you use the word *soaking* in a sentence to show me you know what it means?

C. The pots and pans were soaking in the sink.

Fifth-Grade Child: changed

I. What does the word *changed* mean?

C. If you like jelly beans when you're little, and then when you're older, you hate jelly beans, you change.

I. OK, what do you mean by the word *change* there?

C. That it's different.

I. Can you tell me any other meaning for the word *changed?*

C. You can change money from paper into coins.

I. What else could you tell me about the word *changed?*

C. That's all.

I. OK. Could you use the word *changed* in a sentence to show me you know what it means, K.?

C. The man changed his two-dollar bill into eight quarters.

Fifth-Grade Child: *sourer*

    I. The next word is *sourer.* What does the word *sourer* mean?

    C. Like you eat something and it tastes really like, not sweet . . . like you can hardly keep it in your mouth. It's like a lemon. A lemon tastes like that. And gum . . . and then there's other gums and they taste really sour . . . sourer.

    I. OK. Can you tell me anything more about the word *sourer?*

    C. Say you have something . . . say you have a lemon and it's sour and you have something . . . a plum . . . and it's sourer than the lemon. So it's really worse than the lemon. It's really bad to eat.

Although the PS responses for inflected words usually manifested a "part to whole" pattern at all age levels—children most often discussed the root word by itself and then got credit for knowledge of the whole word—there were a few cases exemplifying a "parts to whole" pattern in which the child explicitly discussed both the root word and the inflectional suffix in achieving credit for knowledge of the word. All cases that manifested a "parts to whole" pattern in the randomly selected transcripts occurred only in discussions with the fifth-grade children. The examples below come from two fifth-grade children who, when discussing the inflected word *changed,* first considered the root word *change* and then explicitly mentioned the past inflection and indicated that they knew the semantic effect that it has on the root word:

Fifth-Grade Child: *changed*

    I. What does the word *changed* mean?

    C. Like if . . . maybe if you're wearing something, like you can change it, like you can change your clothes, like that's one meaning, like you can do that, and also for *change* you can mean a change of weather or something like that too, like something is like it is then, and then it changes, like it goes different, like all of a sudden.

    I. OK. Can you tell me anything more about the word *changed?*

    C. Well, sometimes it has an *-e-d* on it, and that would mean that you already did change.

Fifth-Grade Child: *changed*

    I. What does the word *changed* mean?

    C. If you fell in the mud, you'd go changed your clothes . . . change them. Or something like if you changed the rules of a game or you change your name . . . like it's different—you can only change something that's different.

    I. OK. That's *change.* Now the word *changed.* What's different about the word *changed,* D.?

    C. No *-d* on change. Just like if you fell in the mud, you could get changed.

Few instances of a seemingly explicit use of analogy for inflected words were noted, and those possible cases that were observed involved the 10-year-olds. In the following example, it seems possible that this fifth-grade child was attempting to work out the meaning of *dishing* by analogy to the similarly inflected word *fishing*. Both the semantic relatedness of the two words and the fact that *fishing* rhymes with *dishing* may have contributed to his choice of the former in trying to interpret the latter:

Fifth-Grade Child: dishing
> *I.* What does the word *dishing* mean?
> *C.* A man was dishing the dish to north so he could get the channel.
> *I.* Mmm.
> *C.* On his TV, he was dishing it around.
> *I.* Mmm.
> *C.* Um, I was thinking of *fishing*. Like he is fishing it out. Um, dishing. He dished the applesauce and ice cream out of his bowl and put it in his mouth. He dished it out. . . .
> *I.* Do you think you could give me a sentence using the word *dishing* to show me you know what it means?
> *C.* The boy was dishing his ice cream and applesauce out of the small bowl to give to his baby sister . . . to feed it to his baby sister. . . .
> [*Multiple-choice question answered correctly.*]

Derived Words

As was the case with inflected words, the most common approach to derived words that showed evidence of morphological problem solving and that was used by children of all ages was to begin by discussing the corresponding root word. If not attained through a correct response to the multiple-choice question, final credit for derived words was also often achieved through appropriate use in an illustrative sentence, although some of the older children, in particular, were occasionally able to provide general definitions. Derivational affixes were rarely explicitly discussed by themselves except in a few instances by some fifth-grade children, so most responses to derived words manifested a "part to whole" pattern. Although in responding to some multimorphemic derived words some of the older children began by discussing a derived word embedded in the whole word (e.g., *hopeless* for *hopelessness* or *admission* or *readmission*) rather than the corresponding root words (e.g., *hope* or *admit*), these responses also exemplified a "part to whole" pattern because just one component (in this case, the embedded derived word) was usually discussed by itself before credit was given for knowledge of the whole word.

In the first two examples, it can be seen that these first graders mainly discussed the root words *still* and *separate,* although they did eventually get credit for knowing the derived words by answering the multiple-choice questions correctly:

First-Grade Child: *stillness*

I. The next word is *stillness.* What does the word *stillness* mean?

C. Like you were walking around and, like you, like you went like this [*the child gets up, walks around, and then stops when she says "like this"*]. That would be still.

I. OK. What does it mean if you're still?

C. It means that maybe you have, like maybe your back hurts or something. . . .

I. Is there anything else you can tell me about the word *stillness?*

C. Like, if you're running, like if you were running, you'd stand still.

I. OK, and if you'd stand still, M., what does that mean if you're standing still?

C. It means that you're not doing anything.

I. Could you use the word *stillness* in a sentence to show me you know what it means?

C. If your back hurts and you're, you're just walking and your back starts to hurt, then you, you just stand still.

[*Multiple-choice question answered correctly.*]

First-Grade Child: *separately*

I. Can you tell me what the word *separately* means?

C. Yup.

I. OK.

C. *Separately* means when your mother and father are separate.

I. Mmm.

C. *Separate* means when your sisters and you kept on fighting and you're separate. Like one's right here. They live here. And then out west, live your other sister.

I. OK. Can you tell me anything else about the word *separately?*

C. No, but I'll do it in a sentence.

I. OK.

C. There once . . . there once was a brother and a sister, and they were always fighting. So one moved. One moved where they lived [*giggles*]. And one moved out west, west, west. That's all.

[*Multiple-choice question answered correctly.*]

In the next example, after illustrating the meaning of *separates* and *separate,* a first-grade child was finally able to get credit for the derived word *separately* by using it appropriately following the request for a sentence:

First-Grade Child: *separately*

I. The next word is *separately*. What does the word *separately* mean?

C. It's like . . . when you're doing math and counting up money and someone's trying to copy you, the teacher separates you like um. . . . For instance the person that was copying you goes to the amusement center and . . . the other one stays here. It just depends who is the bad one and who is the good one.

I. Mmm. Is there anything more you could tell me about what the word *separately* means?

C. It's like when you have a divorce, you don't see each other and sometimes you . . . I mean you don't live together and you live downstairs with the child. You're separate.

I. OK. Do you think you could use the word *separately* in a sentence to show me you know what it means?

C. My mom lives separately now.

In the following example, after discussing and defining the root word *muck*, a first-grade child eventually received credit for *mucky* by using it appropriately in several sentences. These sentences were produced, not in response to a request for one, but during the definition phase of the procedure in response to the question, "Is there anything you can tell me about the word *mucky?*"

First-Grade Child: *mucky*

I. The next word is *mucky*.

C. Muck!

I. What does the word *mucky* mean?

C. Some people go in and the cows go in muck.

I. What is *muck*, N.?

C. It's sand with lots of water in it.

I. Is there anything you can tell me about the word *mucky?*

C. Mucky. Sometimes children get mucky. I got mucky one time. . . . My pants were all mucky. My boots were mucky, too.

In the next example, another first-grade child was also able to get credit for the derived word *mucky* in the definition phase of the procedure, although she did so by referring to the root word *muck*, which is why it was coded as showing evidence of morphological problem solving. Interestingly, and atypically for first-grade children, after using an appropriate illustrative sentence for *mucky*, the child was, with probing, eventually able to define it as "muddy":

First-Grade Child: *mucky*

I. What does the word *mucky* mean?

C. Mucky means when you walk in the muck and you slip and you get all mucky.

I. OK, L., and when you said "you walk in the muck," what did you mean by the word *muck?*
C. Well, you're walking in the mud.
I. And when you said you slip in it and get all mucky, what did you mean by the word *mucky?*
C. Muddy.
I. And what do you mean by *muddy?*
C. It means you're getting all filthy dirty.

In the next example, in discussing *separately,* a third-grade child first mentioned and defined the root word *separate* but then was able to get credit by using *separately* correctly in a sentence during the definition phase of the procedure in response to a request to tell more about the word *separately:*

Third-Grade Child: *separately*
I. The next word is *separately.* What does the word *separately* mean?
C. If . . . I was standing beside . . . one friend and he walked away, then you'd be separate, and *separately* means not together, that you're apart.
I. That's about the word *separate;* now can you tell me more about the word *separately?*
C. Those two people grew up separately.

The next two examples, both taken from grade 5 children, illustrate responses to the word *priesthood.* Both children began by describing *priest* but eventually received credit for *priesthood.* The first used the word reasonably appropriately in a sentence. The second also used it reasonably appropriately as well as attempting to define it in a more general way:

Fifth-Grade Child: *priesthood*
I. What does the word *priesthood* mean?
C. It's where somebody is a priest, a very religious person.
I. OK. Can you tell me anything more about the word *priesthood?*
C. No.
I. And when you say that someone is a priest, what do you mean by the word *priest?*
C. It's a person that dresses in black or brown, and they're very religious.
I. OK. Could you use the word *priesthood* in a sentence to show me you know what it means?
C. Priesthood, to some people, is a very important step in their life.

Fifth-Grade Child: *priesthood*
I. What does the word *priesthood* mean?
C. It could mean like . . . a priest is a special person that could

work at a vicarage, like those are houses, they're like a little building, and *priesthood* might mean that you are a priest and that you're like working, like being in priesthood to be a priest. . . .

I. Do you think you'd be able to use it in a sentence to show me you know what it means?

C. Maybe it's like I'm in the priesthood part of my life.

I. When you say, "I'm in the priesthood part of my life," what do you mean by *priesthood* there?

C. That you are a priest, that you might be in a stage of being a priest.

[*Multiple-choice question answered correctly.*]

The next two examples, also illustrating a "part to whole" pattern, are cases in which two fifth-grade children responded to the multimorphemic derived words *unbribable* and *magnetization* by first discussing the corresponding root words *bribe* and *magnet*. The first child ultimately received credit for *unbribable* by illustrating its meaning and using it appropriately in sentences. The second appeared to attempt a general definition, then used a somewhat appropriate sentence, and finally confirmed his understanding of the word *magnetization* by answering the multiple-choice question correctly:

Fifth-Grade Child: unbribable

I. The next word is *unbribable*. What does the word *unbribable* mean?

C. Um . . . people try to bribe you, and sometimes like they try to . . . say somebody had like $2,500.00 maybe and someone . . . say their friend who never cared for them or something . . . they would give you flowers and chocolates and they would say, "I want to be your friend," and all that, but they're just trying to bribe you. But *unbribable*, they won't do it, they just, you won't fall for it anymore. Like you won't get bribed; you'll be unbribable. You'll say no.

I. OK. Can you tell me anything more about the word *unbribable*?

C. Like I'm probably unbribable because I don't let anybody bribe me or anything to take my toys and money or something away. So like I wouldn't let them do it to me. I'd just say like, "I can't. I'm unbribable."

Fifth-Grade Child: magnetization

I. What does the word *magnetization* mean?

C. It's where you have a magnet . . . a little thing that sticks to metal and it's when a whole bunch of that sticks to metal.

I. Can you tell me anything more about the word *magnetization*?

C. Mmm . . . no.

I. Could you use it in a sentence to show me you know what it means?

C. Because of the magnetization with my suit and my refrigerator, I could not go to my appointment at my doctor's.
[*Multiple-choice question answered correctly.*]

There were instances in which children would begin by attempting to discuss the entire derived word, often using an illustrative sentence, but would then discuss the corresponding root word before achieving full credit. Such cases might be viewed as exemplifying a "whole to part" pattern, a variation on the more typical "part to whole" pattern illustrated by the preceding responses. In the example given below, after saying that he had never heard of *unbribable* before, a fifth-grade child proceeded to use it in a sentence. Subsequently, he received credit for knowing it after using and eventually defining the root word *bribe*:

Fifth-Grade Child: *unbribable*
I. What does the word *unbribable* mean?
C. Never heard of that word. . . .
I. OK. Do you think you might be able to use it in a sentence to show me you know what it means?
C. The boy was unbribable.
I. OK. When you say "the boy was unbribable," what do you mean by the word *unbribable?*
C. That you can't bribe him with anything.
I. And when you say you can't bribe him with anything, what does it mean to bribe?
C. Um . . . sort of like talking him into something by using things.
I. OK. Can you give me an example?
C. Um . . . I might talk you into giving me a phone number by giving you a piece of gum.

As noted above, when discussing derived words with more than one affix, some of the older children would sometimes begin by discussing a derived word embedded within the multimorphemic word and then eventually get credit for the entire word. Such cases reveal a "part to whole" pattern, but the part in this case is a derived word rather than a root word, as in the more typical pattern. In the examples presented below, two fifth-grade children began discussing the multimorphemic words *hopelessness* and *readmission* in terms of the embedded derived words *hopeless* and *admission*. Their responses suggest that the embedded, singly derived words may have been "psychologically basic" for them but that the multimorphemic words on which they were being tested were figured out through morphological analysis and composition. The first child finally received credit for *hopelessness* when she used it appropriately in a sentence. After the second child illustrated the meaning of *admission*, she attempted to illustrate the meaning of *readmission* and to use it in a sentence before confirming her knowledge by answering the multiple-choice question correctly:

Fifth-Grade Child: hopelessness

I. What does the word *hopelessness* mean?

C. *Hopeless,* OK, *hopelessness. Hope-less-ness....* They're hopelessness. Well, *hopeless,* I know what that means.

I. Mmm.

C. If you're hopeless, you're um, like the girl was hopeless at playing the piano.

I. Mmm.

C. *Hopelessness. Hopelessness.* And I've heard the word *hopeless,* but I've never heard the word *hopelessness.*

I. OK. Well, can you tell me what the word *hopeless* means?

C. *Hopeless,* like, it's, you're hopeless at something, you're, you could never do it, like if you want to try and learn to play something like you're hopeless at playing at it, you can't but it's too bad but you can't. You're hopeless, you can't do that . . . [*continues to describe* hopeless *and give examples of being* hopeless.]

I. Is there anything else you could tell me about the word *hopelessness?*

C. The boy thought that it was hopeless, so he just told everybody that it was just plain ordinary hopelessness.

Fifth-Grade Child: readmission

I. What does the word *readmission* mean?

C. Like it could mean something like if you were to go to a movie and you pay your admission and that means you pay to get in or something, maybe like you might have to . . . like if you want . . . like say the movie's too scary and you leave, then you might have to pay again, like it may mean again like over again.

I. Can you tell me anything more about what the word *readmission* means?

C. No.

I. Can you use the word *readmission* in a sentence to show me you know what it means?

C. I had to pay readmission because the movie was too scary.

[*Multiple-choice question answered correctly.*]

In the following example, a fifth-grade child attempted to define the multimorphemic word *magnetization* in terms of the embedded derived word *magnetize,* which he then, in turn, defined in terms of the root word *magnet:*

Fifth-Grade Child: magnetization

I. What does the word *magnetization* mean?

C. It means like you magnetize something and it works or something like that.

I. What do you mean by the word *magnetize,* J.?

C. Like um, like you have a magnet. And then, then you put copper wire around something else and you like magnetize it, like um like it's a magnet, it turns into a magnet too, like a steel thing. And then you could pick up nails or something, beer caps.

I. OK. Can you tell me what you mean by the word *magnet,* J.?

C. Well, it's something that picks up steel things like nails, stuff like that. And that's about all.

I. Is there anything else you can tell me about the word *magnetization?*

C. No.

I. No. Do you think you may be able to use the word *magnetization* in a sentence?

C. No.

[*Multiple-choice question answered correctly.*]

One could view the preceding example as illustrating a "parts to whole" pattern because the child discussed both *magnet* and *magnetize* in working out the meaning of *magnetization.* However, it is not a case of treating a derivational affix explicitly by itself. Such cases were infrequent and, in the randomly selected transcripts that were studied in detail, occurred only in discussions with the oldest group of children. In the following four examples, the responses illustrate a "parts to whole" pattern because the child discussed explicitly either a root word or an embedded derived word *and* a derivational affix en route to getting credit for knowing the whole derived word. In the first example, the child discussed the derivational prefix *semi-* after discussing the root word *liquid* in constructing the meaning of *semiliquid.* In the second example, the child mentioned the derivational suffix *-let* before correctly guessing the meaning of the word *treelet.* In the third example, the child discussed the prefix *in-* and the root word *earth* in figuring out the meaning of *inearth.* Although this child construed this word as a literal compound, *Webster's Third* treats it as a derived word consisting of the prefix *in-* and the root word *earth* with the archaic meaning of "bury" or "inter." In the fourth example, the child explicitly discussed the suffix *-less* after discussing the embedded derived word *foundation* in working out the meaning of *foundationless:*

Fifth-Grade Child: *semiliquid*

I. What does the word *semiliquid* mean?

C. It could mean like a different . . . like *liquid* is a wet substance like, but *semi-* could mean half, like half liquid or something. Like something could be half liquid, half solid, like maybe ice cream . . . on top of pop or something.

I. Can you use the word *semiliquid* in a sentence to show me you know what it means?

C. The dessert was semiliquid.
[*Multiple-choice question answered correctly.*]

Fifth-Grade Child: *treelet*
I. What does the word *treelet* mean, J.?
C. *Treelet?*
I. Yeah, *treelet.*
C. Like is it *t-r-e-e?*
I. Mmm, *l-e-t.*
C. OK. Maybe it means like a tree and maybe like for Christmas you can put lights on it. . . .
I. Can you tell me anything more about the word *treelet?*
C. Is it *-let* or *-lit?*
I. Actually, it's *-let*, J., *treelet.*
C. I'm not sure about this, but it might mean a baby tree. . . .

Fifth-Grade Child: *inearth*
I. What does the word *inearth* mean?
C. *Inearth?*
I. Mmm.
C. It means like you're going in, and *earth* is what we're on right now. . . . It's inside the earth. Like if you dig a big, big hole and you put a piece of metal in the hole and then you bury it back up. . . . I was going to say no, that I don't know, but then when you think, think, you can just split the word out, because most words are just two words put together.
[*Multiple-choice question answered correctly.*]

Fifth-Grade Child: *foundationless*
I. The next word is *foundationless.* What does the word *foundationless* mean?
C. I know what a foundation is. Like when you build a house you have a foundation, but if you don't have it, you're foundationless because you don't have it. Most houses have a foundation because they have to start it in the ground and they gradually build up. But if you don't have one, you just kind of like have some smooth ground and start the house by there.
I. Can you tell me anything more about the word *foundationless?*
C. Like maybe just a foundation is all the dirt and like the bottom kind of. If you didn't have dirt in the foundation, it would be like . . . it's *-less* . . . it's not there anymore. Like it never was probably, it's just foundationless.

Clear cases of the explicit use of analogy to words of similar morphological form, like the explicit discussion of affixes, were found to be infrequent in dealing with derived words and tended to occur mainly in the interviews with the fifth-grade children. It had been noted that a few fifth-grade children appeared to work out the meaning of *treelet* by analogy to *piglet,* as in the example cited previously. In the first example presented below, another fifth-grade child eventually received credit for *treelet,* apparently through analogy to the word *riverlet.* In the second example, a fifth-grade child eventually received credit for the word *priesthood* in the multiple-choice phase of the procedure, after apparently trying to figure out its meaning by analogy to *childhood:*

Fifth-Grade Child: treelet

I. The next word is *treelet.* What does the word *treelet* mean?

C. I don't know, but I'll guess.

I. OK.

C. Treelet. Well, I know what a riverlet is.

I. Mmm.

C. That's a river.

I. Mmm.

C. But off of it will come a little, little creek or a riverlet. Um a treelet, um, that could be, there was the tree. . . .

I. Mmm.

C. . . . And a little branch sprouted out. A treelet, ya, just a big tree and then another, a branch was forming a treelet.

I. Is there anything else you could tell me about the word *treelet?*

C. Um . . . a treelet would probably be very small . . . and about as skinny as a small straw . . . and little buds would start to spread out . . . and the little treelet would get bigger and bigger and then it wouldn't be a treelet anymore.

[*Multiple-choice question answered correctly.*]

Fifth-Grade Child: priesthood

I. What does the word *priesthood* mean?

C. Priest, I know what a priest is.

I. Mmm.

C. It's like a pastor or somebody like that. And *-hood,* a childhood.

I. Mmm.

C. Maybe when you grow up you have a good childhood. Oh. *Priesthood.* Um. Like you might grow up when you're a child with a priest, and you'll have a good prie-, priesthood. And you'll know lots of stuff from the Bible and everything. Like you'll know verses and chapters, and you'll know all the days, and you'll go to church, and stuff like that.

I. OK. I'm not sure I understand what you're saying. Are you saying like if you're a child and you grow up with a priest, that's priesthood?

C. [*Nods yes.*]

I. OK. Is there anything else you could tell me about the word *priesthood?*

C. No. I just guessed that one 'cause I've never heard it before.

I. Could you use the word *priesthood* in a sentence to show me you know what it means?

C. No.

I. OK.

[*Multiple-choice question answered correctly.*]

Literal Compounds

Across all grades, the majority of children's PS responses to literal compounds (about two-thirds of the instances in the randomly selected transcripts) exemplified a "parts to whole" pattern because the child most often explicitly defined or discussed separately two (or more) of the words making up a literal compound en route to achieving credit for knowledge of the entire compound. Often, credit for literal compounds was finally achieved when the children, especially the older ones, defined them in a general way by putting together the meanings of the constituent words in a reasonable fashion. This is in contrast to inflected and derived words for which children more often ultimately achieved credit by using them in illustrative sentences.

A developmental trend—suggested by reading all the transcripts and confirmed by the detailed examination of the randomly selected transcripts—was an increase with age and grade in the tendency explicitly to define or discuss more than one of the words making up a literal compound. With respect to the randomly selected transcripts, slightly less than half the first-grade responses for literal compounds manifested a "parts to whole" pattern, whereas a clear majority of the responses of the third- and fifth-grade children did so. The PS responses of the children in the first grade were almost equally likely to reveal a "part to whole" pattern, with just one component word being discussed explicitly and separately before credit for knowledge of the whole compound was given. For example, consider the following discussion with a first-grade child about the literal compound *low-level.* This 6-year-old girl used the word *low* separately and implied some knowledge of it, but she did not use the word *level* separately. When she did mention the entire literal compound *low-level,* she seemed to be thinking of it as synonymous with *low.* However, she did eventually get credit for *low-level* by responding correctly to the multiple-choice question:

First-Grade Child: *low-level*

I. What does the word *low-level* mean?

C. Like when you're building with some building bricks and you . . . build them so low.

I. And what do you mean when you say *low?*

C. Um, I mean they're very, very low. . . .

I. Can you tell me anything else about the word *low-level,* L.?

C. Yup. Some things are l- . . . , in low levels.

I. And what does that mean if they are in low levels?

C. They're very, very small.

I. OK. Could you use the word *low-level* in a sentence to show me you know what it means?

C. Yup. There once was a baby. She was always very low. She would never, ever grow . . . even if she was a mother. She would never, ever grow. She was always very low.

I. OK, L. That was a good sentence using the word *low,* but could you try to use the word *low-level* in a sentence?

C. OK. There once was a little baby. She was so low-level. When she was a mommy she was still so low-level. [*Laughs.*] . . .

[*Multiple-choice question answered correctly.*]

Another example of explicitly discussing only one component word by itself in a literal compound occurred in a conversation with a 6-year-old girl about the word *western saddle,* in which she explicitly described and defined only *saddle.* However, she did eventually get credit for *western saddle* by answering the multiple-choice question correctly:

First-Grade Child: western saddle

I. The word is *western saddle.* Can you tell me what the word *western saddle* means?

C. Like if you didn't have a saddle on a horse.

I. Mmm.

C. You'd put one on and then you could ride on your horse.

I. Can you tell me a little more about the word *saddle?*

C. Like it's a thing that you sit on. And it goes around your horse's tummy. And then, and you put a blanket under it, so the horse doesn't get hurt on its back. . . .

I. Could you use the word *western saddle* in a sentence to show me you know what it means? . . .

C. Hum. You ride on a horse with a saddle. You put the saddle on your horse, then you get on the horse and then you ride. . . . [*The child discusses only* saddle *even though the interviewer requests using* western saddle *in a sentence a number of times.*]

[*Multiple-choice question answered correctly.*]

In the next example, a first-grade child explicitly mentioned both component words in the literal compound *western saddle* separately. *Saddle* was mentioned by itself and eventually defined. *Western* was also mentioned by itself, and, although it was not defined, the child eventually referred to a cowboy's western saddle in her sentence, which also represents an advance over the description of *western saddle* by the first-grade child presented above:[25]

First-Grade Child: western saddle

I. The next word is *western saddle.* What does the word *western saddle* mean?

C. Like you have some horses. And you put some saddles on them.

I. OK.

C. Or when you're in western. And you might—like you know those ways that you put horses at the end. And you put saddles on them. That's another word what it means. . . . A saddle is one of those things you put on a horse's back so you can stay on it.

I. Can you tell me more about the word *western saddle?*

C. I don't know any more.

I. OK. Do you think you could use the word *western saddle* in a sentence to show me you know what it means?

C. Mmm. There once was a horse. And he, um, his, his ah, I'll just say his cowboy, his cowboy never ever bought a saddle for him. One day the cowboy went on his horse without his western saddle, and he kept on falling off! Then one day the cowboy got a saddle. He put it on the horse so he can go for a ride. He went on the horse and had a ride, and he never fell off again.

The next two examples are cases in which first-grade children discussed both component words making up the literal compounds *western saddle* and *milk cow* separately before getting credit for knowing them. They also show that even 6-year-olds can sometimes generate somewhat general definitions of these literal compounds, something they rarely do for inflected or derived words:

First-Grade Child: western saddle

I. What does the word *western saddle* mean?

C. Western saddle means it's western, and that means kind of like cowboy, and they put the saddle on a horse.

I. And when you say they put a saddle on a horse, what do you mean by the word *saddle?*

C. A saddle is something that can be leather, and it's like a mat that you put on a horse except it has these things at the bottom to put your feet on them.

I. Can you tell me more about the word *western saddle?*

---

[25] In our original coding of responses for this word, we had decided that expression of the knowledge that cowboys use saddles was adequate to receive credit for *western saddle,* provided, of course, that the child also indicated that she knew what a saddle was.

C. Western saddle means something like the saddle you put on a horse but only western people use it.

First-Grade Child: *milk cow*

I. What does the word *milk cow* mean?

C. Well, some farmers milk the cows. And then they make chocolate milk, or just normal milk, you drink. . . . Some cows have spots. Some are brown. Some are white. Some are black.

I. Can you tell me anything else about the word *milk cow*?

C. Well, they give you chocolate milk.

I. Mmm.

C. They give you normal milk.

The older children usually defined, described, or discussed each component word in a literal compound separately en route to getting credit for knowing it. Often, they would seem to retrieve the meaning of each component word separately and then construct the meaning of the literal compound by putting the meanings together in what seemed to them to be a reasonable fashion, as the following five examples taken from fifth-grade children illustrate. Notice also that, in most of the examples, these children were able to generate general definitions of the literal compounds (e.g., "It's a flower that's very, very red like a cardinal" for *cardinal flower;* "Well, I guess a maned sheep is a sheep with a mane" for *maned sheep*), something they did only occasionally for inflected and derived words:

Fifth-Grade Child: *cardinal flower*

I. How about the word *cardinal flower?* What does the word *cardinal flower* mean?

C. *Cardinal flower?*

I. Mmm.

C. Well, I know what a cardinal is; it's a bird. And a car- . . . a flower is a flower that grows, a pretty flower. So my guess is, *cardinal flower* um. . . . It's a flower that's very, very red like a cardinal. A cardinal flower, ya.

I. OK.

C. It's a type of flower.

Fifth-Grade Child: *maned sheep*

I. The next word is *maned sheep.*

C. *Maned.*

I. Hmm.

C. *Sheep.* A mane is a thing on a horse. I guess it can be on a sheep too. And then a sheep where we get wool from. It's a real fuzzy fat animal with little legs.

I. Mmm.

C. So a maned sheep. Well, I guess a maned sheep is a sheep with a mane.

I. Hmm.

C. And if, if you know what a mane is, like a mane on a horse. Like their head comes up and then just along their neck and the back of their head, like it's real hair, like hair, and it usually comes down to around here [*the child points to his throat*].

I. OK. Do you think you'd be able to use the word *maned sheep* in a sentence to show me you know what it means?

C. There was a flock of sheep, but there was only one sheep that was maned.

I. OK.

C. That had a mane.

I. OK, R. Now try to keep the words *maned sheep* together in your sentence.

C. OK. The mane, the maned sheep was the last one to get buzzed.

Fifth-Grade Child: live-born

I. What does the word *live-born* mean?

C. Well, *live* means that it's living and it breathes. And it's born . . . it's a tiny little baby and it's brought into the world. . . .

I. Could you use the word *live-born* in a sentence?

C. Some animals have their babies *live-born,* but others have them in eggs first.

Fifth-Grade Child: western saddle

I. What does the word *western saddle* mean?

C. OK, a saddle is something that you put on a horse or a bull or something. And you use that to help you to ride a horse or whatever you're riding on. And *western* is like a direction.

I. OK. What else can you tell me about the word *western saddle?*

C. Sometimes it tells you whereabouts the thing maybe came . . . like western Canada or something.

I. OK. And when you say "western Canada," could you tell me something about what kind of a saddle it would be?

C. Well, a western saddle is mainly made out of leather.

I. And how can you tell whether it's a western saddle or not?

C. Sometimes two saddles look alike, but most of the time there's like a seal or a stamp on it to tell you. And sometimes it's the style.

I. OK. And what does the word *western* mean?

C. Something from up west.

I. And when you say "up west," can you tell me something about that place? What is it known for? How do you know you're up west?

C. Well, if you have a compass, you have west on the compass.

I. Is there anything you would see up west that you wouldn't see in other places?

C. Cowboys and cowboy hats.

Fifth-Grade Child: *Japanese crab*

 I. What does the word *Japanese crab* mean?

 C. It might mean like a little creature like a crab, and it might come from Japan. I'm not sure; I never heard of it before.

 I. OK. When you say it might mean a crab, what do you mean by the word *crab?*

 C. It's like a little animal and like I'm not sure how they say it, little things, like they have claws and all that, and they live in water and out of water, and they're really small, some of them are.

 I. OK. When you say they might come from Japan, what do you mean by *Japan?*

 C. Well, maybe there's certain kinds of crabs, and from a certain place there may be like a different type of crab, and so they come from Japan.

 I. OK. And when you say they come from Japan, what does the word *Japan* mean?

 C. That's like a place that like it's kind of different from ours but it's in the world and it has different stuff from us, like it has different crabs, like it's a place where you live. . . .

 [*Multiple-choice question answered correctly.*]

There were also some cases in which a child would begin by trying to define the whole literal compound, often in a general way, and often by reordering its component words in some reasonable fashion. Then, he or she would define or describe the component words. Three examples of this variation, all from interviews with fifth-grade children, are presented below:

Fifth-Grade Child: *milk cow*

 I. What does the word *milk cow* mean?

 C. Is it like um, like you were milking a cow or something?

 I. Aaah. . . .

 C. Ah, oh! A cow that gives milk.

 I. And when you say "a cow," what do you mean by the word *cow?*

 C. Um *cow* is um like a whole bunch of cows are cattle. . . . It has four legs, and a small tail, and m- most, um, cows are milk cows, and they're brown and white.

 I. And when you said that it's a cow that gives milk, what did you mean by the word *milk?*

 C. Like um, some, like, it's white and um, you can drink it with your cereal and that.

Fifth-Grade Child: *cardinal flower*

 I. What does the word *cardinal flower* mean?

 C. Well it might mean . . . I'm kind of guessing but I think . . . it might mean like a type of a flower, maybe it's red because cardinals are red.

I. Mmm.

C. I'm not sure, but I'm just saying it might be a flower that's red.

I. OK. When you say it's a flower that's red, what do you mean by the word *flower?*

C. That's like a plant that grows, and it could be in different colors. I'm just saying it's red.

I. OK. Do you think you can use the word *cardinal flower* in a sentence to show me you know what it means?

C. I picked a cardinal flower for my Mom.

[*Multiple-choice question answered correctly.*]

Fifth-Grade Child: maned sheep

I. What does the word *maned sheep* mean?

C. Um. *Maned sheep* means, a, I'll give it a try, um . . . a sheep with a mane.

I. Can you tell me what you mean by the word *mane?*

C. Like fuzzy part around your head or something.

I. OK. And can you tell me what you mean by the word *sheep?*

C. Um, like an animal, that has wool. It's probably wild.

There were few cases of children seeming to work out the meaning of morphologically complex words by explicit analogy to words of similar morphological form, especially in the case of literal compounds. The only possible instances noted for literal compounds in the randomly selected transcripts were for the word *low-level,* for which a few children earned credit by contrasting it with *high-level.* Although the few relatively clear cases of the explicit use of analogy for other types of complex words (derived and inflected words) tended to occur only in the interviews with the fifth-grade children, even a few of the younger children mentioned *high-level* in discussing *low-level.* For example, one 6-year-old boy said, "*Low-level* means in an apartment there's high levels and low," en route to getting credit eventually. A few of the fifth-grade children expressed their knowledge of *low-level* by quite explicitly contrasting it with *high-level,* as the following excerpt illustrates:

Fifth-Grade Child: low-level

I. The next word is *low-level.* Can you tell me what the word *low-level* means?

C. OK. My father was scared when we went up the CN Tower, so he stayed on the low, what was it? *Lower level?*

I. Just *low-level.* . . .

C. Um, um *high-level,* it's above the ground.

I. Mmm.

C. Or wherever you are, on the moon, whatever.

I. [*Laughs.*]

C. It's the highest part.

I. Mmm.

C. And then the low-level is the low part.

I. Mmm.

C. Like in an airport.

I. Mmmm.

C. You could be up on the top, on . . . the high-level, and you could be boarding the plane on the ground, on the low-level. . . .

I. Can you tell me where the low-level is?

C. Um, it's at the bottom . . . on the ground or pretty near the ground . . . you're low, low as the ground, and the high-level is up top. Like not near the low-level. . . .

Apart from such possible cases involving the word *low-level,* explicit use of analogy for literal compounds was rare.

Treating Idioms as Literal Compounds

It is of interest to note that children often appeared to attempt to construct the meanings of idioms through morphological problem solving in ways that were similar to the ways in which they treated literal compounds. In doing so, they typically came up with reasonable ideas of what the idioms might mean but usually failed to receive credit in such cases because *Webster's Third* defines them in terms of their idiomatic meanings only. The first three examples of treating idioms like literal compounds are taken from conversations with third-grade children. In the first example, a child came up with the hypothesis that *moneybags* are bags to fill with money. Although this is a reasonable hypothesis, credit was not given because *Webster's Third* defines the word as "a person having or believed to have considerable wealth." In the second example, the child reasoned that *twenty questions* means a score of queries. Again, this is a perfectly sensible response, but credit could not be given since *Webster's* defines *twenty questions* only as "a game in which one player or team tries to determine from yes and no answers to not more than 20 questions what word or object the others have chosen to be guessed." In the third example, the child reckoned that *strange woman* meant an unfamiliar female adult, which again is reasonable enough but could not be credited because *Webster's* defines this term of biblical origin as "a female prostitute":

Third-Grade Child: *moneybags*

I. What does the word *moneybags* mean?

C. Well, it means that money goes in the bags, and they have like

dollar signs on them, and usually people bring moneybags to rob banks and stuff. . . . And they keep moneybags full of money in safes. . . .
[*Multiple-choice question answered incorrectly.*]

Third-Grade Child: twenty questions
I. What does the word *twenty questions* mean?
C. *Twenty questions* means if someone's to ask you something um twenty . . . something different twenty times.
I. Can you tell me anything more about the word *twenty questions*?
C. Yes. I'm having more than twenty questions. . . .
[*Multiple-choice question answered incorrectly.*]

Third-Grade Child: strange woman
I. What does the word *strange woman* mean?
C. If I were to walk down a street, and I saw someone that I don't know, that would be a strange woman. . . . It's someone that you don't know and it's a woman . . . not a man. . . .
[*Multiple-choice question answered incorrectly.*]

The next five examples are taken from interviews with fifth-grade children for whom the tendency to treat idioms as literal compounds was quite common. In the first two examples, two 10-year-olds attempted to define *twenty questions* and *strange woman* in a fashion similar to the third graders' attempts presented above. In the third example, the child defined *dust bowl* as a bowl to put dust into; credit could not be given because *Webster's Third* defines the word as "a region that suffers from prolonged droughts and dust storms." In the fourth example, the child defined *eleventh hour* (defined by *Webster's* as "the latest possible time") as eleven o'clock. In the fifth, the child defined *softheaded* literally as meaning having a soft head, whereas *Webster's* defines it in terms of the idiomatic meaning "having a weak, unrealistic or uncritical mind":

Fifth-Grade Child: twenty questions
I. The next word is *twenty questions*. What does the word *twenty questions* mean?
C. Um, like, like there's a whole bunch of questions, and you number them, and there's twenty of them.
I. Mmm.
C. You, ah, answer them.
I. OK. That is one meaning for the word *twenty questions,* J. Do you think you'd be able to think of another meaning for *twenty questions*?
C. No.
I. No? Do you think you might be able to use the word *twenty questions* in a sentence to show me you know what it means?
C. Ya.

I. OK.

C. The boy had twenty questions.

Fifth-Grade Child: *strange woman*

I. What does the word *strange woman* mean?

C. It's somebody you don't know, and it's the opposite of a man. It's a lady, and you don't know her, so she's a stranger to you.

I. OK. Can you tell me any other meanings for the word *strange woman?*

C. That she's maybe different.

I. OK. Could you use the word *strange woman* in a sentence to show me you know what it means?

C. The strange woman walked down the street pretending to carry her imaginary dog.

Fifth-Grade Child: *dust bowl*

I. The next word is *dust bowl.* What does the word *dust bowl* mean?

C. *Dust bowl* means like, um, a bowl that you use for dust. . . .

I. Do you think you could use *dust bowl* in a sentence to show me you know what it means?

C. Yes.

I. OK.

C. We used the dust bowl for, um, putting the dust into it.

Fifth-Grade Child: *eleventh hour*

I. OK. What does the word *eleventh hour* mean?

C. *Eleventh hour?*

I. Mm-mmm.

C. OK. Like we have hours on our clock, and it's like when it's the last hour, or one of the last, and like it's before 12 o'clock midnight, and it could be either P.M. or A.M., and *P.M.* means a certain time of the day when it's past noon, and *A.M.* means before noon.

I. Mm-mmm. Can you tell me more about the word *eleventh hour?*

C. *Eleventh* is the number, and *hour* is the part of the day, it has sixty minutes in it.

I. OK. Can you use the word *eleventh hour* in a sentence to show me you know what it means?

C. I go to bed in the eleventh hour.

Fifth-Grade Child: *softheaded*

I. What does the word *softheaded* mean? *Softheaded.*

C. That you have a very soft head.

I. OK. Can you tell me anything more about the word *softheaded?*

C. No.

I. Could you use it in a sentence to show me you know what it means?

C. After the operation on his skull, he got very softheaded.

Some of the older children would sometimes start by treating an idiom as a literal compound but would eventually get credit for knowing its idiomatic meaning (as listed in *Webster's Third*). For example, in the following discussion about the idiom *softheaded,* the child ultimately went beyond a literal interpretation to a reasonably good approximation of its idiomatic meaning:

Fifth-Grade Child: *softheaded*
    I. OK, J. The next word is *softheaded.* What does the word *softheaded* mean?
    C. Like a head is on people or animals and lots of insects or something, they may be softheaded like their head is very soft.
    I. OK.
    C. Or they're not very smart or something.

In the next dialogue, a fifth-grade child attempted to figure out the idiom *dust bowl* but then rejected his construction as implausible. When asked the multiple-choice question, he was able to choose the correct idiomatic meaning for it (worded as "an area that has no rain and heavy winds for long periods of time"), even though one of the wrong answers in the multiple-choice test was "a container which people use to keep sand in":

Fifth-Grade Child: *dust bowl*
    I. What does the word *dust bowl* mean?
    C. *Dust bowl?*
    I. Mmm. . . .
    C. Well, dust is, like, is like little dirt in the air that it'll, it'll collect on things.
    I. Mmm.
    C. Dust. And a bowl is like you eat your cereal out of it.
    I. Mmm.
    C. A dust bowl. Wouldn't be dust in a bowl I don't think.
    I. Mmm.
    C. So I don't know.
    I. OK. Do you think you might be able to use it in a sentence to show me you know what it means?
    C. No. These ones are getting tougher.
    [*Multiple-choice question answered correctly.*]

In the next example, the fifth grader began by treating the idiom *twenty questions* as a literal compound but then chose the correct idiomatic meaning on the multiple-choice question (worded as "a guessing game in which one person tries to determine what someone else has in mind"), commenting that she was in fact familiar with the game twenty questions but that she had forgotten about it before having been asked the multiple-choice question:

Fifth-Grade Child: *twenty questions*

    I. OK. What does the word *twenty questions* mean?

    C. It could mean like questions like things that are asked by people.

    I. Mm-mmm.

    C. Twenty might mean that you're asking them twenty questions.

    I. OK. Can you tell me anything more about the word *twenty questions?*

    C. Twenty's a number, and it's the amount of questions you can ask.

    I. Can you use it in a sentence to show me you know what it means?

    C. The teacher asked us twenty questions in the afternoon.

    [*Multiple-choice question answered correctly.*]

    I. Have you ever played that game?

    C. Ya, I just forgot about that.

Summary of Impressions of Children's PS Responses

Most inflected and derived words coded as indicating morphological problem solving appeared to manifest a "part to whole" pattern in which just the root word, or occasionally in multimorphemic derived words an embedded derived word, was explicitly defined or discussed prior to attaining credit for the entire word. Children often ultimately achieved final credit for such words either by answering the multiple-choice question correctly or by casting them appropriately into illustrative sentences rather than by defining them in a general way. Only the oldest children occasionally showed a "parts to whole" pattern for such words, by explicitly discussing affixes as well as their constituent root words. Literal compounds typically manifested a "parts to whole pattern," with each component word being explicitly discussed or defined before credit for the entire literal compound was attained. Credit for literal compounds was often finally achieved when children defined them, frequently in a general way, by putting the meanings of the component words together in some reasonable fashion. The tendency to treat each word in a literal compound explicitly increased with development but was relatively common even for the youngest children interviewed. The explicit use of analogy, narrowly defined as expressing knowledge of a complex word by relating it to another complex word of similar morphological form, was, like the explicit discussion of affixes, found to be infrequent, and the few relatively convincing cases of it occurred mainly in the responses of the fifth-grade children.

Although this study is not ideally designed to reveal the precise nature of the processes used by children in figuring out word meanings through morphological knowledge, I discuss its possible implications for our understanding of such processes and the possibilities that it might hold for future

113

research in the final chapter of this *Monograph*. I do believe that the examples given above, and many similar instances found in the transcripts, strongly suggest that children often use morphological knowledge to synthesize complex word meanings and that it is important to acknowledge this in attempting to understand the nature of vocabulary development. The impression that children are predisposed to exploit their knowledge of morphology in constructing word meanings seems supported by the fact that they often appeared to treat idioms like literal compounds. Although credit for knowing them was not achieved in most such cases, the fact that the children often treated idioms such as *dust bowl, moneybags,* and *softheaded* as though they could be understood through morphological analysis and composition suggests that, when children have not previously learned such words (and presumably other kinds of words) by rote, they will often use morphological knowledge in an attempt to construct meanings for them.

Obviously, not all word meanings for which children received credit in this study were constructed through morphological knowledge. The vast majority of root words and idioms that they understood could not have been comprehended on the basis of such knowledge, and, for some inflected words, derived words, and literal compounds, there was no evidence that credit was achieved through morphological analysis and composition. Words not figured out by means of morphological knowledge presumably had been previously learned and somehow stored in long-term memory as raw sound-concept associations. In the final section of this chapter, an attempt is made to partition estimates of total recognition vocabulary at each grade level into two subestimates, corresponding roughly to how many words children may have actually learned and how many were potentially knowable through morphological problem solving. The former, which are offered as approximating "psychologically basic vocabulary," are then used as a basis for estimating the rate of actual word learning prior to and during the early and middle elementary school years.

APPROXIMATING PSYCHOLOGICALLY BASIC VOCABULARY

The PS and NE classifications allowed us to partition the raw scores and estimates for each child's total main entry vocabulary knowledge into two types: (i) those words for which there was (for raw scores), or would have been had it been feasible to test all main entries in the dictionary (for estimates), evidence of morphological problem solving and (ii) those for which there was or would have been no such evidence. The mean raw scores and mean estimates for each type of vocabulary knowledge (as well as for total entries known) at each of the three grades are shown in Table 13. The vocabulary growth functions for three types of estimates based on the data

TABLE 13

MEAN RAW SCORES AND ESTIMATES FOR KNOWN WORDS CLASSIFIED AS SHOWING
EVIDENCE OF MORPHOLOGICAL PROBLEM SOLVING (PS), AS SHOWING NO SUCH EVIDENCE
(NE), AND FOR TOTAL MAIN ENTRY VOCABULARY AT EACH GRADE

WORD TYPE	GRADE 1		GRADE 3		GRADE 5	
	Raw Score	Estimate	Raw Score	Estimate	Raw Score	Estimate
Problem solving (PS)	7.09	4,225	13.96	8,318	33.84	20,164
No evidence of problem solving (NE) ...	10.36	6,173	18.62	11,094	33.28	19,830
Total	17.45	10,398	32.58	19,412	67.12	39,994

presented in this study are shown in Figure 4. The top function depicts all main entries known, the bottom function all known root words and idioms (or what might be called "linguistically basic" vocabulary), and the middle function words for which there would have been no evidence of morphological problem solving. This middle function is offered here as a first approximation to the growth function for "psychologically basic" vocabulary.

It should be noted, of course, that this middle function is just an approximation of "psychologically basic" or "learned" vocabulary since there may have been instances in which a child was problem solving mentally but not expressing it in words. Such a child's NE score would have led to overestimation of his or her "psychologically basic" vocabulary. On the other hand, there may have been times when NE scores might have resulted in underestimation of "psychologically basic" vocabulary because children, on occasion, may have mentioned the morphological parts of a word in defining it as a kind of metalinguistic display of morphological knowledge, rather than because they needed to analyze it to figure out its meaning. Still, on the basis of the evidence at hand, the middle function in Figure 4 represents our best guess regarding the growth of "psychologically basic" or learned vocabulary.

A MANOVA with grade, sex, and SES as the independent variables and the PS and NE raw scores as the dependent variables showed a significant multivariate effect for grade, $F(4, 166) = 47.29$, $p < .001$. Subsequent univariate F tests indicated significant grade effects for words coded both PS, $F(2, 84) = 125.18$, $p < .001$, and NE, $F(2, 84) = 56.03$, $p < .001$. The only other significant multivariate F was for SES, $F(2, 83) = 3.50$, $p < .035$, which univariate F tests revealed to hold for words coded as NE, $F(1, 84) = 6.65$, $p < .012$, but not for words coded as PS, $F(1, 84) = 1.73$, N.S. Upper-SES children were credited with knowing 23.06 NE and 19.37 PS words on average, whereas the corresponding values for lower-SES children were, respectively, 18.44 and 17.23.

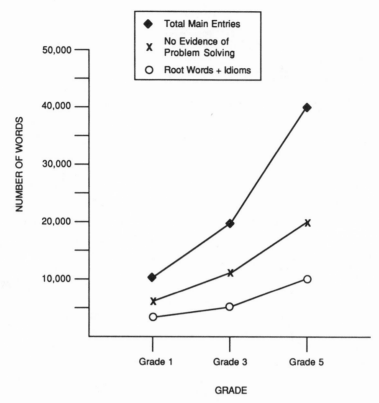

FIG. 4.—Functions showing mean estimated number of words known at each grade for root words + idioms, for total main entries, and for vocabulary for which there would have been no evidence of problem solving, offered here as an approximation to learned or "psychologically basic" vocabulary.

TABLE 14

ESTIMATED RATES OF VOCABULARY GROWTH IN WORDS PER DAY
(Problem-Solving Analysis)

Word Type	Grade 1– Grade 5	1.5 Years– Grade 1	Grade 1– Grade 3	Grade 3– Grade 5
Problem solving (PS)	10.64	2.26	5.50	15.83
No evidence of problem solving				
(NE)	9.38	3.26	6.63	12.13
Total	20.02	5.52	12.13	27.96

Trend analyses on the total PS scores (collapsing across sex and SES) as a function of grade revealed a significant quadratic, $F(1, 93) = 18.64$, $p < .001$, as well as a significant linear component. For individual word types coded as PS, the quadratic component was not significant for inflected words, but it was for derived words, $F(1, 93) = 19.71$, $p < .001$, and for literal compounds, $F(1, 93) = 7.71$, $p < .007$. Similar analyses on the NE scores yielded significant linear components but nonsignificant quadratic components in each case.

ESTIMATED RATES OF VOCABULARY GROWTH IN WORDS PER DAY FOR PS WORDS VERSUS NE WORDS

Estimated rates of growth for both types of vocabulary under discussion during different developmental periods are shown in Table 14; these were calculated as before. Table 14 indicates not only that the rates of growth for the two types of vocabulary increase as children get older but also that there is a shifting pattern in terms of the relative rapidity of the rates associated with them with increasing age. Specifically, from 1½ years to grade 1, and from grade 1 to grade 3, the estimated rates of vocabulary development are higher for NE than for PS words. However, the estimated rates for PS words are higher from grade 3 to grade 5 and for the total period from grade 1 to grade 5 than the corresponding estimated rates for NE words. This shifting pattern suggests that, with development, morphological problem solving plays an increasingly important role in contributing to total rate of growth of recognition vocabulary.

At last, approximate estimates of the rate of *word learning* during different developmental periods can be offered on the basis of this study. These are shown in the second row of entries in Table 14, which correspond to the number of new known words per day that we estimate would have manifested "no evidence of problem solving" had all the main entries in *Webster's Third* been tested. Of course, the qualifications regarding the possibility that NE scores might at times have led to overestimates or underestimates of "psychologically basic" vocabulary must be kept in mind. Nevertheless, to the extent that it is reasonable to assume that NE words are "psychologically basic" and have actually been previously learned, Table 14 suggests that, for children such as those interviewed in the present study, the rate of *word learning* between grade 1 and grade 5 is in the neighborhood of 9.38 words per day. Similarly, it suggests that prior to grade 1 it is about 3.26 words per day, that between grade 1 and grade 3 it is about 6.63 words per day, and that from grade 3 to grade 5 it is about 12.13 words per day.

VII. VOCABULARY DEVELOPMENT
AND THE GROWTH OF MORPHOLOGICAL KNOWLEDGE

The main findings of this study will now be summarized and discussed from the perspective of the goals of this research, the questions about vocabulary development that motivated it, and the predictions generated from the review of the literature presented in Chapter III. Most important, an attempt will be made to interpret these findings with respect to the light they shed on our understanding of vocabulary development during childhood. Future avenues of research that might further illuminate the nature of vocabulary acquisition will also be suggested.

DEVELOPMENTAL CHANGES IN
ESTIMATED RECOGNITION VOCABULARY SIZE

Our results indicate that vocabulary knowledge develops at a remarkable rate during the early and middle elementary school years, as others have also suggested (e.g., Anderson & Freebody, 1981; Beck & McKeown, in press; Miller, 1977, 1978a, 1981, 1986a, 1986b, 1988, 1991; Miller & Gildea, 1987; Nagy & Anderson, 1984; Nagy & Herman, 1987; White et al., 1989; Wysocki & Jenkins, 1987). The present research yielded average estimates of approximately 10,000, a little less than 20,000, and approximately 40,000 words (main entries in *Webster's Third*) in the recognition vocabularies of first-, third-, and fifth-grade children, respectively. These estimates were based on children's knowledge of a sample of words taken from an unabridged dictionary that was larger than samples used in previous research, one that was shown to be unbiased in terms of frequency of occurrence and distribution according to morphological type. Criteria for word knowledge that were neither too stringent nor too lax were used, and, even under the more conservative criteria, the average estimates at the three grade levels were not greatly reduced.

Although these estimates may seem large, they are not out of line with those of other researchers who also tested children on samples of words from unabridged dictionaries (for reviews, see, e.g., Anderson & Freebody, 1981; Nagy & Anderson, 1984; and Nagy & Herman, 1987). The present investigation was most similar to those conducted by Templin (1957) and Smith (1941). Its estimates for main entry—or what these researchers called "basic"—vocabulary knowledge are slightly higher than Templin's but somewhat lower than Smith's for children in grades 1 and 3. Templin's median estimates of 7,800 and 17,600 main entries known by first- and third-grade children, respectively, are often cited in the literature; she also reported mean estimates of 8,500 and 18,200, respectively, for these two grade levels. In the present research, means have been used as opposed to medians (for statistical reasons), and a comparison of mean estimates from the two studies reveals them to be reasonably close: Templin's estimates are slightly lower, but her first- and third-grade children were about 8 months younger on average than those interviewed in this study. Although Lorge and Chall (1963) found that Seashore and Eckerson's (1940) sample of words was somewhat biased in favor of frequently occurring words, estimates obtained in this study (to which this criticism does not apply) are of the same order of magnitude as those in Templin (1957), which are based on her careful study conducted with the Seashore-Eckerson Recognition Vocabulary Test. (Of course, since Templin did not test children in grade 5, comparisons can be made only at grades 1 and 3.) It is possible that the fact that *Webster's Third* contains more main entries (we estimated about a quarter of a million words) than Funk and Wagnalls's *New Standard Dictionary* (1937) (for which Seashore and Eckerson, 1940, estimated about 166,000 words) may have offset the bias in Seashore and Eckerson's sample to some extent. In any event, there is considerable consistency in these estimates, which is particularly notable because they involved the testing of different generations of children, in different geographic locations, on different samples of words taken from different dictionaries.

The estimates for main entry vocabulary knowledge arising from this study are somewhat less consistent with those of Smith (1941). Her estimates of main entry (or what she called "basic") vocabulary size were somewhat higher than ours for children in grades 1 and 3 (hers were about 16,500 and 24,000 and ours 10,398 and 19,412 words, respectively). However, hers was somewhat lower than ours for children in grade 5 (hers was about 28,000 and ours 39,994), albeit her estimate of between 40,000 and 50,000 words in total vocabulary knowledge at grade 5, which includes both main entries and subentries (she reported a median estimate of about 43,000 words and a mean estimate of about 49,000), was higher than ours for main entries. As noted earlier, Smith sometimes used hints in testing the children and gave partial credit if they then showed knowledge of the word. Also, it is not clear whether she corrected her multiple-choice questions for guessing. (Templin found that, without such correction, her estimates for first-

and third-grade children more closely approximated Smith's, although they still remained lower.) These somewhat lax procedures may partially account for Smith's higher estimates for grades 1 and 3; they do not explain, however, why her estimate for fifth-grade children was somewhat lower than that of the present study.

Two possibly relevant thoughts about this discrepancy are as follows. First, although Smith tested children in grades 1 and 3 individually and orally, as both we and Templin did, by grade 5 she switched to written tests given to children in groups, a change in method that may have attenuated the children's performance. Second, an informal comparison of Funk and Wagnalls's *New Standard Dictionary,* used by Smith, and of *Webster's Third,* used in the present research, suggests that, although derived words are common as main entries in both dictionaries, they appear to be relatively more so in *Webster's.* Since a major finding of the present study was that fifth-grade children did particularly well on derived words in comparison with the younger children, this difference between the two dictionaries from which words were sampled for the two studies may partially account for the comparatively larger estimates achieved by our fifth-grade children and the smaller ones obtained by our younger children.

The fifth-grade children did especially well in the present study, and a trend analysis revealed a significant quadratic effect for main entries known as a function of grade that was not apparent in Smith's data. If the positive acceleration in vocabulary knowledge suggested by this study proves to be a reliable finding, it may be partly accounted for by the relatively large increases in known derived words and also literal compounds that occurred between grade 3 and grade 5 (each of these word types showed a quadratic effect); this may in turn reflect children's increasing ability to figure out such words through morphological problem solving. However, significant quadratic effects were also found for both root words and idioms, words that usually cannot be figured out through morphological problem solving but must be learned. The positive acceleration that we observed for such words could reflect the fact that schoolchildren often start to read more extensively and independently after about grade 3, and this may enhance vocabulary learning (Miller, 1991; Miller & Gildea, 1987; Nagy & Herman, 1987; White et al., 1989).

However, two more recent related studies, conducted with different children and using different samples of 433 and 435 main entries, have now been completed. One (with Teresa Alexander) revealed that, although children in grades 1 and 5 performed very similarly to those in the present study, third-grade children did somewhat better, with the result that the increase in main entry vocabulary knowledge from grade 1 to grade 5 appeared to be more nearly linear; a trend analysis of the data showed no significant quadratic effect. The other study (with Nancy Malloy) did reveal such an effect, although the positive acceleration in the growth of vocabulary knowledge that it suggested was not quite as pronounced as that suggested by the present study. Other analyses of the data from both these more recent studies have confirmed the vast majority of findings obtained in the present one, with this one exception. Hence, the significant quadratic effects found in the present investigation will not be emphasized in the remainder of this chapter as much as the other findings, such as the overall changes in vocabulary knowledge between grade 1 and grade 5, which the more recent studies have consistently confirmed. Whether or not the growth of vocabulary knowledge is positively accelerated between grade 1 and grade 5 remains to be established by further research. It does seem relatively clear, however, that rate of vocabulary development is more rapid in the early and middle elementary school years than it is in the preschool years (see the discussion of the rate of vocabulary development below; also compare Carey's, 1978, estimated rates of vocabulary development during the preschool years with those of Miller, 1977, for the early school years, both of which are based on Templin's, 1957, findings).

The present estimates of main entry vocabulary knowledge may seem large, but, if anything, they may actually underestimate children's total vocabulary knowledge. They are estimates of the average number of the roughly quarter of a million different main entry words in *Webster's Third* within the children's recognition vocabularies. The children were not tested on subentries or for their knowledge of polysemous meanings or for the number of homographs that they might have known for the main entries for which they received credit. Moreover, although *Webster's Third* was the largest synchronic dictionary of modern-day English at the time of the inception of this research (Landau, 1984), it does not contain all the words in English (Gove, 1981). (It excludes, e.g., most proper nouns and many idioms.) Thus, the estimates being discussed refer to the number of main entry words in *Webster's Third* for which children such as those interviewed in the present study know at least one meaning; further research will be necessary to indicate to what extent these estimates would increase if knowledge of subentries, polysemous meanings, homographs, proper nouns, and other words not in *Webster's* were studied as well. Although, in discussing the present results, I will for simplicity's sake sometimes refer to knowledge of "words" and of "vocabulary," it should be kept in mind that I will usually be referring to knowledge of words that are main entries in *Webster's*.

VOCABULARY DEVELOPMENT IN TERMS OF MORPHOLOGICALLY DEFINED WORD TYPES

We partitioned each child's raw score and estimate for main entries known into five subscores and subestimates on the basis of the number of root words, inflected words, derived words, literal compounds, and idioms that the child knew, a partitioning that enabled a more qualitative analysis of the children's recognition vocabulary knowledge. Although knowledge of each of these types of words increased with age and grade, the extent of vocabulary knowledge varied considerably from word type to word type, as evinced by the highly significant word-type effect revealed by the ANOVA on the raw scores. For example, idioms were the least extensively known of all word types at each grade. Moreover, relative knowledge of the different word types also varied as a function of grade, as indicated by the highly significant grade × word type interaction. For example, in grade 1, root words were associated with the highest raw scores and estimates, followed by inflected words and literal compounds. Significantly less extensively known in grade 1 were derived words. By grade 3, however, derived words were associated with the highest raw scores and estimates and by grade 5 with by far the highest.

Developmental changes in relative knowledge of the different word types were especially clearly shown by the analysis of proportion$_1$ scores, in which the fraction of total main entry vocabulary knowledge accounted for by each word type was computed for each child. The proportion of vocabulary knowledge accounted for by root words decreased between grade 1 and grade 5, as did the proportion for inflected words. The proportion for literal compounds did not change significantly. In contrast, the proportion of vocabulary knowledge accounted for by derived words increased substantially over this period, representing on the average about 16% of recognition vocabulary in grade 1 and almost 40% of such knowledge by grade 5. The proportion of vocabulary knowledge accounted for by idioms also increased significantly, but, at each grade level, it was significantly smaller than the corresponding proportions for every other word type. Thus, recognition vocabulary not only grows quantitatively during the early and middle elementary school years but also changes qualitatively in terms of the relative contributions made by different word types to total main entry vocabulary knowledge at different grade levels.

In the second proportional analysis (on proportion$_2$ scores), the percentage of all words of a given type in the sample that was known by each child was examined. Although these proportions increased significantly with age and grade for all word types, an analysis of variance again revealed a significant word-type effect and a significant grade × word type interaction. In this case, inflected words were associated with the highest proportion$_2$ scores at all grade levels. The earlier analyses did not suggest that children knew more inflected words than any other type in absolute terms, but, because the sample contained relatively few main entry inflected words, the proportion of such words in the sample that were known by the children was highest at all ages. Idioms were associated with the lowest proportion$_2$

scores at all grade levels. The grade × word type interaction was accounted for in part by the relatively rapid rise in proportion$_2$ scores for derived words between grade 1 and grade 5. For example, whereas in grade 1 children knew a significantly higher proportion of the root words in the sample than they did of derived words, by grade 5 they knew a significantly higher proportion of the derived words than of the root words.

In spite of the somewhat different patterns that resulted from transforming the raw scores into the two proportional measures, all analyses revealed a relatively rapid increase in knowledge of derived words in the early and middle elementary school years. They all indicated that, although known to some degree in grade 1, derived words were not as widely known at that age as other word types, with the exception of idioms; however, by grade 5, they were much more extensively known—more so, in fact (in terms of raw scores, estimates, and proportion$_1$ scores), than any other morphologically defined word type. Thus, the first basic prediction outlined in Chapter III, namely, that derived words would manifest particular growth from grade 1 to grade 5, was confirmed. What was somewhat surprising about these findings was the extent to which comprehension of derived words contributed to total main entry vocabulary knowledge in the older and particularly the fifth-grade children.

These results are consistent with those of others whose research suggests that, by the beginning of the school years, children should have considerable knowledge not only of root words but also of inflected words (e.g., Berko, 1958; Brown, 1973; Cazden, 1968; de Villiers & de Villiers, 1973; Kuczaj, 1977; Marcus et al., 1992; Mervis & Johnson, 1991; Munson & Ingram, 1985) and of literal compounds (e.g., Berko, 1958; Clark, 1981, 1983a; Clark & Berman, 1987; Clark et al., 1985; Clark & Hecht, 1982; Derwing & Baker, 1979) but that, although they do have some knowledge of derived words (Bowerman, 1982; Clark & Cohen, 1984; Clark & Hecht, 1982; Gordon, 1989), it is less extensive at the beginning of formal education and develops considerably during the elementary school years (Derwing, 1976; Derwing & Baker, 1979, 1986; Tyler & Nagy, 1989; White et al., 1989; Wysocki & Jenkins, 1987; see also Freyd & Baron, 1982). This study revealed that even first-grade children have some, that third-grade children have considerable, and that fifth-grade children have extensive knowledge of derived words.

These findings, combined with the results of the morphological problem-solving analyses to be discussed below, seem more consistent with those of investigators who have found knowledge of derived words and of derivational morphology to be present to a considerable extent in the early and middle elementary school years (e.g., Gordon, 1989; Tyler & Nagy, 1989; see also Bowerman, 1982; Clark & Cohen, 1984; Clark & Hecht, 1982) than with those of others (e.g., Freyd & Baron, 1982; Wysocki & Jenkins, 1987) whose research might be interpreted as suggesting that knowledge of derivational morphology does not develop much until the later elementary school years and, even then, only in a limited fashion. Tyler and Nagy (1989) were probably right when they suggested that certain extraneous task demands may have prevented the children studied by Freyd and Baron (1982) and Wysocki and Jenkins (1987) from showing the extent of their knowledge of derived words and of derivational morphology. Still, the findings of the present research are consistent with these two studies in that analogous developmental trends were found in all instances, with the qualification that the current study suggests a greater knowledge of derived words and of derivational morphology at earlier ages than is suggested by the other two. For example, Freyd and Baron found that superior word learners had especially good knowledge of derived words compared to average word learners; on the assumption, which I think is justifiable, that in the present investigation it is the fifth-grade children who are the (relatively) superior word learners, there is a kind of confirmation of these authors' finding since the fifth-grade children in this study also had an especially good knowledge of derived words as compared to the younger children.

VOCABULARY DEVELOPMENT AND MORPHEMIC COMPLEXITY

When total main entry raw scores and estimates were partitioned according to level of morphemic complexity into monomorphemic, bimorphemic, and multimorphemic words and idioms, knowledge of each word type was shown to increase significantly with age and grade, but significant effects were also found for word type and the interaction between grade and word type. The word-type effect revealed by the ANOVA on raw scores reflected the fact that, across grade, sex, and SES level, some word types were much more extensively known than others. Bimorphemic words were associated with significantly higher raw scores and estimates at each grade level than words of any other type classified according to morphemic complexity. This finding, among others, reinforces the point that elementary school children's main entry vocabulary knowledge consists of more than just *basic words* or *root words*, even though these terms have often been used to refer to their knowledge of main entries in unabridged dictionaries. Idioms, on the other hand, were associated with lower raw scores and estimates than words of any other type at each grade level, and, apart from the comparison between idioms and multimorphemic words known by the first-grade children, these differences were also significant in all cases. The grade × word type interaction reflected in part the relatively rapid rise in multimorphemic words known as a function of grade. In grade 1, knowledge of such words was significantly less than knowledge of monomorphemic words and not significantly greater than knowledge of idioms; by grade 5, however, knowledge of multimorphemic words was significantly greater than knowledge of idioms and not significantly different from knowledge of monomorphemic words (in terms of raw scores and estimates, they were virtually identical).

When the fraction of each child's total main entry vocabulary knowledge accounted for by each type of word as classified according to level of morphemic complexity (proportion$_1$) was analyzed, developmental changes in the relative contributions made by the different word types to recognition vocabulary became especially clear. The proportion of vocabulary knowledge accounted for by multimorphemic words increased significantly between grade 1 and grade 5, whereas the proportion accounted for by monomorphemic words decreased significantly. (The proportion accounted for by bimorphemic words decreased slightly overall, although it was highest at all grade levels; the proportion accounted for by idioms increased slightly, but it was always lowest.)

When the data were analyzed in terms of the percentage of all words in the sample of a given type known by each child (proportion$_2$), it was found that, at each grade level, the proportion of known bimorphemic words was significantly greater and the proportion of known idioms significantly less than that for every other word type. In addition, however, a highly significant grade × word type interaction was found, which was accounted for partly by the relatively rapid increase in the percentage of known sample words that were multimorphemic. In grade 1, this percentage was significantly less than that for monomorphemic words; however, in grade 5, the percentage of multimorphemic sample words known was significantly greater than the corresponding percentage for monomorphemic words.

These findings (obtained on raw scores, estimates, and both proportions) support the second basic prediction outlined in Chapter III, namely, that knowledge of multimorphemic words would be associated with particular growth between grade 1 and grade 5. According to each of these analyses, multimorphemic words were not extensively known in grade 1 but were considerably more extensively known by grade 5. Of course, even by grade 5, and even in terms of proportion$_2$ scores (which take into account the different numbers of each type of word in the sample), knowledge of multimorphemic words was still substantially less than that of bimorphemic words. This might in part reflect the fact that more cognitive effort must be expended in analyzing multimorphemic words into their components and synthesizing a meaning from them, at least for those complex words figured out through morphological problem solving.

These findings are consistent with the view that language development can be characterized in terms of increasing complexity in general and morphological complexity in particular (e.g., Brown, 1973; Clark, 1983b; Slobin,

1973; Wells, 1984). More specifically, they are consistent with the hypothesis advanced by Eve Clark and her colleagues that lexical development follows the principle of simplicity of form, that, as children get older and learn more about a language, they go beyond morphologically simpler forms and increasingly add more complex forms to their lexical knowledge (e.g., Clark & Berman, 1987; Clark et al., 1986).

Of course, even first-grade children in this study had considerable knowledge of bimorphemic words, and knowledge of bimorphemic words was more extensive than knowledge of monomorphemic words as well as of other word types in our youngest children, as it was in our older children. But the first-grade children in this study were not linguistic novices; they had several years of language development behind them and, according to our data, already knew thousands of words. It is not surprising that they knew many bimorphemic words because research with younger preschool children has shown that they have good productive knowledge of many bimorphemic inflected words (e.g., Berko, 1958; Brown, 1973; Cazden, 1968; de Villiers & de Villiers, 1973; Kuczaj, 1977; Marcus et al., 1992), that they produce and comprehend a substantial number of two-term endocentric compounds (e.g., Berko, 1958; Clark, 1981, 1983a; Clark & Berman, 1987; Clark et al., 1985; Clark & Hecht, 1982; Derwing & Baker, 1979), and even that they produce and comprehend some bimorphemic derived words with relatively productive affixes (e.g., Clark, 1981; Clark & Cohen, 1984; Clark & Hecht, 1982). The present study also suggests that first-grade children have relatively extensive knowledge of bimorphemic words (although this knowledge continues to grow dramatically until grade 5 at least) but that they have substantially less extensive knowledge of multimorphemic words, especially in contrast with the fifth-grade children, whose knowledge of such words appears to be considerable.

One can hypothesize with some confidence that studies of much younger children would reveal a phase in very early language development in which the child's lexicon would consist primarily of monomorphemic words. Studies of children's vocabularies during the "one word at a time" stage generally suggest this (e.g., Benedict, 1979; Bloom, 1973; Bruner, 1983; Clark, 1983b; Greenfield & Smith, 1976; Halliday, 1975; Huttenlocher, 1974; Leopold, 1939; Nelson, 1973; Piaget, 1962). Although reduplicated words (e.g., [bʌbʌ] for *bottle;* [dædæ] for *father*) and diminutives (e.g., [kIti] for *cat;* [mʌmi] for *mother*) are common among the first words produced by children, it is unlikely that the reduplicated syllable in the former or the diminutive ending [-i] in the latter usually have morphological value for children during the earliest phase of language development (Ingram, 1974; see also Berko, 1958; Derwing & Baker, 1979). Munson and Ingram (1985) have reported the case of an English-speaking child who, at about 2 years of age, produced some reduplicative prefixes for certain lexical stems in which the prefix appeared to have morphological value (meaning roughly "more"). However, this occurred toward the end of the "one word at a time" stage, after the child had acquired several monomorphemic words. Brown (1973) found that, in the first stage of grammatical development after the one-word stage, when children's MLU (mean length of utterance in terms of morphemes) is between 1 and 2, their words are not generally overtly marked with inflections or derivational affixes and that the few words that they do produce in the form of compounds (e.g., *birthday*) should be treated as monomorphemic because there was no evidence of their having been composed from independent root words. Brown found that only in the second stage of grammatical development, when the child's MLU is between 2 and 2.5, do inflections and other "modulators of meaning" begin to appear. Recently, two studies have reported cases of English-speaking children producing words with certain common English inflections prior to the onset of word combinations. Mervis and Johnson (1991) documented a case of a boy producing the plural morpheme as an inflectional suffix on words before the end of the one-word stage and prior to the onset of syntax. They also mentioned that the past, progressive, possessive, and diminutive inflections had been produced by this boy, as well as by his younger brother, before the beginning of word combinations. Munson and Ingram (1985) also reported a child using the plural and possessive morphemes as well as the reduplicative morpheme described above prior to the production of two-word utterances. Therefore, it may be that some children *begin* to acquire morphology prior to the onset of syntax. Nevertheless, in each of these studies, bimorphemic words were not produced until toward the end of the one-word stage, well after the children had acquired several monomorphemic words (see Mervis, 1987; Mervis & Johnson, 1991; Munson & Ingram, 1985).

Thus, although the current study focused on older children (6–10-year-olds in grades 1–5), its results are consistent with a broader view of lexical development in which the child's vocabulary knowledge increases in terms of morphological complexity: words are primarily monomorphemic in the earliest phase of language development, knowledge of bimorphemic words increases substantially during the preschool years and beyond, and knowledge of multimorphemic words increases substantially after the child has gone to school.

WORDS KNOWN THROUGH MORPHOLOGICAL PROBLEM SOLVING VERSUS PSYCHOLOGICALLY BASIC VOCABULARY

The findings of this study indicate that the development of recognition vocabulary knowledge during the early and middle school years is quite dramatic, as has been suggested recently by many other researchers. But to show knowledge of a word on a recognition vocabulary test does not necessarily imply that that word had been learned previously or that it is "psychologically basic" in the sense of having been stored in long-term memory as a unitary whole. The analyses (discussed above) of how total main entry vocabulary knowledge breaks down into different morphologically defined types of words show that more than half the known words at each grade level were morphologically complex (inflected words, derived words, and literal compounds), and the meanings of some of these words might therefore have been figured out through what I have called "morphological problem solving." As pointed out in Chapter II, to get root words or idioms right on a vocabulary test would seem to imply, in most cases, that such words had been learned before because it is not usually possible to figure out their meanings without such prior learning. But this is not necessarily the case for the morphologically complex words. One might figure out some, but not necessarily all, such words through morphological analysis and composition, even if they had never been learned or represented as distinct entries in the mental lexicon before. Therefore, the total average estimates of recognition vocabulary of approximately 10,000, 20,000, and 40,000 words in grades 1, 3, and 5, respectively, presumably include some words that are known in the sense that they have actually been learned before and their meanings can be retrieved when necessary and some words that are known or, more precisely, *potentially knowable* in the sense that they could be decoded through morphological knowledge. If this argument is valid, then it would seem that a relatively large number of the roughly 3,000, 5,000, and 10,000 root words and idioms that we estimated were known on average by the children in grades 1, 3, and 5, respectively, had actually been learned by them before. But some of the other words estimated to be in their recognition vocabularies may not have been learned but rather may have been potentially knowable, or potentially recognizable, through morphological analysis and composition.

With that in mind, and having noticed some relatively clear instances of morphological problem solving and other cases in which evidence of such problem solving was completely absent, we coded what each child said for each credited word in terms of whether any such evidence could be seen (see Chap. VI). We found evidence of morphological problem solving at all grade levels, but we also found that the proportion of words for which such evidence existed increased as a function of grade. The percentage of main entries known for which there was evidence of morphological problem solving increased significantly, from 40% in grade 1 to 51% in grade 5, on average. Restricted to just the known morphologically complex words, the percentage increased, again significantly, from 56% in grade 1 to 65% in grade 5. This latter finding suggests that the increase in the extent of morphological problem solving is independent of the increase in the number of complex words relative to other words known as a function of age and grade.

The evidence suggesting that there was some morphological problem solving at all grades and that the extent to which it was used increased with development confirms the third basic prediction outlined in Chapter III. A somewhat surprising finding that resulted from these analyses, however, was that the extent of evidence of morphological problem solving for inflected words was not much higher than that for derived words and lower than that for literal compounds. We had expected to find more evidence of morphological problem solving for both inflected words and literal compounds than for derived words since the literature suggests that children acquire productive knowledge of each of the former kinds of words earlier than they do productive knowledge of the latter (see Chap. III). However, an examination of the inflected words for which children received credit indicated that these were often relatively common words, such as *soaking, changed,* and *reports,* and that they therefore might actually have been learned before, making the use of morphological problem solving unnecessary (although, given what is known about the acquisition of English inflections, one would predict that the children could have analyzed such words morphologically if they had needed to do so). Future research will be necessary to confirm this finding and to clarify its implications.

The finding of some evidence of morphological problem solving for each of the three morphologically defined word types even in the first-grade children is consistent with the results of others who have shown productive knowledge of inflections (e.g., Berko, 1958; Brown, 1973; Cazden, 1968; de Villiers & de Villiers, 1973; Kuczaj, 1977; Marcus et al., 1992), of endocentric compounds (e.g., Berko, 1958; Clark, 1981, 1983a; Clark & Berman, 1987; Clark & Hecht, 1982; Clark et al., 1985; Derwing & Baker, 1979), and of some derivational affixes (e.g., Bowerman, 1982; Clark & Cohen, 1984; Clark & Hecht, 1982; Gordon, 1989) prior to the onset of formal education (grade 1). This finding also suggests that, if not interpreted cautiously, some investigations could lead to underestimation of the extent to which morphological analysis, even of derived words, may be used by children at the beginning of the elementary school years (e.g., Freyd & Baron, 1982; Wysocki & Jenkins, 1987) because of the difficult task demands inherent in the tests used in such research (as Tyler & Nagy, 1989, have suggested). However, consistent with the findings of these and other studies (e.g., Derwing, 1976; Derwing & Baker, 1979, 1986; Tyler & Nagy, 1989; White et al., 1989), our results also suggest that knowledge of morphology and the extent to which children engage in morphological analysis increase significantly during the elementary school years.

On the basis of these analyses, we partitioned each child's total raw scores for main entries known into two types: words for which there was evidence of morphological problem solving and those for which there was none. This led to a partitioning of the estimates of total main entries known in the dictionary into two subestimates: those for which—if tested—the children would be likely to show morphological problem solving and those for which they would not. The average subestimates for words for which there would be evidence of morphological problem solving rose from 4,225 in grade 1 to 20,164 in grade 5, whereas the average subestimates for words for which there would be no such evidence rose from 6,173 in grade 1 to 19,830 in grade 5. The latter subestimates were offered as first approximations to learned or "psychologically basic" vocabulary.

If these approximations are of the right order of magnitude, they suggest that, on average, the children in grades 1, 3, and 5 had actually learned in the neighborhood of 6,000, 11,000, and 20,000 of the main entry words in *Webster's Third,* respectively (see Fig. 4 above). However, for reasons discussed in Chapter VI, these figures may either overestimate or underestimate "psychologically basic" or "previously learned" vocabulary to some degree since they are based on an analysis of the knowledge *expressed* by children during the interviews. Future research will be necessary to determine the extent to which the middle function shown in Figure 4 accurately depicts the growth curve for "psychologically basic" vocabulary. For now, it is offered as only a first approximation.

In any event, these analyses strongly suggest that morphological problem solving occurs to some degree at all ages and that the extent to which it occurs increases as a function of age and grade. I believe that they support the need to distinguish between words that have actually been learned before and words that may not have been learned but rather figured out through morphological knowledge, especially when interpreting the performance of children (or adults) on a recognition vocabulary test. And, when estimates of total recognition vocabulary knowledge are derived from such performance, I believe that these analyses emphasize the need to distinguish between words for which there are distinct representations in the mental lexicon and words that are not so represented but are rather *potentially knowable* through morphological analysis and composition.

RATE OF VOCABULARY DEVELOPMENT

Following Miller (1977), Carey (1978), and others (cf. Nagy & Herman, 1987), and on the basis of the average estimates of main entries and of specific types of words known at each grade level, we computed estimates of rates of vocabulary growth in terms of new words known or knowable per day for four different age/grade ranges: grade 1–5, 1.5 years to grade

1, grade 1–3, and grade 3–5. These are estimated average rates for the age/grade ranges specified and do not presuppose that, within each such developmental period, the rate is constant. (For example, the average rate of vocabulary growth might increase within a particular period as a function of age.) Further, because this was not a longitudinal study, these rates of growth were not actually observed in particular children, who would show individual differences and might manifest more variability in terms of spurts and lags than was revealed by this investigation. Thus, the estimated rates are for "average" children of the kind interviewed in this study, and they are based on the assumption that there were no significant cohort effects that might have had a major effect on vocabulary knowledge. (It would indeed be interesting to conduct longitudinal research along the lines of the present study, but longitudinal research is also associated with such problems as increasing sophistication in taking tests and subject loss.) Most of the previous estimates of rate of vocabulary growth during the preschool and elementary school years have also been based on cross-sectional research and involve similar qualifications and assumptions (e.g., Carey, 1978; Clark, 1983a, 1983b, 1987; Jones et al., 1991; Keil, 1983; Markman, 1987; Miller, 1977, 1978a, 1981, 1986a, 1986b, 1988, 1991; Miller & Gildea, 1987; Nagy & Herman, 1987; Waxman & Kosowski, 1990).

Moreover, in estimating the rates of vocabulary growth in the preschool years, we assumed (following Carey, 1978) that vocabulary knowledge was minimal prior to 18 months (see also Piaget, 1962). In fact, children often do acquire some words prior to 18 months of age, perhaps about 50 or so in production (e.g., Nelson, 1973) and up to two or three times as many in comprehension (e.g., Benedict, 1979). However, these numbers are quite small given the size of the estimates with which we are dealing, and it has often been noted that larger gains in vocabulary growth are typically observed in children starting at about $1\frac{1}{2}$ years of age (e.g., Gopnik & Meltzoff, 1987). Because Carey had assumed that vocabulary knowledge is minimal prior to 18 months, and because we wanted to compare our estimated rates of vocabulary growth during the preschool years with hers, we made this assumption also.

The results of these analyses suggest what seem like rather high estimates, particularly for total main entries per day. For example, from $1\frac{1}{2}$ years to grade 1, the estimated rate of growth of known or knowable new main entries per day was about 5.5 words; from grade 1 to grade 5, it was estimated to be substantially higher, about 20 words per day; and so on. Although these estimated rates may seem high, they are not inconsistent with those of some other researchers; in fact, where comparable, they are actually quite compatible with those derived originally by Carey (1978) for preschool children and by Miller (1977) for children between grade 1 and grade 3, both of whom based their estimates on Templin's (1957) data.

Carey's estimated rate of about 5 main entry words a day during the preschool years corresponds fairly well with ours of about 5.5 words per day, and Miller's estimated rate of about 14.5 main entry words per day between grade 1 and grade 3 corresponds fairly well with ours of a little more than 12 words per day during this period.

These seemingly large estimated rates of vocabulary growth are illuminated to some extent by partitioning them into rates for the specific types of words that make up total main entry recognition vocabulary knowledge. For example, the total of about 20.02 words per day between grade 1 and grade 5 breaks down into specific estimates of about 3.00 root words, 1.92 inflected words, 9.67 derived words, 3.86 literal compounds, and 1.57 idioms per day, and the total of 5.52 words per day during the preschool years breaks down into about 1.64 root words, 1.46 inflected words, 0.95 derived words, 1.39 literal compounds, and 0.08 idioms per day. Other estimated rates for specifically defined word types for various developmental periods can be found in Tables 7, 11, and 14 above.

These analyses are of interest not only because they suggest that rate of vocabulary growth increases as children get older (which appeared to be true to some extent for every word type examined in this study) but also because of the shifting patterns that they suggest for the relative rapidity of the rates for different word types during different developmental periods. For example, the morphological word type analysis indicated that, during the period from 1½ years to grade 1, root words were associated with the highest estimated rate, followed by inflected words and literal compounds; however, between grade 1 and grade 5, derived words were associated with the highest rate by a considerable margin. When rates were analyzed for words of different levels of morphemic complexity, bimorphemic words were associated with the highest rates and idioms with the lowest at all the developmental periods, but a shifting pattern was observed for the remaining two word types. Monomorphemic words were associated with a much higher rate than multimorphemic words during the period from 1½ years to grade 1; in contrast, the estimated rate for multimorphemic words was somewhat higher than that for monomorphemic words between grade 1 and grade 5. When the children's responses were coded for evidence of morphological problem solving (PS) or the lack thereof (NE), the estimated rate for all main entries that would be coded NE was higher for the period from 1½ years to grade 1; however, for the period from grade 1 to grade 5, the estimated rate for words that would be coded as PS was higher, suggesting that, with development, morphological problem solving plays an increasingly important role in contributing to total rate of growth of recognition vocabulary.

In terms of the distinction between "psychologically basic" (or actually learned) vocabulary and words that are potentially knowable through morphological problem solving, this last analysis was especially revealing. The point made earlier about how our estimates of known words for which there would be no evidence of problem solving might underestimate or overestimate learned or "psychologically basic" vocabulary to some degree should be kept in mind here as well; nevertheless, to the extent that they do correspond to "psychologically basic" vocabulary, the estimated rates shown in the second row of Table 14 suggest that the rate of actual word learning is about nine words a day between grade 1 and grade 5, about three words a day during the preschool years, and so on.[26]

It is interesting to note that, in a totally independent research project that took quite a different approach, Nagy and Herman (1987) have estimated that, during the school years, children *learn* about 3,000 distinct words per year, which converts to an estimated rate of about eight words per day (see also Nagy & Anderson, 1984). Nagy and Herman (1987) developed this estimate by recalibrating the estimates of recognition vocabulary produced by various other researchers for children in grade 3 and adolescents in grade 12,[27] so their analysis applies to an overlapping but somewhat later developmental period than the present one. Still, their estimate of about eight words learned per day during the elementary and high school years is interestingly similar to ours of approximately nine words for the early and middle elementary school years. It is also of interest that, although this estimate is somewhat lower than Miller's earlier ones for the rate of

[26] These approximate rates of actual word learning represent the average estimated numbers of new words that children would have learned sufficiently well per day to be able to satisfy criteria of word knowledge such as those used in the present research. It is well known that a child's knowledge of any given word can vary from a vague recognition that it has been encountered before to a fairly precise understanding of its meaning (Curtis, 1987). Word meanings undergo gradual change in the course of development (e.g., Vygotsky, 1986), as some of my previous research (e.g., Anglin, 1977, 1978, 1985), and that of many others, has suggested. As Carey (1978) and Miller (1978a, 1986a) have argued, it is likely that the learning process for any given word is not completed in a single day and that a child will, in fact, be gradually learning more and more about the meanings of a large number of words over extended developmental periods. According to the present research, children between grade 1 and grade 5 may have learned on average approximately nine additional words per day well enough to satisfy our criteria, preschoolers approximately three additional words, and so on.

[27] Following Nagy and Anderson (1984), these researchers assumed that the word stock of English consists of about 88,500 distinct word families, i.e., sets of words that are morphologically related to one another in such a way that learning one word in the set would likely allow understanding of the other words in it (e.g., *persecute, persecution, persecutor, persecuted, persecutions*, etc.). Nagy and Herman (1987) used this value to recalibrate estimates of recognition vocabulary produced by several other investigators whose research had implicitly assumed very different values for the total number of distinct words in English. From these revised estimates, they derived their estimated rate of word learning of about 3,000 words per year during the grade school and high school years.

word learning during the school years (e.g., Miller, 1977, 1978a, 1981, 1986a), it is closer to his more recent estimates. For example, the present estimate of approximately nine words learned per day by elementary school children falls between those of about 13 words per day presented by Miller and Gildea (1987) and of about seven presented by Miller (1988), and it is very close to Miller's (1991) most recent estimate of a little more than 10 words a day learned during the school years.

Not all recent investigations concerned with the acquisition of English vocabulary have concluded that the rate of vocabulary learning in schoolchildren is as high as 8 to 10 words per day. Indeed, three rather thorough and interesting recent studies (D'Anna et al., 1991; Dupuy, 1974; and Goulden et al., 1990) have suggested that the rate of word learning during the school years is of the order of only two or three words per day. It is therefore relevant to consider here why the rates of word learning that these studies suggest are so much lower than those suggested by the present and other related studies (e.g., Miller, 1991; Nagy & Anderson, 1984; Nagy & Herman, 1987).

Dupuy (1974), whose goal was to develop what he called a "basic word vocabulary test," began by drawing a large sample of 2,400 main entry words from the 1961 edition of *Webster's Third*, using criteria that were very similar to those used in the present investigation. He then pared this sample down to 123 "basic" words in the following way. First, he eliminated from the list all compounds of two or more words and hyphenated entries, all proper words (those for which the 1961 *Webster's* indicated that the first letter was always, usually, or sometimes capitalized), and all abbreviations. The remaining 1,360 words were then checked in three other dictionaries and any that were not found in each eliminated, leaving 381 words. These words were then checked in *The Random House Dictionary of the English Language* (1966) and any that were indicated to be foreign, archaic, slang, informal, or technical eliminated, leaving 307 words. These remaining words were then classified as either derived (for the exact definition of *derived words* used, see Dupuy, 1974, p. 6) or basic, and all derived words were then eliminated, leaving the final set of 123 basic words. Thus, a basic word in Dupuy's study was operationally defined as "a single word form and not a proper name, abbreviation, affix, or letter with a main entry common to the four major American dictionaries whose referent terms furnish a comprehensive definition, and it is not subordinate to another basic word form of the same term or classified as foreign, archaic, slang, or technical. This procedure also eliminates simple, regular, or common variations of basic word forms such as words formed with affixes, plurals, comparatives, adjectives, verb forms, etc." (Dupuy, 1974, p. 6). Dupuy estimated that there were 12,300 such basic words in the 1961 edition of *Webster's*.

Dupuy then tested children from the elementary and high school years on this set of 123 "basic" words using multiple-choice questions in a written format, correcting for guessing. Dupuy argued that, because of the written test format, the data for children in grades 1 and 2 should be interpreted very cautiously and that oral tests would have been more suitable at these grade levels. He found that, by grade 3, children knew an average of 14.4 of the 123 basic words; assuming a total population of 12,300 such words, this converts to an estimate of approximately 1,440 known basic words. He found that, by grade 12, students knew an average of 78 of the 123 basic words, which converts to an estimate of approximately 7,800 known basic words. Thus, in the 9 years between grade 3 and grade 12, average esti- mated basic vocabulary size had increased by about 6,360 words, which works out to about 707 words per year (cf. Nagy & Herman, 1987) or a little less than two words per day.

Dupuy's study was conducted carefully, and it was not his goal to esti- mate total vocabulary knowledge or rate of total vocabulary development in schoolchildren. Rather, his goal was to develop a test of what he called "basic words," which would allow absolute estimates of such vocabulary knowledge in grade school and high school children. Nevertheless, his study is often cited in current work that is more directly concerned with rate of total vocabulary development in children, and I think that it is important to clarify why his estimates of vocabulary knowledge and the corresponding estimated rate of vocabulary development are so much lower than those presented in this *Monograph* and in some other recent studies. The main reason is that, in defining *basic words* as he did, Dupuy eliminated the vast majority of words that occur as main entries in *Webster's Third*. His definition of *basic words* includes only a restricted subset of morphologically simple words or what in the present study are called "root words." According to his estimates, of the quarter of a million main entries or so listed in *Webster's* unabridged dictionary, only about 12,300 would qualify as basic. This means that only 12,300 basic words would be estimated to be known in the unlikely event that someone taking his test were to get credit for knowing them all. It is no wonder that his estimates are lower than those presented here and elsewhere.

Similar comments can be made about two more recent studies by Goul- den et al. (1990) and by D'Anna et al. (1991) that have also estimated vocab- ulary size but that, unlike Dupuy's, explicitly discuss the implications of the research reported for our understanding of rate of vocabulary growth. Goulden et al. began by selecting three large samples of main entries from the 1961 edition of *Webster's Third* as well as a sample from a recent addition to it.[28] The samples were then classified as base words, proper words, com- pound words, derived words, and "others." These classifications were dis-

---

[28] For a description of the "recent addition," see n. 9 above.

cussed in some detail in Chapter IV, where it was shown that, if one takes into account the somewhat different categories used in their research and in the present investigation, the proportions of main entries accounted for by different word types in the two studies are consistent with one another. Goulden et al. then eliminated proper words, compound words, derived words, and "others," leaving just the base words (primarily morphologically simple or what I have called "root" words, with some excluded). They estimated that there were less than 58,000 such words in the population from which they sampled.

Twenty native speakers of English, all of whom were university graduates, were tested for their knowledge of the base words in the samples using a modified version of the "yes/no" or checklist method, in which respondents are asked to indicate whether they know a word. Their data were converted to estimates that ranged from 13,200 to 20,700, with an average of 17,200 base words known. The authors indicate that the latter estimate corresponds to an average rate of acquisition of about two to three words a day and argue that their findings suggest that rate of vocabulary growth has been overestimated considerably by others (e.g., Miller & Gildea, 1987) and that direct teaching of English vocabulary to foreign students who have little knowledge of English should be feasible.

As was the case with Dupuy (1974), it seems that a major reason why Goulden et al.'s estimates of vocabulary knowledge and of rate of vocabulary development are lower than those previously discussed is that their definition of *base vocabulary* excluded many entries from *Webster's Third* that others would consider to be words. These authors did not exclude as many entries as Dupuy had, and their estimates are correspondingly higher than his. Still, they did exclude about three-quarters of the different main entry words in *Webster's Third* and, with some exceptions, restricted their tests to primarily morphologically simple or root words. Like Dupuy's study, Goulden et al.'s investigation is in many ways well done and interesting, and its goals were also somewhat different from those of the present research. But, since they use their findings to estimate rate of vocabulary acquisition, I believe that it is important to clarify the primary reason for the different conclusions that we have reached concerning this aspect of vocabulary development.

Finally, a recent study by D'Anna et al. (1991) should also be discussed in this context. These researchers used the *Oxford American Dictionary* (1980), a respected abridged dictionary, but one that is considerably smaller than *Webster's Third*. With a few exceptions, the authors operationally defined *word* in such a way as to exclude several types of main entries in this abridged dictionary, including hyphenated words (e.g., *free-lance*), contractions, interjections, letters and names of letters, multiword entries (e.g., *video cassette*), slang, capitalized entries (e.g., *Talmud*), foreign words, alternate spellings, words beginning with the prefixes *non-*, *re-*, or *un-*, and words identified as "old use." Excluding these types of words, 26,901 main entries remained.

D'Anna et al. then randomly sampled 380 of these main entries and used them to test undergraduate students (of an average age of about 20 years) by means of a rating scale; the students were given credit for knowing the words if they indicated that they thought that they could define them or recognize their meanings if given a multiple-choice test that included the correct and several incorrect meanings. On the basis of these ratings, D'Anna et al. estimated that, on average, the students whom they tested knew about 16,785 out of the population of 26,901 words. This estimate is quite close to that of Goulden et al. (of 17,200 base words) and can also be converted to an estimated rate of vocabulary development of between two and three words a day. D'Anna et al. concluded that vocabulary size and the corresponding rate of vocabulary growth are not as great and that attempts to teach vocabulary directly are therefore not as futile as some (e.g., Miller & Gildea, 1987; Nagy & Anderson, 1984; Nagy & Hei nan, 1987) have suggested. D'Anna et al.'s study is of interest for several reasons. For example, their discussion and analysis of the different types of words found in dictionaries is valuable, as are related discussions and analyses in Dupuy (1974) and Goulden et al. (1990). Moreover, it is important to acknowledge that D'Anna et al.'s research goals were somewhat different from those of others. Like Goulden et al., they were interested in focusing on a core set of basic words that they felt might be especially important to consider in developing programs of direct vocabulary instruction. However, they also use their findings to suggest that some previous estimates of rate of vocabulary development are too high, whereas the present research could be used to argue that theirs may be too low. It is important to keep in mind that, given their choice of dictionary and their definition of what a word is, the number of words in the total population that they were considering in deriving their estimates was about 27,000, which is only slightly more than one-tenth of the different main entry words that we estimate to be listed in *Webster's Third*.

It was mentioned in Chapter II that, as noted by many others, several factors can influence estimates of children's vocabulary size and of rates of vocabulary development, including the source from which the sample of words is drawn, the criteria of knowledge that must be met before credit is given, and the definition of what a word is. Each of these factors is undoubtedly important, and it is hoped that reasonable decisions were made about them in the present study. Both the preceding discussion of research by Dupuy, Goulden et al., and D'Anna et al. and the estimated rate analyses as well as several other analyses presented in this *Monograph* show how the last of these factors—the definition of what a word is—can be especially important in influencing conclusions about estimates of vocabulary size at different points in development, rate of vocabulary growth, and so on. For example, if our definition of a word were to include only monomorphemic root words (as Dupuy's and Goulden et al.'s did), the present research would indicate that first-grade children know an average of about 3,000 words, that fifth-grade children know about 7,500, and that the rate of vocabulary development between grade 1 and grade 5 is about three words per day. By contrast, defining a word as any boldfaced main entry in an unabridged dictionary—including root words, inflected words, derived words, literal compounds, and idioms, provided that they are headwords in the dictionary (cf. Seashore & Eckerson, 1940; Smith, 1941; Templin, 1957)—would lead us to estimate that first-grade children know an average of about 10,000 words, that fifth-grade children know about 40,000, and that the rate of vocabulary development between grade 1 and grade 5 is about 20 words per day.

Each of these ways of defining a word might be valid for some purposes, but they can lead to radically different impressions of the nature of vocabulary development if not treated cautiously. If one is interested in estimating the number of words for which children have established lexical representations and the rate at which such words are learned, the former definition would probably lead to substantial underestimation since, in addition to root words, most known idioms and many known morphologically complex words may have been previously learned; the latter definition would probably lead to substantial overestimation because many of the morphologically complex main entries that occur in an unabridged dictionary and are estimated to be within children's recognition vocabularies may not have been learned but may rather have been potentially knowable through morphological decoding. Although, in the present research, "psychologically basic" vocabulary and the rate of actual word learning were only roughly approximated, the estimates and rates fall between those that would result if one defined words as being root words and those that would result if one defined words as all boldfaced main entries in an unabridged dictionary. According to the present approximations of "psychologically basic" vocabulary, first-grade children may, on average, have established lexical representations for some 6,000 words, fifth-grade children for roughly 20,000, and the rate of word learning between grade 1 and grade 5 may be of the order of about nine words a day.

SEX EFFECTS, SES EFFECTS, AND INDIVIDUAL DIFFERENCES IN VOCABULARY DEVELOPMENT

The main concerns of this research pertained to developmental changes in recognition vocabulary, to the growth of understanding of different morphologically defined types of words, and to how knowledge of morphology and word formation contributes to vocabulary development in the early and middle elementary school years. The design was balanced for sex and SES level primarily in order to allow conclusions to be made on the basis of the performance of relatively representative samples of children rather than on the basis of just one particular subgroup or another. Although sex, SES, and individual differences were not of primary concern, a few comments can be made about them in view of the results of this study.

Apart from two grade × sex interactions (one of them unreplicated when the data were subjected to the logit transformation), there were no significant sex effects in the vast majority of the analyses. Although some studies of language development have found significant sex effects, often in favor of girls, many others have not (e.g., Maccoby & Jacklin, 1974). With respect to vocabulary development, many studies have failed to find significant sex differences after about 2 years of age (Huttenlocher, Haight, Bryk, Seltzer, & Lyons, 1991). The lack of significant gender differences in the present research is consistent with such studies and specifically with Templin (1957) and Dupuy (1974), in which virtually no significant sex differences in the development of recognition vocabulary knowledge in grade school children were found. It is also consistent with the findings of Berko (1958), who observed no consistent sex differences in her study of the acquisition of morphological rules.

On the other hand, several of the analyses did reveal significant SES differences, almost always in favor of upper-SES children. These effects were not huge, however, especially in comparison to the grade effects, word-type effects, and grade × word type interactions that were usually large and highly significant. Templin (1957) also found SES effects, in favor of upper-SES children, in her study of the development of recognition vocabulary. One of the most interesting findings regarding SES differences in the present study emerged from the MANOVA with grade, sex, and SES level as independent variables and with the raw scores for words coded as showing versus not showing evidence of morphological problem solving (see Chap. VI). The multivariate effect for SES in this analysis was significant, but the univariate analyses revealed that this effect was significant only for words coded NE, not for those coded PS. If this finding were to prove replicable, it might be interpreted as indicating that, while upper-SES children may learn somewhat more words on average, they are not significantly more capable of morphological analysis and composition than lower-SES children. However, further research is required to confirm this finding and, if confirmed, to shed light on its meaning.

Individual differences were generally considerable (see also Beck & McKeown, in press; Graves, 1986; Miller & Gildea, 1987; Nagy & Herman, 1987; Smith, 1941; Templin, 1957), and the extent of such differences tended to increase with grade. For example, not only did the mean raw scores and estimates for total main entry vocabulary knowledge increase as a function of age and grade, but so did their standard deviations, particularly between grade 3 and grade 5; this tended to be true of the raw scores and estimates for particular word types as well. As a statistical precaution, therefore, all the ANOVAs and MANOVAs on the raw scores reported in Chapters V and VI were redone on their square root transformations, but the significant effects were so robust that none was lost after the scores had been transformed. The increase with age and grade in the variability of vocabulary knowledge suggested by this investigation and by other research (e.g., Miller, 1988; Stanovich, 1986) merits further study. For example, it would be interesting to know whether this increased variability may be in part a consequence of the kind of "Matthew effect" discussed by Stanovich (1986), whereby children who have relatively large vocabularies early on encounter relatively little difficulty in learning to read, enjoy doing so, and end up reading a lot with increasingly large gains in their vocabulary knowledge as a result, whereas children who early on have relatively small vocabularies encounter more trouble learning to read, enjoy the experience less, and end up reading very little with the resulting negative effect of learning fewer and fewer words relative to those children who are reading a lot.

SUGGESTIONS FOR FUTURE RESEARCH AND GENERAL THEORETICAL IMPLICATIONS

Additional research will be necessary to confirm the results of this study and to extend them in various ways, including ones that might shed light on the processes underlying vocabulary development (see below). With respect to confirming the findings of this investigation, it would be desirable to establish their generalizability by replicating them with different children at these age and grade levels, using different samples of words taken from an unabridged dictionary, and creating these with different sampling procedures. With respect to extensions of this line of research, several areas merit investigation. As Huttenlocher et al. (1991) point out, it seems likely that, over the full range of development, the vocabulary growth curve is S shaped, with rate of vocabulary development eventually decelerating after an initial acceleration phase. The present study suggests that the deceleration phase does not begin on average until sometime after 10 years of age. Research with older children, adolescents, and adults would help clarify the nature of the vocabulary growth curve over the full span of development. If possible, it would be interesting to study recognition vocabulary knowledge in younger children as well, using procedures similar to those of the present study. It would also be valuable to investigate recognition vocabulary knowledge in different groups, such as children with reading disabilities or other types of language impairment, bilingual children, or children enrolled in language immersion programs.

Another interesting extension of the current work would be to examine children's knowledge of subentries and of other kinds of words, such as proper names, that are not included in *Webster's Third*. A particularly important but challenging area for future research lies in studying how knowledge of homographs and of polysemous meanings contributes to total vocabulary knowledge at different age and grade levels. It seems likely that knowledge of conversion or "zero derivation," as when the noun *work* is derived from the verb *work*, is a relatively early acquisition in contrast with other aspects of derivational morphology (e.g., Clark, 1981, 1982; Derwing & Baker, 1986) but that some polysemous meanings, even of common words, are acquired comparatively late in development (e.g., Asch & Nerlove, 1960).

The only qualitative analyses of children's vocabulary knowledge that were undertaken in the present study focused on the kinds of morphologically defined word types that they knew and on the quality of morphological knowledge that they expressed at different age and grade levels. It would be well worthwhile to study the quality of children's vocabulary knowledge in other ways as well. Evidence has been reported of a developmental shift from representations of word meanings in which characteristic features predominate to representations in which defining features become more central for particular lexical domains (see esp. Keil, 1987; Keil, 1989, chaps. 4–7; Keil & Batterman, 1984). For example, younger children might think of a kin term such as *uncle* as a man who visits and brings them presents on their birthdays, whereas older children might think of an uncle as a brother of either of their parents (Keil, 1987, 1989; Keil & Batterman, 1984; see also Benson & Anglin, 1987; Chambers & Tavuchis, 1976; Danziger, 1957; Haviland & Clark, 1974; Piaget, 1928). Researchers have also noted a developmental trend in the definitions of words from various domains that proceeds from the expression of functional and/or somewhat concrete properties to the expression of superordinate categories and defining properties (e.g., Al-Issa, 1969; Anglin, 1978, 1985; Feifel & Lorge, 1950; Litowitz, 1977; Nelson, 1978, 1985; Watson, 1985; Wolman & Barker, 1965). Although most of the definitions produced by the children in the present study appeared to be at least somewhat general, particularly if the use of *you* were to be counted as general (e.g., for *closet*, "You put your clothes in it"), there was evidence of a developmental increase in the expression of superordinate concepts in their definitions (e.g., for *closet*, "A closet is a *small room* where clothes are kept," or, "A *place* where you put your clothes"). More systematic analysis of children's expressed knowledge of words in studies such as the present one along these and related dimensions would be of interest. It is of course necessary to remember that the knowledge that children express in their definitions of words may not always show everything they know (see, e.g., Anglin, 1985; Macnamara, 1982; Watson, 1985; but see also Nelson, 1985), which is one reason why children in this study were given the additional opportunity to show their knowledge of the words in sentence and multiple-choice tests.

The present study examined children's *recognition vocabulary knowledge;* it would be enlightening in future research to study children's *productive vocabulary knowledge* for a representative sample of words drawn from an unabridged dictionary as well. There is evidence that, early in development, children's comprehension vocabularies are larger than their production vocabularies (e.g., Benedict, 1979) and also that older children's understanding of morphologically complex words is in advance of their ability to produce them (e.g., Clark & Berman, 1987; Clark & Hecht, 1982). As Tyler and Nagy (1989) have suggested, some types of morphological knowledge are required for the production of morphologically complex words, particularly derived words, that are not required for their comprehension. One reason why this may be so is that different derivational affixes with roughly the same meaning are used in different words in English. For example, there are several prefixes that can have the meaning "not" (White et al., 1989). Thus, we say *unhappy,* but *disenchanted,* but *immobile,* but *invincible,* but *irreverent,* but *atypical,* conventionally in English. Children do not need to choose the correct affix to recognize such words as they do if they are required to produce them. For these and other reasons, it seems likely that children's productive vocabularies would be found to be smaller than their recognition vocabularies. It would be interesting to see whether actually learned or "psychologically basic" vocabulary more closely approximates productive vocabulary than does total recognition vocabulary.

It might also be profitable to pursue some of the potential educational applications of this line of research. The children in the present study from grades 3 and 5 had received a modest amount of instruction on word attack skills in their language arts classes, including a little on how to break some inflected words, some simple compounds, and a few derived words into parts. And this instruction may, indeed, have helped them in the present study. But, as in many schools today, the emphasis was on the "whole language approach," and their training on the morphological structure of English words was not extensive. In view of the present findings, it would be useful to see whether programs of instruction specifically designed to teach morphology and word formation more comprehensively might enhance vocabulary knowledge. Some preliminary work along these lines has been done (for a review, see Graves, 1986, pp. 76–77; see also Graves & Hammond, 1980; Pressley, Levin, & McDaniel, 1987, pp. 120–122; White et al., 1989; Wysocki & Jenkins, 1987), with some positive results, indicating that more ambitious programs of instruction of this nature might indeed be both feasible and beneficial.[29]

Finally, further research will be required to elucidate the processes underlying the rapid growth of vocabulary knowledge that seems to occur during the early and middle elementary school years. In general, three kinds of such processes are currently receiving considerable attention: (1) a growing ability to infer the meanings of words through morphological analysis, or what I have called morphological problem solving (see, e.g., Nagy & Anderson, 1984; Tyler & Nagy, 1989; White et al., 1989; Wysocki & Jenkins, 1987); (2) direct instruction of vocabulary in school (see, e.g., Beck & McKeown, in press; Beck et al., 1982; McKeown et al., 1983); and (3) learning words and their meanings from context, especially during reading activities (see, e.g., Miller, 1988, 1991; Miller & Gildea, 1987; Nagy & Anderson, 1984; Nagy et al., 1987; Nagy & Herman, 1987). Below I discuss the first of these processes and its relation to the development of potentially knowable vocabulary and, then, briefly, the way in which and the extent to which each of the three processes might contribute to word learning and the growth of psychologically basic vocabulary.

Morphological Analysis and
the Growth of Potentially Knowable Vocabulary

The emphasis in the present research has to some extent been on the growing use of morphological knowledge in contributing to vocabulary development, and this research does suggest that morphological problem solving contributes substantially to the growth of vocabulary knowledge. For example, in spite of the qualifications discussed about them, the final analyses presented in Chapter VI suggest that in the neighborhood of half the estimated 40,000 main entries in *Webster's Third* in the average recognition vocabularies of fifth-grade children are knowable to them because of their ability to decipher their meanings through morphological analysis and composition. The relevance of morphological decoding to vocabulary growth suggested by this research points to the importance of clarifying the precise nature of the development of knowledge of morphology and of word formation. A great deal of progress has been made, much of it recently, in this

---

[29] One potentially promising educational approach might be to teach children about morphology and word formation in terms of *morphologically related word families*. For example, they might be taught how, through knowledge of root words (e.g., of *bake*) and of morphological rules, many related inflected words (e.g., *bakes, baking, baked*), derived words (e.g., *baker, bakery*), and compounds (e.g., *bakeshop, baking powder, clambake, half-baked*) can be understood (see Miller, 1991; Nagy & Anderson, 1984).

regard (e.g., Berko, 1958; Bowerman, 1982; Brown, 1973; Cazden, 1968; Clark, 1981, 1982, 1983a, 1983b; Clark & Berman, 1987; Clark & Cohen, 1984; Clark et al., 1985; Clark & Hecht, 1982; Clark et al., 1986; Derwing, 1976; Derwing & Baker, 1979, 1986; de Villiers & de Villiers, 1973; Freyd & Baron, 1982; Gordon, 1989; Kuczaj, 1977; MacWhinney, 1978; Marcus et al., 1992; Mervis & Johnson, 1991; Munson & Ingram, 1985; Nagy & Anderson, 1984; Tyler & Nagy, 1989; White et al., 1989; Wysocki & Jenkins, 1987). Still, further research illuminating the nature of and the mechanisms responsible for the growth of knowledge of the inflectional, derivational, and compounding rules of English (as well as of other languages) is clearly warranted.

Of direct relevance to further understanding of the findings reported in this *Monograph* would be future research aimed at clarifying the exact nature of the processes that enable children of different ages to figure out different types of complex words on the basis of morphological knowledge. Although it was acknowledged that this study was not ideal for illuminating such processes in detail, the transcripts were studied to see whether the patterns in how children expressed their knowledge of complex words coded as indicating evidence of morphological problem solving would suggest clues as to the nature of such processes, clues that might be useful to consider in future, more specifically process-oriented research. Several examples illustrating the typical patterns observed in this study were presented in the previous chapter. Although there was a developmental trend toward greater explicitness in discussing more than one morphological component for all complex word types, there was also some basis for distinguishing inflected and derived words, on the one hand, from literal compounds, on the other. Most often, inflected and derived words manifested a "part to whole" pattern in which children explicitly discussed just the embedded root word separately before achieving credit for knowing the whole word; in contrast, literal compounds most often manifested a "parts to whole" pattern because children usually explicitly discussed two or more of their component words separately before achieving final credit for knowing them.

Clear evidence both of the explicit use of analogy narrowly defined as expressing knowledge of a morphologically complex word by relating it to another complex word of similar morphological form (e.g., *piglet* for *treelet*) and of the explicit analysis of affixes (e.g., discussing the suffix -*let* in working out the meaning of *treelet*) was found to be infrequent, and the few relatively clear cases occurred mainly in the responses of the fifth-grade children. It is certainly possible that, at a tacit level, the use of analogy or the separate analysis of affixes was more common than was manifested in the statements made by the children. Indeed, these processes are clearly candidates for what makes it possible for children to compose the meanings of derived and inflected words, following an analysis of their embedded constituent words (Derwing & Skousen, in press; MacWhinney, 1978; Marcus et al., 1992; Pinker, 1991; Tyler & Nagy, 1989; White et al., 1989). However, the data resulting from this study—the knowledge expressed by children—did not reveal much direct evidence for either of them. On the other hand, some relatively clear examples of each process were observed in the fifth-grade children showing that both are possible and confirming the impression that children will exploit different strategies to figure out the meanings of complex words at different times. Further research will be necessary to establish how often such processes are used tacitly and which might be more important at different age levels for different word types.

A potentially significant clue to how children may often compose the meanings of words with affixes was the observation that, after they had described the meanings of the corresponding root words, children frequently finally achieved credit for many inflected and derived words by casting them into illustrative sentences in a grammatically appropriate fashion (e.g., "A lemon is *sourer* than an orange"; "Those two people grew up *separately*"). It was relatively uncommon and generally seemed difficult for a child to produce a general definition of a whole inflected or derived word, although this did occur occasionally, especially for some of the older children for some derived words (e.g., "A treelet might be a baby tree"). Freyd and Baron (1982) and Wysocki and Jenkins (1987) have also noted the difficulty that grade school children have in defining derived words in a general way and their tendency to compose such definitional attempts in terms of only the corresponding root words. Children seemed more capable of defining literal compounds in a general way, often after they had defined their constituent words separately (e.g., "A *cardinal flower* is a flower that is very, very red like a cardinal"). This impression is consistent with separate studies of the definitions produced by these children conducted by Carla Johnson, Sheri Skwarchuk, and me, in which we have found that children at all ages are better able to provide general definitions of literal compounds than of derived or inflected words.

Thus, there is some suggestion in these data that children often figure out literal compounds by identifying the meanings of their constituent words and then constructing definitions of the whole literal compounds by putting the constituent word meanings together in some plausible way. On the other hand, the data suggest that children more often figure out an inflected or derived word by isolating its corresponding root word, identifying its meaning, and then casting the whole inflected or derived word appropriately into an illustrative sentence. Thus, after an analysis of their root words, the ability to figure out words with affixes may ultimately often hinge on children's skill at constructing grammatically correct illustrative sentences more than is the case for literal compounds. Additional research

145

will be necessary to confirm this impression and to clarify more precisely the possible roles played by sentence construction abilities and grammatical knowledge when children compose the meanings of inflected and derived words.

The interviews suggested that what children do articulate, and therefore what they presumably find most salient, in the process of constructing complex word meanings through morphological knowledge are *whole words* that are constituents of the complex words. In the vast majority of all responses coded as showing evidence of morphological problem solving, children explicitly, and often early, discussed one (in the case of inflected and derived words and some literal compounds) or more (in the case of most literal compounds) constituent whole words en route to attaining credit for knowing the complex words; they rarely discussed affixes or other bound morphemes explicitly. Thus, although the data from this study are not ideal for illuminating the processes underlying morphological problem solving in detail, they lend credence to the view that these processes are in some sense "word based."

They also suggest that children's ability to engage in morphological problem solving will depend in part on their ability to disembed a constituent word from a complex word. A prediction that follows from this for derived words in particular is that children should engage in morphological problem solving more often for derived words in which the pronunciation of the embedded root words is not affected by derivational affixes (e.g., *treelet, amendable, modernish*), rendering them relatively transparent, than for derived words in which the pronunciation of the corresponding root words has undergone a transformation (e.g., *competitive, hideosity, cynicism*), rendering them relatively opaque. Presumably, it is easier to perceive and disembed the root word in the former type of derived word, when its phonemic structure and stress are unchanged, than in the latter, when its phonemic structure and/or stress have been altered. The transparent/opaque distinction is captured to some extent by the distinction discussed by linguists and psycholinguists (e.g., Aronoff, 1976; Chomsky & Halle, 1968; Gordon, 1989; Kiparsky, 1982, 1983; Selkirk, 1982; Tyler & Nagy, 1989) between derived words with neutral and derived words with nonneutral derivational affixes in them (as described in Chap. III above). Words with neutral affixes are usually transparent, whereas words with nonneutral affixes are often opaque. In a separate study on the data from this *Monograph*, Jill Seim and I have indeed found that the proportion of known derived words that were coded as showing evidence of morphological problem solving was much higher for words with neutral affixes and for words that are transparent than for words with nonneutral affixes and for words that are opaque. Future research investigating children's analysis of transparent and opaque words or of words with neutral and nonneutral affixes might be very useful in illuminating the processes involved in figuring out derived words through what I have called morphological problem solving (cf. Gordon, 1989; Tyler & Nagy, 1989).

The tendency in grade school children to try to figure out words through morphological analysis was particularly clear in their attempts to define idioms, which they often interpreted quite reasonably as though they were literal compounds, construing *strange woman* as a peculiar lady, *money-bags* as bags full of money, *dust bowl* as a bowl for putting dust into, and so on. Idioms were the least well known of all word types at each grade level, although, by grade 5 in particular, many children were able to define a few correctly. Children are known to interpret many figurative expressions such as metaphors, proverbs, and phrasal idioms literally (Owens, 1992), and it may be that their inclination to take a morphological problem-solving approach to lexical idioms and to treat them like literal compounds contributes to their difficulty with them. Occasionally, in the case of some relatively "transparent" idioms (Gibbs, 1987), it may be that such an approach might provide a base from which the child could guess their nonliteral meanings, possibly through metaphorical reasoning. This may have been how the 10-year-old who first hypothesized that *softheaded* might mean having a soft head, but then speculated that it might mean "not very smart or something," was able to guess its idiomatic meaning. But most lexical idioms could not be understood in this way; rather, because their meanings are not given by the combined meanings of their component words, they would usually have to be learned by rote. Even in some instances where they had been previously learned, children's inclination to treat them as literal compounds might interfere with their correct idiomatic interpretation. Recall the child who interpreted *twenty questions* as a score of queries when asked definition and sentence questions; it was not until she was given the multiple-choice test that she was able to remember having played the game twenty questions and to get credit for this idiom. Future investigations examining how children are able to go beyond literal interpretations of lexical idioms and to learn their nonliteral meanings would be well worthwhile.

Word Learning and the Growth of Psychologically Basic Vocabulary

Although this research suggests that morphological decoding contributes substantially to the dramatic total growth of lexical knowledge, it does not account for it all. For example, it does not account for the growth of knowledge of most idioms, as discussed above, and most root words since these generally cannot be analyzed into morphological components in a semantically revealing way. According to the present study, the fifth-grade children knew on average approximately 10,000 root words and idioms, the vast majority of which had presumably been previously learned.

Learning Morphologically Complex Words

Some of the known morphologically complex words may also have been learned previously, making morphological problem solving unnecessary for their comprehension. I have emphasized here and elsewhere that not all known complex words are necessarily figured out through morphological decoding and that some may have been previously learned and represented in the mental lexicon as distinct entries. Indeed, this possibility is what necessitated the coding of the responses of the children for complex words as to whether there was evidence of morphological problem solving in order to produce approximations of psychologically basic and potentially knowable vocabulary. There are at least two possible reasons why some complex words might be learned, making morphological analysis unnecessary for their comprehension. First, some inflected words (e.g., *bored, soaking*) and many derived words (e.g., *nonsense, decision, studious*) and literal compounds (e.g., *birthday, playground, sunburn*) might often be learned initially as unanalyzed wholes in much the same way as root words are. Second, other words that may have initially required morphological problem solving for their comprehension may subsequently become sufficiently familiar that they too are eventually learned and stored in long-term memory. The very act of figuring out a word through morphological analysis might contribute substantially to its learning since such analysis exemplifies the type of deep processing that has been shown to facilitate remembering (Craik & Lockhart, 1972). In spite of the qualifications concerning them, the final results presented in Chapter VI suggest that in the neighborhood of one-third of the complex words (or about 10,000 of them) and in the neighborhood of half of all the main entries (or about 20,000 of them) in the average fifth-grade child's total estimated recognition vocabulary may actually have been previously learned, that is, represented in the mental lexicon as distinct entries.

Direct Instruction of Vocabulary

It seems unlikely that many of the words actually learned by children are acquired as the result of direct vocabulary instruction in the classroom. Generally, very little time is devoted to such direct instruction in the schools that the children in the present study attended, as in most others (Graves, 1986, 1987; Nagy & Herman, 1987). And attempts to develop programs of direct vocabulary instruction have involved the teaching of only a relatively modest number of words, no more than a few hundred. For example, in one of the most ambitious and thorough attempts to teach vocabulary directly to grade school children, Beck et al. (1982) taught the meanings of 104 words intensively to children in grade 4 over a 5-month period. Although instructed children gave evidence of having learned the words and of being able to process them in tasks reflecting reading comprehension to a greater extent than carefully matched control children, the number of words acquired as a result of this intensive training was not great relative to the thousands of words per year that children seem to learn on average anyway without the benefit of such training. Thus, direct instruction of vocabulary seems unlikely to account for a large proportion of the vocabulary learning that occurs during the school years (which is not to say that such instruction may not still be valuable).

Contextual Learning

A factor that seems more likely to account for a substantial amount of the word learning that occurs in schoolchildren is the incidental learning of words and their meanings from context and, especially after grade 3 or so, during reading activities (Miller, 1988, 1991; Miller & Gildea, 1987; Nagy & Anderson, 1984; Nagy et al., 1987; Nagy & Herman, 1987; Stanovich, 1986). Recent research does show beyond a reasonable doubt that children from grade 3 and up do learn new word meanings from context during reading (e.g., Graves, 1986; Nagy et al., 1987; Nagy & Herman, 1987). Nagy, Anderson, and Herman have demonstrated that, even though the probability of actually learning a novel word from a single exposure in text may be as low as 1 in 20, if a child reads regularly, he or she still might acquire a lot of new words in this way (Nagy et al., 1987; Nagy & Herman, 1987; Nagy, Herman, & Anderson, 1985). For example, it is not unusual for a child in grade 5 to read a million words of text per year (Nagy & Anderson, 1984; Nagy et al., 1987; Nagy & Herman, 1987; White et al., 1989). This would be accomplished if the child spent 25 min a day reading at a rate of 200 words per minute for 200 days a year (Nagy & Herman, 1987) or 40 min a day reading at a rate of 125 words per minute for 200 days a year, etc. Nagy and Herman (1987) estimate that up to 30,000 of these million words might be unfamiliar and that, if 1 out of 20 of them were learned, this would account for up to 1,500 new words learned per year. Of course, this example is based on several assumptions and a fair amount of extrapolation (Graves, 1986). Children during the middle school years might on average learn fewer words in this way (Nagy & Herman, 1987), but then again they might learn more (Nagy et al., 1985). And there are considerable individual differences in the amount of reading done by children in the middle elementary school years, which would result in substantial variation in the number of words that they would actually acquire in this way (Miller, 1988; Nagy et al., 1987; Nagy & Herman, 1987; Stanovich, 1986). Still, it is clear that children during the middle school years could learn a substantial number of new words through regular reading.

This line of argument suggests that further studies of children's ability to infer and learn word meanings from context during reading activities would be fruitful, although a considerable amount of such research has recently been done (e.g., Drum & Konopak, 1987; Elshout-Mohr & van Daalen-Kapteijns, 1987; Jenkins, Stein, & Wysocki, 1984; Miller & Gildea, 1987; Nagy et al., 1987; Nagy & Herman, 1987; Nagy et al., 1985; Sternberg, 1987; see also Werner & Kaplan, 1952).

Of course, even according to the estimates provided by Nagy et al. (1987) and Nagy and Herman (1987), regular reading will not account for all the words that the present research suggests children learn between grade 1 and grade 5, particularly in the early elementary school years, when reading is less extensive. But several other factors may also influence the learning of vocabulary during these years, such as participating in conversation with parents, siblings, friends, and others, learning from lessons and discussions in the classroom, watching and listening to television, listening to the radio, and so on. As does acquiring words through reading, each of these possible factors involves the learning of words and their meanings from context, although in these cases the context involves speech, as opposed to print, and, with the exception of such activities as listening to the radio, often includes nonlinguistic as well as linguistic elements. Thus, research on children's ability to infer and learn new word meanings from context when the words are heard in speech would also be illuminating in view of the results of the present study (cf. Brown, 1957; Brown & Berko, 1960; Carey, 1978; Carey & Bartlett, 1978; Dockrell & Campbell, 1986).

CONCLUSION

As indicated at the outset of this *Monograph*, the learning of a first language by children is a remarkable phenomenon. Many of the basics of syntax and phonology are acquired tacitly by most children during the preschool years. The pragmatic, communicative, and conversational skills of children are also impressive, although their development is relatively protracted, extending through the school years and beyond. The present research suggests that vocabulary development and semantic development are quite remarkable as well. Six-year-olds have recognition vocabularies of thousands of words. According to this study, children toward the latter half of grade 1 could potentially recognize in the neighborhood of about 10,000 words (main entries in *Webster's Third*), implying an average rate of recognition vocabulary growth of about 5.5 words per day during the preceding years of language development. Even more impressively, toward the latter half of grade 5, 10-year-olds could potentially recognize in the neighborhood of 40,000 such words, which converts to an average rate of growth of recognition vocabulary knowledge of roughly 20 words per day between grade 1 and grade 5. Like the development of pragmatic, communicative, and conversational skills, and to some extent in contrast with syntactic and phonological development, vocabulary growth appears to be relatively protracted; although it is impressive during the preschool years, in some respects it is even more dramatic during the early and middle elementary school years.

Of course, a major point of this study is that, although the growth of lexical knowledge is impressive, not all words that are recognized by children have necessarily been learned by them before. Many of the words on which children were tested were morphologically complex—inflected words, derived words, and literal compounds; children at all grade levels knew considerable numbers of each of these types of words, although derived words were associated with particular growth between grade 1 and grade 5. Moreover, for substantial numbers of these complex words, children appeared to achieve credit for knowing them through the use of morphological analysis and composition, or morphological problem solving. Our analyses suggested that, of the roughly 10,000 words in the average first-grade child's estimated recognition vocabulary, some 4,000 may not actually have been learned before but were rather potentially knowable through the use of morphological analysis and composition; of the 40,000 words or so in the average fifth-grade child's estimated recognition vocabulary, approximately half may have been potentially knowable through morphological decoding. This still leaves about 6,000 and 20,000 words that the first- and fifth-grade children, respectively, had presumably learned previously and encoded as distinct entries in the mental lexicon. Thus, although the average rate of growth of recognition vocabulary knowledge in the first years of language development preceding the latter half of grade 1 may be about 5.5 words per day, the average rate of actual word learning during this time is perhaps in the neighborhood of 3 or 4 words per day; and, although the average rate of growth of known or potentially knowable vocabulary between grade 1 and grade 5 may be on the order of about 20 words per day, the average rate of actual word learning during these years is more likely to be about 9 or 10 words per day.

The emphasis in this *Monograph* has been on the possible role played by morphological knowledge in contributing to vocabulary development, on the different kinds of morphologically defined word types known at different age and grade levels, and on the distinction between knowing words through morphological problem solving and knowing them because they have been previously learned. In no way is the latter distinction meant to diminish the child's accomplishments in the realms of vocabulary and semantic development. Rather, it is hoped that this study clarifies the nature of these impressive achievements somewhat. The current findings as well as other considerations suggest that children have at least two complex, burgeoning, powerful kinds of abilities that they use in developing vocabulary knowledge. First, they presumably have a powerful ability to learn words by inferring their meanings from oral and, in all likelihood increasingly during the school years, from written contexts and somehow to develop representations of these words and their meanings in long-term memory. Although this skill was not directly studied in the present research, as argued earlier some such ability would seem necessary to account for the thousands of words that children appear to actually learn during the preschool and the early and middle elementary school years. Second, they also appear to have an increasingly powerful ability to analyze the morphological structure of complex words so as to figure out their meanings, which they can apply to words that they have not actually learned before. Thus, the child's vocabulary knowledge is enhanced increasingly by morphological knowledge, that is, by tacit or explicit knowledge of the rules of morphology and word formation.

THE 196 WORDS ON WHICH CHILDREN WERE TESTED, WITH COMMENTS ON THEIR MORPHOLOGICAL CLASSIFICATIONS

The 196 words on which children were tested in this study are shown in Table A1 (which follows the text of this appendix). The morphological classifications are shown to the right of each word. In Table A1, the symbols are defined as follows: R = root word; IW = inflected word; D = derived word with one derivational affix; C = literal compound made of two root words; I = idiom; DD = derived word with two derivational affixes; DDD = derived word with three derivational affixes; DDDD = derived word with four derivational affixes; D_{IW} = derived word with an inflectional suffix; CC = literal compound made of three root words; CCC = literal compound made of four root words; C_D = literal compound made of one root word and one derived word with a derivational affix; C_{IW} = literal compound made of one root word and one inflected word; CC_{IW} = literal compound made of two root words and one inflected word; CC_D = literal compound made of two root words and one derived word with a derivational affix; C(I) = literal compound made of one root word and one idiom; 2CFs = word made of two combining forms (see below); CF + D = word made of a combining form and a derivational affix. For definitions of and the rationale for the various morphological classifications, see Chapters II and IV.

As described in Chapter IV, interrater reliability for the morphological classifications of these words was 96% in terms of the five major classifications (root words, inflected words, derived words, literal compounds, and idioms) and 95% when the more stringent criterion of perfect agreement of both type and subtype was employed. Most decisions were relatively straightforward, particularly because *Webster's Third* lists affixes and combining forms as well as words. However, there were some borderline cases that are discussed below.

Word 10, *enjoyable*, was classed as D, a derived word with one derivational affix, *-able;* although *en-* is included in *Webster's Third* as a prefix, none of the meanings listed for this prefix corresponded to the *en-* in *enjoy* or *enjoyable*, and we could not think of or find other words beginning with *en-* other than *enjoy* and its derivatives with the relevant meaning. Thus, *enjoyable* was not classified as doubly derived (DD) on the grounds that one could not derive the meaning of *enjoy* from morphological components. Word 37, *northwest coast indian* was classified as CCC instead of CCC$_D$ since the sense of *indian* in it is not derived from *India*. Word 47, *titanosaurus*, was classified as a root word even though *-saurus* is a common ending in the names of many dinosaurs and is listed in *Webster's Third* as a combining form meaning "lizard." The problem is that *titano-* is not listed in *Webster's Third* with the relevant meaning and does not appear in other words with this meaning. Thus, one could not derive the meaning of this word from morphological components, and, hence, it was classified as a root word. Word 51, *wild lilac*, was classified as an idiom as opposed to a literal compound because a wild lilac is not a lilac that has escaped cultivation and grown wild. A wild lilac belongs to a different genus of plants (*Ceanothus*) than does a lilac (*Syringa*) and, indeed, to a different botanical family. Hence, it was decided that a definition of *wild lilac* as a lilac that has grown wild or that has escaped cultivation would not be accepted as correct, and it was therefore classified as an idiom. On the other hand, word 58, *cardinal flower*, was classified as a literal compound since it was decided to accept "red flower" as a definition of this word because cardinal flowers are red and because a salient property of cardinals, the birds, is their brilliant red color.

These last two borderline cases (*wild lilac, cardinal flower*) illustrate the point that our classification decisions in such cases were often determined ultimately by what we decided would be reasonable to accept as definitions of the words. Word 146, *hematology*, is composed of two bound morphemes called "combining forms" (2CFs) listed in *Webster's* (*hemato-*, meaning "blood," and *-logy*, meaning "theory" or "science"; hence, *hematology* is the science of blood). Words such as this are interesting since they have no root words or free morphemes in them. As Bauer (1983) notes, such words are borderline cases, being similar in some respects to derived words and in others to compounds. Following Bloomfield (1933), who treated words without a free form and more than one bound form as derived words, we classified this word as derived as well (and as bimorphemic since it consists of two morphemes). One could classify such words as compounds with equal justification (e.g., Adams, 1973). Such words were not common in the sample, and, in general, children did not know them, so this classification decision has little bearing on the results of this study.

In the 196 words on which children were tested, one other word, word 187, *duarchy*, consisted of two combining forms (*du-* and *-archy*, both listed as combining forms in *Webster's Third*), and one, word 185, *hominidae*, consisted of a combining form (*homin-*, meaning "man" or "human") and a suffix (*-idae*, meaning "members of the family of"). Each of these words was also classified as derived and as bimorphemic for the purposes of analysis. Finally, word 191, *grandfer* (defined in *Webster's Third* as English dialect for *grandfather*), was classified as a root word since *fer* was not listed separately as a word in *Webster's Third* with the meaning of "father" and since it would not be possible to derive the meaning of *grandfer* from morphological components.

TABLE A1

THE 196 WORDS ON WHICH CHILDREN WERE TESTED IN THIS STUDY,
ORDERED FROM SIMPLEST TO MOST DIFFICULT

	Morphological Classification		Morphological Classification
1. *closet*	R	42. *foundationless*	DD
2. *soaking*	IW	43. *unbribable*	DD
3. *elastic*	R	44. *loft*	R
4. *changed*	IW	45. *hermit*	R
5. *plenty*	R	46. *unreluctant*	D
6. *outgrow*	C	47. *titanosaurus*	R
7. *reports*	IW	48. *custom-made*	C
8. *improve*	R	49. *pep*	R
9. *forgotten*	IW	50. *priesthood*	D
10. *enjoyable*	D	51. *wild lilac*	I
11. *milk cow*	C	52. *workable*	D
12. *mucky*	D	53. *talkativeness*	DD
13. *live-born*	C	54. *accusal*	D
14. *stillness*	D	55. *newsbeat*	C
15. *western saddle*	C_D	56. *inearth*	D
16. *sourer*	IW	57. *peasant*	R
17. *baits*	IW	58. *cardinal flower*	C
18. *flop*	R	59. *cousinly*	D
19. *serviced*	IW	60. *competitive*	D
20. *fenderless*	D	61. *maned sheep*	C_{IW}
21. *knotless*	D	62. *boomless*	D
22. *low-level*	C	63. *off-camera*	C
23. *scene*	R	64. *parole*	R
24. *separately*	D	65. *raspberry rose*	C
25. *occasion*	R	66. *carrying-on*	I
26. *firesafe*	C	67. *hopelessness*	DD
27. *towering*	IW	68. *strange woman*	I
28. *Japanese crab*	C_D	69. *quarrelsomeness*	DD
29. *incomparable*	DD	70. *corresponding*	IW
30. *treelet*	D	71. *rational*	R
31. *polyester*	R	72. *clark*	R
32. *recklessly*	DD	73. *loose cover*	C
33. *modernish*	D	74. *extremeness*	D
34. *suspicious*	D	75. *redefine*	D
35. *doubting Thomas*	I	76. *meadow pea*	I
36. *dishing*	IW	77. *back along*	C
37. *northwest coast indian*	CCC	78. *staggerer*	D
38. *advisable*	D	79. *semiliquid*	D
39. *readmission*	DD	80. *eleventh hour*	I
40. *preservable*	D	81. *ingatherer*	DD
41. *untrusty*	DD	82. *waahoo*	R

TABLE A1 (*Continued*)

	Morphological Classification		Morphological Classification
83. *twenty questions*	I	140. *iodide*	D
84. *seabound*	C	141. *limbic system*	I
85. *amendable*	D	142. *thusness*	D
86. *softheaded*	I	143. *exhaust-gas-analyzer*	CC_D
87. *adhesive*	D	144. *gathering coal*	I
88. *sparrow-tail*	C	145. *causationist*	DD
89. *wittily*	DD	146. *hematology*	2CFs
90. *retailing*	IW	147. *hypertonicity*	DDD
91. *trail boss*	C	148. *frugalness*	D
92. *noncommunicable*	DD	149. *lay over*	I
93. *skunk cabbage*	I	150. *thing in action*	I
94. *bare-eyed cockatoo*	CC_{IW}	151. *referendum*	R
95. *malarial fever*	C_D	152. *disburden*	D
96. *underprize*	C	153. *convocate*	R
97. *moneybags*	I	154. *spousal*	D
98. *waspishly*	DD	155. *devonshire*	R
99. *ropey*	D	156. *cynicism*	D
100. *ashfall*	C	157. *alphabetico-classed catalog*	I
101. *dust bowl*	I	158. *airplay*	C
102. *explorational*	DD	159. *centenary*	R
103. *Indian robin*	C_D	160. *insatiable*	DD
104. *right at*	I	161. *disreputation*	DD
105. *ebony brown*	C	162. *hideosity*	D
106. *magnetization*	DD	163. *rembrandtish*	D
107. *overfulfill*	C	164. *oppositive*	D
108. *delaying action*	I	165. *pyro*	R
109. *steady state*	C	166. *erosible*	D
110. *universalness*	DD	167. *patriarchic*	D
111. *zero hour*	I	168. *capital gain*	I
112. *yew green*	C	169. *abstractionism*	DD
113. *pump cylinder*	C	170. *pubescent*	D
114. *jovial*	R	171. *hourglass stomach*	C(I)
115. *brights*	IW	172. *rehabilitant*	DD
116. *viridine green*	C	173. *pony league*	I
117. *continuous kiln*	C_D	174. *driveling*	IW
118. *share-out*	C	175. *derisible*	D
119. *unfooted*	D_{IW}	176. *missive*	R
120. *golden spoon*	I	177. *salinification*	DD
121. *clerkship*	D	178. *evulse*	R
122. *motor carriage*	I	179. *subconical*	DD
123. *confidential communication*	I	180. *sadomasochist*	C_D
124. *slicking*	IW	181. *denervate*	DD
125. *lady's slipper*	I	182. *nectarian*	D
126. *impassibility*	DDD	183. *calorimeter*	D
127. *brother-in-arms*	CC_{IW}	184. *voice part*	I
128. *ritual murder*	I	185. *hominidae*	CF + D
129. *bluenosed*	I	186. *filled board*	C_{IW}
130. *head and front*	I	187. *duarchy*	2CFs
131. *combat fatigue*	I	188. *drammatico*	R
132. *supposition*	D	189. *shoemake*	R
133. *chuckleheaded*	I	190. *organdy*	R
134. *limby*	D	191. *grandfer*	R
135. *bushelage*	D	192. *freshet*	R
136. *vegetive*	D	193. *jiggered*	IW
137. *gamey*	D	194. *break back*	C
138. *chateau grey*	I	195. *intransitivity*	DDD
139. *despiritualization*	DDDD	196. *ruff out*	C

NOTE.—For definitions of the symbols used to identify morphological classifications, see the first paragraph of this appendix.

REFERENCES

Adams, V. (1973). *An introduction to modern English word-formation.* London: Longman.

Al-Issa, I. (1969). The development of word definitions in children. *Journal of Genetic Psychology,* **114,** 25–28.

Anderson, R. C., & Freebody, P. (1981). Vocabulary knowledge. In J. T. Guthrie (Ed.), *Comprehension and teaching: Research reviews.* Newark, DE: International Reading Association.

Anglin, J. M. (1977). *Word, object, and conceptual development.* New York: Norton.

Anglin, J. M. (1978). From reference to meaning. *Child Development,* **49,** 969–976.

Anglin, J. M. (1980). Acquiring linguistic skills: A study of sentence construction in preschool children. In D. R. Olson (Ed.), *The social foundations of language and thought: Essays in honor of Jerome S. Bruner.* New York: Norton.

Anglin, J. M. (1985). The child's expressible knowledge of word concepts: What preschoolers can say about the meanings of some nouns and verbs. In K. E. Nelson (Ed.), *Children's language* (Vol. **5**). Hillsdale, NJ: Erlbaum.

Aronoff, M. (1976). *Word formation in generative grammar.* Cambridge, MA: MIT Press.

Asch, S. E., & Nerlove, H. (1960). The development of double function terms in children: An exploratory investigation. In B. Kaplan & S. Wapner (Eds.), *Perspectives in psychological theory: Essays in honor of Heinz Werner.* New York: International Universities Press.

Au, T. K., & Glusman, M. (1990). The principle of mutual exclusivity in word learning: To honor or not to honor? *Child Development,* **61,** 1474–1490.

Barnett, V. (1974). *Elements of sampling theory.* London: Edward Arnold.

Bates, E. (1976). *Language and context.* New York: Academic.

Bauer, L. (1983). *English word-formation.* New York: Cambridge University Press.

Beck, I. L., & McKeown, M. G. (in press). Conditions of vocabulary acquisition. In P. D. Pearson (Ed.), *The handbook of reading research* (Vol. **2**). New York: Longman.

Beck, I. L., McKeown, M. G., & Omanson, R. C. (1987). The effects and uses of diverse vocabulary instructional techniques. In M. G. McKeown & M. E. Curtis (Eds.), *The nature of vocabulary acquisition.* Hillsdale, NJ: Erlbaum.

Beck, I. L., Perfetti, C., & McKeown, M. G. (1982). The effects of long-term vocabulary instruction on lexical access and reading comprehension. *Journal of Educational Psychology,* **74,** 506–521.

Benedict, H. (1979). Early lexical development: Comprehension and production. *Journal of Child Language,* **6,** 183–200.

Benelli, B., Arcuri, L., & Marchesini, G. (1988). Cognitive and linguistic factors in the development of word definitions. *Journal of Child Language,* **15,** 619–635.

Benson, N., & Anglin, J. M. (1987). The child's knowledge of English kin terms. *First Language, 7*, 41–66.

Berko, J. (1958). The child's learning of English morphology. *Word, 14*, 150–177.

Blishen, B. R., & McRoberts, M. A. (1976). A revised socioeconomic index for occupations in Canada. *Canadian Review of Sociology and Anthropology, 13*, 71–79.

Bloom, L. (1973). *One word at a time: The use of single word utterances before syntax.* The Hague: Mouton.

Bloomfield, L. (1933). *Language.* New York: Henry Holt.

Bowerman, M. (1979). The acquisition of complex sentences. In P. Fletcher & M. Garman (Eds.), *Language acquisition* (1st ed.). New York: Cambridge University Press.

Bowerman, M. (1982). Reorganizational processes in lexical and syntactic development. In E. Wanner & L. Gleitman (Eds.), *Language acquisition: The state of the art.* New York: Cambridge University Press.

Brinton, B., & Fujiki, M. (1984). Development of topic manipulation skills in discourse. *Journal of Speech and Hearing Research, 27*, 350–358.

Brown, F. (1983). *Principles of educational and psychological testing.* New York: CBS.

Brown, R. (1957). Linguistic determinism and the part of speech. *Journal of Abnormal and Social Psychology, 55*, 1–5.

Brown, R. (1973). *A first language.* Cambridge, MA: Harvard University Press.

Brown, R. (1980). The maintenance of conversation. In D. Olson (Ed.), *The social foundations of language and thought.* New York: Norton.

Brown, R., & Berko, J. (1960). Word association and the acquisition of grammar. *Child Development, 31*, 1–14.

Brown, R., & Hanlon, C. (1970). Derivational complexity and order of acquisition in child speech. In J. R. Hayes (Ed.), *Cognition and the development of language.* New York: Wiley.

Bruner, J. S. (1983). *Child's talk.* New York: Norton.

Carey, S. (1978). The child as word learner. In M. Halle, J. Bresnan, & G. A. Miller (Eds.), *Linguistic theory and psychological reality.* Cambridge, MA: MIT Press.

Carey, S. (1983). Constraints on the meanings of natural kind terms. In T. B. Seiler & W. Wannenmacher (Eds.), *Concept development and the development of word meaning.* New York: Springer.

Carey, S. (1988). Lexical development—the Rockefeller years. In W. Hirst (Ed.), *The making of cognitive science: Essays in honor of George A. Miller.* New York: Cambridge University Press.

Carey, S., & Bartlett, E. J. (1978). Acquiring a single new word. *Papers and Reports on Child Language, 15*, 17–29.

Carroll, J., Davies, P., & Richman, B. (1971). *Word frequency book.* New York: American Heritage.

Cazden, C. (1968). The acquisition of noun and verb inflections. *Child Development, 39*, 433–448.

Chall, J. S., & Dale, E. (1950). Familiarity of selected health terms. *Educational Research Bulletin, 39*, 197–206.

Chambers, J. C., & Tavuchis, N. (1976). Kids and kin: Children's understanding of American kin terms. *Journal of Child Language, 3*, 63–80.

Chomsky, N. (1965). *Aspects of the theory of syntax.* Cambridge, MA: MIT Press.

Chomsky, N. (1970). Remarks on nominalization. In R. Jacobs & P. Rosenbaum (Eds.), *Readings in English transformational grammar.* Waltham, MA: Ginn.

Chomsky, N. (1975). *Reflections on language.* New York: Pantheon.

Chomsky, N., & Halle, M. (1968). *The sound pattern of English.* New York: Harper & Row.

Clark, E. V. (1981). Lexical innovations: How children learn to create new words. In W. Deutsch (Ed.), *The child's construction of language*. London: Academic.

Clark, E. V. (1982). The young word-maker: A case study of innovation in the child's lexicon. In E. Wanner & L. Gleitman (Eds.), *Language acquisition: The state of the art*. New York: Cambridge University Press.

Clark, E. V. (1983a). Convention and contrast in acquiring the lexicon. In T. B. Seiler & W. Wannenmacher (Eds.), *Concept development and the development of word meaning*. New York: Springer.

Clark, E. V. (1983b). Meanings and concepts. In J. H. Flavell & E. M. Markman (Eds.), P. H. Mussen (Series Ed.), *Handbook of child psychology: Vol. 3. Cognitive development*. New York: Wiley.

Clark, E. V. (1987). The principle of contrast: A constraint on language acquisition. In B. MacWhinney (Ed.), *Mechanisms of language acquisition*. Hillsdale, NJ: Erlbaum.

Clark, E. V., & Berman, R. A. (1987). Types of linguistic knowledge: Interpreting and producing compound nouns. *Journal of Child Language, 14,* 547–567.

Clark, E. V., & Cohen, S. R. (1984). Productivity and memory for newly formed words. *Journal of Child Language, 2,* 611–625.

Clark, E. V., Gelman, S. A., & Lane, N. M. (1985). Compound nouns and category structure in young children. *Child Development, 56,* 84–94.

Clark, E. V., & Hecht, B. F. (1982). Learning to coin agent and instrument nouns. *Cognition, 12,* 1–24.

Clark, E. V., Hecht, B. F., & Mulford, R. C. (1986). Coining complex compounds in English: Affixes and word order in acquisition. *Linguistics, 24,* 7–29.

Clark, H. H., & Clark, E. V. (1977). *Psychology and language: An introduction to psycholinguistics*. New York: Harcourt Brace Jovanovich.

Cohen, J., & Cohen, P. (1975). *Applied multiple regression/correlation analysis for the behavioral sciences*. Hillsdale, NJ: Erlbaum.

Cole, M., & Cole, S. (1993). *The development of children* (2d ed.). New York: W. H. Freeman.

Collins, W. A., & Kuczaj, S. A. (1991). *Developmental psychology*. New York: Macmillan.

Colvin, C. M. (1951). A re-examination of the vocabulary question. *Elementary English, 28,* 350–356.

Conway, F. (1967). *Sampling: An introduction for social sciences*. London: Allen & Unwin.

Cowie, A. P., & Mackin, R. (Eds.). (1975). *Oxford dictionary of current idiomatic English* (Vol. 1). London: Oxford University Press.

Cowie, A. P., Mackin, R., & McCaig, R. (Eds.). (1983). *Oxford dictionary of current idiomatic English* (Vol. 2). London: Oxford University Press.

Craik, F. I. M., & Lockhart, R. S. (1972). Levels of processing: A framework for memory research. *Journal of Verbal Learning and Verbal Behavior, 11,* 671–684.

Curtis, M. E. (1987). Vocabulary testing and vocabulary instruction. In M. G. McKeown & M. E. Curtis (Eds.), *The nature of vocabulary acquisition*. Hillsdale, NJ: Erlbaum.

D'Anna, C., Zechmeister, E., & Hall, J. (1991). Toward a meaningful definition of vocabulary size. *Journal of Reading Behavior, 23,* 109–122.

Danziger, K. (1957). The child's understanding of kinship terms: A study in the development of relational concepts. *Journal of General Psychology, 91,* 213–232.

Derwing, B. (1976). Morpheme recognition and the learning of rules for derivational morphology. *Canadian Journal of Linguistics, 21,* 38–66.

Derwing, B., & Baker, W. (1979). Recent research on the acquisition of English morphology. In P. Fletcher & M. Garman (Eds.), *Language acquisition* (1st ed.). New York: Cambridge University Press.

Derwing, B., & Baker, W. (1986). Assessing morphological development. In P. Fletcher

& M. Garman (Eds.), *Language acquisition* (2d ed.). New York: Cambridge University Press.

Derwing, B., & Skousen, R. (in press). Real-time morphology: Symbolic rules or analogical networks? In *Proceedings of the Berkeley Linguistic Society* (Vol. **15**). Berkeley, CA: Berkeley Linguistic Society.

de Villiers, J. G., & de Villiers, P. A. (1973). A cross-sectional study: The development of grammatical morphemes in child speech. *Journal of Psycholinguistic Research*, **2**, 267–278.

Dockrell, J., & Campbell, R. (1986). Lexical acquisition strategies in the preschool child. In S. A. Kuczaj & M. C. Barrett (Eds.), *The development of word meaning*. New York: Springer.

Dore, J. (1979). Conversation and preschool language development. In P. Fletcher & M. Garman (Eds.), *Language acquisition* (1st ed.). New York: Cambridge University Press.

Drum, P. A., & Konopak, B. C. (1987). Learning word meanings from written context. In M. G. McKeown & M. E. Curtis (Eds.), *The nature of vocabulary acquisition*. Hillsdale, NJ: Erlbaum.

Dupuy, H. (1974). *The rationale, development, and standardization of a basic word vocabulary test* (DHEW Publication No. HRA74-1334). Washington, DC: U.S. Government Printing Office.

Elshout-Mohr, M., & van Daalen-Kapteijns, M. M. (1987). Cognitive processes in learning word meanings. In M. G. McKeown & M. E. Curtis (Eds.), *The nature of vocabulary acquisition*. Hillsdale, NJ: Erlbaum.

Feifel, H., & Lorge, I. (1950). Qualitative differences in the vocabulary responses of children. *Journal of Educational Psychology*, **41**, 1–18.

Flavell, J., Botkin, P., Fry, C., Wright, J., & Jarvis, P. (1968). *The development of role-taking and communication skills in children*. New York: Wiley.

Flavell, J., Miller, P., & Miller, S. (1993). *Cognitive development* (3d ed.). Englewood Cliffs, NJ: Prentice-Hall.

Fraser, B. (1970). Idioms within transformational grammar. *Foundations of Language*, **6**, 22–42.

Freyd, P., & Baron, J. (1982). Individual differences in acquisition of derivational morphology. *Journal of Verbal Learning and Verbal Behavior*, **21**, 282–295.

Funk & Wagnalls. (1937). *New standard dictionary of the English language* (unabridged ed.). New York: Funk & Wagnalls.

Gathercole, V. C. (1987). The contrastive hypothesis for the acquisition of word meaning: A reconsideration of the theory. *Journal of Child Language*, **14**, 493–532.

Gibbs, R. (1987). Linguistic factors in children's understanding of idioms. *Journal of Child Language*, **14**, 569–586.

Gopnik, A., & Meltzoff, A. (1987). The development of categorization in the second year and its relation to other cognitive and linguistic developments. *Child Development*, **58**, 1523–1531.

Gordon, P. (1989). Levels of affixation in the acquisition of English morphology. *Journal of Memory and Language*, **28**, 519–530.

Goulden, R., Nation, P., & Read, J. (1990). How large can a receptive vocabulary be? *Applied Linguistics*, **11**, 341–363.

Gove, P. B. (1981). Preface. In *Webster's third new international dictionary of the English language*. Springfield, MA: G. & C. Merriam.

Graves, M. (1986). Vocabulary learning and instruction. *Review of Research in Education*, **13**, 49–89.

Graves, M. (1987). The roles of instruction in fostering vocabulary development. In

M. G. McKeown & M. E. Curtis (Eds.), *The nature of vocabulary acquisition*. Hillsdale, NJ: Erlbaum.

Graves, M., Brunetti, G., & Slater, W. (1982). The reading vocabularies of primary grade children of varying geographic and social backgrounds. In J. A. Harris & L. A. Harris (Eds.), *New inquiries in reading research and instruction*. Rochester, NY: National Reading Conference.

Graves, M., & Hammond, H. (1980). A validated procedure for teaching prefixes and its effect on students' ability to assign meaning to novel words. In M. L. Kamil & A. V. Moe (Eds.), *Perspectives on reading research and instruction*. Washington, DC: National Reading Conference.

Greenfield, P., & Smith, J. (1976). *The structure of communication in early language development*. New York: Academic.

Greenhouse, S. W., & Geisser, S. (1959). On methods in the analysis of profile data. *Psychometrika*, **24**, 95–112.

Halle, M. (1973). Prolegomena to a theory of word-formation. *Linguistic Inquiry*, **4**, 3–16.

Halliday, M. (1975). *Learning how to mean: Explorations in the development of language*. London: Edward Arnold.

Harris, J. R., & Liebert, R. M. (1991). *The child* (3d ed.). Englewood Cliffs, NJ: Prentice-Hall.

Haviland, S. E., & Clark, E. V. (1974). This man's father is my father's son: A study of the acquisition of English kin terms. *Journal of Child Language*, **1**, 23–47.

Hetherington, E., & Parke, R. (1993). *Child psychology: A contemporary viewpoint* (4th ed.). Toronto: McGraw-Hill.

Hockett, C. (1958). *A course in modern linguistics*. New York: Macmillan.

Howell, D. C. (1987). *Statistical methods for psychology* (2d ed.). Boston: Duxbury.

Huttenlocher, J. (1974). The origins of language comprehension. In R. L. Solso (Ed.), *Theories in cognitive psychology: The Loyola symposium*. Potomac, MD: Erlbaum.

Huttenlocher, J., Haight, W., Bryk, A., Seltzer, M., & Lyons, T. (1991). Early vocabulary growth: Relation to language input and gender. *Developmental Psychology*, **27**, 236–248.

Ingram, D. (1974). Phonological rules in young children. *Journal of Child Language*, **1**, 49–64.

Ingram, D. (1986). Phonological development: Production. In P. Fletcher & M. Garman (Eds.), *Language acquisition* (2d ed.). New York: Cambridge University Press.

Jackendoff, R. (1975). Morphological and semantic regularities in the lexicon. *Language*, **51**, 639–671.

Jenkins, J. R., Stein, M., & Wysocki, K. (1984). Learning vocabulary through reading. *American Educational Research Journal*, **21**, 767–787.

Jones, S. S., Smith, L. B., & Landau, B. (1991). Object properties and knowledge in early lexical learning. *Child Development*, **62**, 499–516.

Just, M. A., & Carpenter, P. A. (1987). *The psychology of reading and language comprehension*. Newton, MA: Allyn & Bacon.

Katz, J. J., & Postal, P. M. (1963). Semantic interpretation of idioms and sentences containing them. *MIT Research Laboratory of Electronics Quarterly Progress Report*, No. 70, 275–282.

Keil, F. (1983). Semantic inferences and the acquisition of word meaning. In T. B. Seiler & W. Wannenmacher (Eds.), *Concept development and the development of word meaning*. New York: Springer.

Keil, F. (1987). Conceptual development and category structure. In U. Neisser (Ed.), *Concepts and conceptual development*. New York: Cambridge University Press.

Keil, F. (1989). *Concepts, kinds, and cognitive development*. Cambridge, MA: MIT Press.

Keil, F., & Batterman, N. (1984). A characteristic to defining shift in the development of word meaning. *Journal of Verbal Learning and Verbal Behavior,* **23,** 221–236.

Kiparsky, P. (1982). From cyclic phonology to lexical phonology. In H. van der Hulst & N. Smith (Eds.), *The structure of phonological representations.* Dordrecht: Foris.

Kiparsky, P. (1983). Word-formation and the lexicon. In F. Ingeman (Ed.), *Proceedings of the mid-America Linguistics Conference.* Lawrence: University of Kansas Press.

Kucera, H., & Francis, W. (1967). *Computational analysis of present day American English.* Providence, RI: Brown University Press.

Kuczaj, S. A. (1977). The acquisition of regular and irregular past tense forms. *Journal of Verbal Learning and Verbal Behavior,* **16,** 589–600.

Landau, S. (1984). *Dictionaries: The art and craft of lexicology.* New York: Scribner's.

Layton, T., & Stick, S. (1979). Comprehension and production of comparatives and superlatives. *Journal of Child Language,* **6,** 511–527.

Leopold, W. (1939). *Speech development of a bilingual child: A linguist's record: Vol. 1. Vocabulary growth in the first two years.* Evanston, IL: Northwestern University Press.

Litowitz, R. (1977). Learning to make definitions. *Journal of Child Language,* **4,** 289–304.

Lorge, I., & Chall, J. (1963). Estimating the size of vocabularies of children and adults: An analysis of methodological issues. *Journal of Experimental Education,* **32,** 147–157.

Lyons, J. (1968). *Introduction to theoretical linguistics.* Cambridge: Cambridge University Press.

Maccoby, E., & Jacklin, C. (1974). *The psychology of sex differences.* Stanford, CA: Stanford University Press.

Macnamara, J. (1982). *Names for things: A study of human learning.* Cambridge, MA: MIT Press.

MacWhinney, B. (1978). The acquisition of morphophonology. *Monographs of the Society for Research in Child Development,* **43**(1–2, Serial No. 174).

Makkai, A. (1972). *Idiom structure in English.* The Hague: Mouton.

Makkai, A. (Ed.). (1975). *A dictionary of American idioms* (rev. ed.). New York: Barron's Educational.

Marchand, H. (1969). *The categories and types of present-day English word-formation* (2d ed.). Munich: Beck.

Marcus, G. F., Pinker, S., Ullman, M., Hollander, M., Rosen, T. J., & Xu, F. (1992). Overregularization in language acquisition. *Monographs of the Society for Research in Child Development,* **57**(4, Serial No. 228).

Markman, E. M. (1987). How children constrain the possible meanings of words. In U. Neisser (Ed.), *Concepts and conceptual development: Ecological and intellectual factors in categorization.* Cambridge: Cambridge University Press.

Markman, E. M. (1989). *Categorization and naming in children: Problems of induction.* Cambridge, MA: MIT Press.

McCarthy, D. (1954). Language development in children. In L. Carmichael (Ed.), *Manual of child psychology* (2d ed.). New York: Wiley.

McGhee-Bidlack, B. (1991). The development of noun definitions: A metalinguistic analysis. *Journal of Child Language,* **18,** 417–434.

McKeown, M. G., Beck, I. L., Omanson, R., & Perfetti, C. A. (1983). The effects of long-term vocabulary instruction on reading comprehension: A replication. *Journal of Reading Behavior,* **15,** 3–18.

McNeill, D. (1987). *Psycholinguistics: A new approach.* New York: Harper & Row.

Merriam-Webster. (1983). *9,000 words.* Springfield, MA: G. & C. Merriam.

Merriman, W. E., & Bowman, L. L. (1989). The mutual exclusivity bias in children's word learning. *Monographs of the Society for Research in Child Development,* **54**(3–4, Serial No. 220).

Mervis, C. B. (1987). Child-basic object categories and early lexical development. In U. Neisser (Ed.), *Concepts and conceptual development: Ecological and intellectual factors in categorization.* Cambridge: Cambridge University Press.

Mervis, C. B., & Johnson, K. E. (1991). Acquisition of the plural morpheme: A case study. *Developmental Psychology, 27,* 222–235.

Miller, G. A. (1977). *Spontaneous apprentices: Children and language.* New York: Seabury.

Miller, G. A. (1978a). The acquisition of word meaning. *Child Development, 49,* 999–1004.

Miller, G. A. (1978b). Semantic relations among words. In M. Halle, J. Bresnan, & G. A. Miller (Eds.), *Linguistic theory and psychological reality.* Cambridge, MA: MIT Press.

Miller, G. A. (1981). *Language and speech.* New York: W. H. Freeman.

Miller, G. A. (1986a). Dictionaries in the mind. *Language and Cognitive Processes, 1*(3), 171–185.

Miller, G. A. (1986b). *How school children learn words* (Report No. 7). Princeton, NJ: Cognitive Science Laboratory, Princeton University.

Miller, G. A. (1988). The challenge of universal literacy. *Science, 241,* 1293–1299.

Miller, G. A. (1991). *The science of words.* New York: Scientific American Library.

Miller, G. A., & Gildea, P. N. (1987, September). How school children learn words. *Scientific American, 257,* 94–98.

Miller, G. A., & Johnson-Laird, P. N. (1976). *Language and perception.* Cambridge, MA: Harvard University Press.

Munson, J., & Ingram, D. (1985). Morphology before syntax: A case study from language acquisition. *Journal of Child Language, 12,* 681–684.

Nagy, W., & Anderson, R. (1984). The number of words in printed school English. *Reading Research Quarterly, 19,* 304–330.

Nagy, W., Anderson, R., & Herman, P. (1987). Learning word meanings from context during normal reading. *American Educational Research Journal, 24,* 237–270.

Nagy, W., & Herman, P. (1987). Depth and breadth of vocabulary knowledge: Implications for acquisition and instruction. In M. G. McKeown & M. E. Curtis (Eds.), *The nature of vocabulary acquisition.* Hillsdale, NJ: Erlbaum.

Nagy, W., Herman, P., & Anderson, R. (1985). Learning words from context. *Reading Research Quarterly, 20,* 233–253.

Nelson, K. (1973). Structure and strategy in learning to talk. *Monographs of the Society for Research in Child Development, 38*(1–2, Serial No. 149).

Nelson, K. (1978). Semantic development and the development of semantic memory. In K. E. Nelson (Ed.), *Children's language* (Vol. 1). New York: Gardner.

Nelson, K. (1985). *Making sense: The acquisition of shared meaning.* New York: Academic.

Nelson, K. (1988). Constraints on word learning? *Cognitive Development, 3,* 221–246.

Owens, R. E. (1992). *Language development: An introduction* (3d ed.). New York: Merrill.

Oxford American dictionary. (1980). New York: Oxford University Press.

Piaget, J. (1926). *The language and thought of the child.* London: Routledge & Kegan Paul.

Piaget, J. (1928). *Judgment and reasoning in the child.* London: Routledge & Kegan Paul.

Piaget, J. (1962). *Play, dreams, and imitation in childhood.* New York: Norton.

Pinker, S. (1991, August). Rules of language. *Science, 253,* 530–535.

Pressley, M., Levin, J., & McDaniel, M. (1987). Remembering versus inferring what a word means: Mnemonic and contextual approaches. In M. G. McKeown & M. E. Curtis (Eds.), *The nature of vocabulary acquisition.* Hillsdale, NJ: Erlbaum.

Random House dictionary of the English language. (1966). New York: Random House.

Rinsland, H. D. (1945). *A basic vocabulary of elementary school children.* New York: Macmillan.

Rosch, E. (1973). On the internal structure of perceptual and semantic categories. In T. E. Moore (Ed.), *Cognitive development and the acquisition of language.* New York: Academic.

Santrock, J. W., & Yussen, S. R. (1992). *Child development: An introduction* (5th ed.). Dubuque, IA: Wm. C. Brown.

Schulman, J., & Havighurst, R. (1947). Relationship between ability and social status in a midwestern community: Size of vocabulary. *Journal of Educational Psychology*, **38**, 437–442.

Seashore, R. H., & Eckerson, L. D. (1940). The measurement of individual differences in general English vocabularies. *Journal of Educational Psychology*, **31**, 14–37.

Selby, S. (1972). The development of morphological rules in children. *British Journal of Educational Psychology*, **42**, 293–299.

Selkirk, E. O. (1982). *The syntax of words*. Cambridge, MA: MIT Press.

Shaffer, D. (1993). *Developmental psychology* (3d ed.). Pacific Grove, CA: Brooks/Cole.

Shibles, B. H. (1959). How many words does a first grade child know? *Elementary English*, **31**, 42–47.

Slobin, D. (1973). Cognitive prerequisites for the acquisition of grammar. In C. Ferguson & D. Slobin (Eds.), *Studies of child language development*. New York: Holt, Rinehart & Winston.

Smith, L. B., Jones, S. S., & Landau, B. (1992). Count nouns, adjectives, and perceptual properties in children's novel word interpretations. *Developmental Psychology*, **28**, 273–286.

Smith, M. E. (1926). An investigation of the development of the sentence and the extent of vocabulary in young children. *University of Iowa Studies in Child Welfare*, **5**, 219–227.

Smith, M. K. (1941). Measurement of the size of general English vocabulary through the elementary grades and high school. *Genetic Psychology Monographs*, **24**, 311–345.

Snow, C. E. (1990). The development of definitional skill. *Journal of Child Language*, **17**, 697–710.

Stanners, R., Neiser, J., Hernon, W., & Hall, R. (1979). Memory representation for morphologically related words. *Journal of Verbal Learning and Verbal Behavior*, **18**, 399–412.

Stanovich, K. E. (1986). Matthew effects in reading: Some consequences of individual differences in the acquisition of literacy. *Reading Research Quarterly*, **21**(4), 360–406.

Sternberg, R. J. (1987). Most vocabulary is learned from context. In M. G. McKeown & M. E. Curtis (Eds.), *The nature of vocabulary acquisition*. Hillsdale, NJ: Erlbaum.

Swinney, D. A., & Cutler, A. (1979). The accessing and processing of idiomatic expressions. *Journal of Verbal Learning and Verbal Behavior*, **18**, 523–534.

Templin, M. (1957). *Certain language skills in children: Their development and interrelationships* (Institute of Child Welfare Monograph Series, No. 26). Minneapolis: University of Minnesota Press.

Terman, L. M. (1918). Vocabulary test as a measure of intelligence. *Journal of Educational Psychology*, **9**, 452–466.

Thorndike, E. L., & Lorge, I. (1944). *The teacher's word book of 30,000 words*. New York: Bureau of Publications, Teachers College, Columbia University.

Trevarthen, C. (1980). The foundations of intersubjectivity: Development of interpersonal and cooperative understanding in infants. In D. Olson (Ed.), *The social foundations of language and thought*. New York: Norton.

Tyler, A., & Nagy, W. (1989). The acquisition of English derivational morphology. *Journal of Memory and Language*, **28**, 649–667.

Urdang, L., & Abate, F. (1983). *Idioms and phrases index*. Detroit: Gale Research/Book Tower.

Vasta, R., Haith, M., & Miller, S. (1992). *Child psychology: The modern science*. New York: Wiley.

Vygotsky, L. S. (1986). *Thought and language* (A. Kozulin, Ed.). Cambridge, MA: MIT Press.

Watson, R. (1985). Towards a theory of definition. *Journal of Child Language,* **12,** 181–197.

Waxman, S. R., & Hatch, T. (1992). Beyond the basics: Preschool children label objects flexibly at multiple hierarchical levels. *Journal of Child Language,* **19,** 153–166.

Waxman, S. R., & Kosowski, T. D. (1990). Nouns mark category relations: Toddlers' and preschoolers' word-learning biases. *Child Development,* **61,** 1461–1473.

Webster's third new international dictionary of the English language. (1961). Springfield, MA: G. & C. Merriam.

Webster's third new international dictionary of the English language. (1981). Springfield, MA: G. & C. Merriam. (The 1981 ed. includes a new Addenda section, listing and defining words that have entered the language since the 1961 ed. appeared)

Wechsler, D. (1949). *Manual, Wechsler Intelligence Scale for Children.* New York: Psychological Corp.

Wells, G. (1984). *Language development in the preschool years.* Cambridge: Cambridge University Press.

Werner, H., & Kaplan, E. (1952). The acquisition of word meanings: A developmental study. *Monographs of the Society for Research in Child Development,* **15**(1, Serial No. 51).

White, T. G., Power, M. A., & White, S. (1989). Morphological analysis: Implications for teaching and understanding vocabulary growth. *Reading Research Quarterly,* **24**(3), 283–304.

Winer, B. J. (1971). *Statistical principles in experimental design.* New York: McGraw-Hill.

Wolman, R. N., & Barker, E. N. (1965). A developmental study of word definitions. *Journal of Genetic Psychology,* **107,** 159–166.

Wysocki, K., & Jenkins, J. R. (1987). Deriving word meanings through morphological generalization. *Reading Research Quarterly,* **22**(1), 66–81.

ACKNOWLEDGMENTS

This research was supported in part by two grants to the author from the Natural Sciences and Engineering Research Council of Canada. I am very grateful to the children who participated in this study, to their parents, and to the teachers and principals at the Bridgeport Public School and the A. R. Kaufman Public School in Waterloo, Ontario, where this research was conducted. I would especially like to thank Marlene Heckman for all the superb work she did in helping prepare the materials for this study and in interviewing the children. I would also like to express my appreciation to Susan Sykes and the Office of Human Research at the University of Waterloo as well as Teresa Alexander, David Bertrand, Anthea Britto, Tracy Cocivera, Mardie Creed, Janice Hansen, Carla Johnson, Nancy Malloy, Shirley Meaning, Jill Seim, and Tracy Versteegh for their assistance during various phases of this research. I am very grateful to George Miller for sharing with me his thoughts and insights during the planning of this research project and to him and Pamela Wakefield for agreeing to write the Commentary. I would also like to thank Joanne Carlisle, Rob Duncan, Carla Johnson, Trudy Landry, Ernie MacKinnon, George Miller, William Nagy, Paul Nation, Sheri Skwarchuk, and the students in my graduate seminar on language development for their very helpful comments on earlier versions of the manuscript. I have benefited from discussing this research with several other people as well, including Margaret Anglin, Gay Bisanz, Jeff Bisanz, Jim Clark, Ed Cornell, Bruce Derwing, Harry Logan, Steve Mackay, Fred Morrison, Keith Nelson, David Olson, David Palermo, Laura Petitto, Diane Poulin-Dubois, Hildy Ross, Michael Ross, Liz Smith, Phil Smith, Endel Tulving, and Laurence Urdang. I am very grateful to Christine Schwendinger for the excellent job she did in typing the manuscript. Finally, I would like to thank Ed Ware, Geoff Fong, Erik Woody, Al Cheyne, Gary Griffin, Dale Griffin, and Jeanette O'Hara-Hines for their advice concerning statistical analyses.

Correspondence should be addressed to Jeremy M. Anglin, Department of Psychology, University of Waterloo, Waterloo, Ontario, Canada, N2L 3G1.

COMMENTARY

ON ANGLIN'S ANALYSIS OF VOCABULARY GROWTH

George A. Miller and Pamela C. Wakefield

Anyone interested in how children learn words will surely be grateful for Anglin's *Monograph.* His meticulous analysis of the contribution of derivational and collocational morphology to the growth of a child's recognition vocabulary will long stand as a landmark, inspiring the comfortable feeling, "No one need do *that* again!" At the outset, therefore, we want to express our admiration for Anglin's contribution—nothing that follows should be interpreted as unappreciative of his considerable accomplishment.

Still, commentators must make comments. We limit ourselves here to two points. First, something must be said about what these units are that Anglin and others have tried to count. Second, we have some observations about the validity of the dictionary-sampling method that Anglin used. Everything we say is said by Anglin, implicitly if not explicitly, but we think that it may help the reader if we say it from a different perspective.

What Is Being Counted?

The lay question, How many words does the average person know? has an apparent plausibility that evaporates as soon as you try to answer it. Your answer must depend on what you are willing to count as a word and on what you are willing to count as knowing. Although the two problems are related, we shall focus primarily on what is being counted. We believe that Anglin is highly skilled at eliciting anything that children might know about

Preparation of this paper was supported in part by a grant from the James S. McDonnell Foundation and in part by grant N00014-91-J-1634 from the Office of Naval Research and the Advanced Research Projects Agency, Information Science and Technology Office. The opinions expressed here are those of the authors and do not represent the views of these sponsors.

a word, but the developmental significance of those results derives from his claims about what he is counting.

Presumably, Anglin is counting words. But what is a word? Many linguists have observed that *word* is not an easy word to define (Di Sciullo & Williams, 1987), but, by limiting ourselves to a single language and ignoring some of the finer points, a simplified definition can serve the present purposes. We propose as our first comment the following definition:

> C1.—A word is an association between a concept and an utterance that plays a syntactic role.

To those who would complain that *concept* is even harder to define than *word* is, the answer must be that, if a concept were not associated with an utterance, no one would utter it. Admittedly, something more than C1 would be needed to distinguish lexicalized concepts (concepts expressed by words) from sentential concepts (concepts expressed by sentences), but, since the concern here is limited to lexicalized concepts, that distinction need not complicate C1.

The point that we want to make is that C1 has clear implications for what you should count when you undertake to count words. It implies, for example, that *dog* and *dogs* are two different words: *a single dog* and *more than one dog* are different concepts, the concepts are associated with different utterances, and the difference has syntactic consequences (number agreement) for the verbs with which they are used. Similarly, *chase, chases, chasing,* and *chased* are different utterances that express different concepts that play different syntactic roles. And the same observation holds for, say, *fast, faster,* and *fastest.* In short, inflectional morphology generates words that, if you accept C1 as your definition of *word,* should be counted as distinct words.

Moreover, according to C1, polysemy also results in distinct words. For example, *poker* is sometimes a fire tool and sometimes a card game. Since the concepts are different, different words must be involved; the fact that both concepts can be expressed by the same utterance does not mean that the utterances are the same word. To count the number of words that a person knows, therefore, you should count every distinct concept-utterance association as a different word. A verb like *take,* for example, has 29 senses in *Webster's Third* (1981), and each sense has several extensions. According to C1, *take* would count as (at least) 29 different English words.

C1 also has clear implications for what we should count as knowing a word. If C1 is accepted, then knowing a word is a matter of (1) having mastered a concept, (2) having learned to pronounce the utterance correctly, (3) having formed an appropriate association between the concept and the utterance, and (4) knowing how to deploy it correctly in grammatical expressions. Although the syntactic role of words is frequently overlooked in vocabulary-estimation studies, the best evidence that 1–3 must have occurred is often obtained by observing 4.

It is clear, however, that those who have attempted to estimate the number of words that a person knows have *not* taken C1 as their definition of the units they are counting. Seashore and Eckerson (1940) ignored inflections in their original study, and nearly everyone who followed assumed that this is the reasonable thing to do. M. K. Smith (1941) gave children credit for knowing a word if they recognized any meaning of the word, so those who followed have also assumed that it is reasonable to ignore polysemy. And most studies have explicitly studied recognition vocabulary, which implies that it is not necessary to test children's ability to produce the word in a grammatical sentence.

If the research tradition here has not counted words as defined by C1, what has it been counting instead? What definition of *word* is being used? The answer is simple: following Seashore and Eckerson (1940), researchers define a *word* as a headword in a dictionary ("boldfaced main entry [flush to the left margin]") or what lexicographers call a *lemma*. The lay question, How many words does the average person know? has been transformed into, How many headwords does the average person recognize? Since there are fewer headwords than there are words, answers to the lay question are figures much smaller than they would have been had C1 been taken as defining the unit to be counted. Those who complain that estimates of recognition vocabulary obtained by the method of dictionary sampling are too large would really have something to complain about were C1 accepted.

Like most other sensible people interested in vocabulary, Anglin assumed that a word is something you find listed in a dictionary, thus taking advantage of more than 200 years of lexicography. And modern dictionaries are organized as alphabetical lists of headwords. Most entries contain information about inflections and polysemy, of course, but the question of vocabulary size is much easier to answer if information given inside the entries can be ignored. Dictionaries, of course, are printed, not spoken, so this strategy assumes that no serious distortion will result from dealing with inscriptions instead of utterances. And, as long as the words are spoken to the person whose knowledge is being tested, it is hard to fault the assumption.

Actually, Anglin has been even more conservative than Seashore and Eckerson. Anglin has defined *word* as a different headword. The word *back*, for example, can be used as a noun, an adverb, an adjective, or a verb; in *Webster's Third*, which Anglin takes as his source, each of these parts of speech is given a separate entry and a separate headword. Anglin ignores differences in the syntactic roles that such a word can play: the four headwords in *Webster's Third* become a single different headword in Anglin's count. That is to say, children would be said to know *back* if they could respond correctly to any meaning of any syntactic use of the word. In this respect, Anglin is consistent with the usual conception of recognition vocabulary. Had he tried to count the children's vocabulary of use, he would have had to assess the children's ability to deploy words correctly in grammatical expressions, and distinctions of syntactic category would have been essential.

Nothing underhanded is going on here. What is counted as a word is explained by Anglin in careful detail and conforms with the best practices of other vocabulary estimators. But a reader should be aware of how and why the lay question, How many words does the average person know? turns into the research question, How many different headwords does the average person recognize? We suspect that an answer to the lay question (if anyone knew how to calculate it) would be more than twice as large as Anglin's answers to the research question.

Is the Sampling Method Accurate?

It has long been known that, the larger the dictionary you sample when creating a test vocabulary, the larger will be your estimate of people's recognition vocabulary. Some have seen this relation as a paradox, others as evidence of some statistical flaw in the sampling method. Yet the explanation is simple. We offer it as our second comment:

C2.—The dictionary-sampling method assumes that the dictionary contains every word that the person being tested can recognize.

The smaller a dictionary is, therefore, the greater the likelihood that C2 will be violated and the recognition vocabulary underestimated. Alternatively, the larger a dictionary is, the greater the likelihood that C2 will be satisfied and the recognition vocabulary not underestimated. Because he understood C2, Anglin began with the largest dictionary of English that he could find.

It is a misuse of the sampling method to apply it when C2 is not fulfilled. To the extent that C2 is violated—to the extent that testees could recognize words that are not included in the dictionary—the sampling method will underestimate their recognition vocabulary. Hence, results obtained by the sampling method should be regarded as lower bounds.

Some thought experiments should help here. Suppose that Anglin's word list was used to estimate the recognition vocabulary of monolingual French children. There might be enough cognates to enable French children to recognize a few words, but the results would undoubtedly indicate that these children have negligible recognition vocabularies (for English). Obviously, the sampling method would greatly underestimate the children's vocabulary—because children who can speak French must know many words that are not included in *Webster's Third*. In this instance, the violation of C2 would be so obvious that it would probably not occur to anyone to use Anglin's list in this manner.

A less extreme violation would occur were Anglin's list used to test children from lower socioeconomic homes—in particular, children whose street vocabulary includes many words that have not found their way into *Webster's Third*. Since the size of a person's academic vocabulary tends to be correlated with intelligence test scores (both predict academic success), underestimating these children's vocabularies might lead to self-fulfilling prophecies of academic failure.

Since C2 is such a basic assumption, we thought it worthwhile to test it. So we used Anglin's *Webster's Third* list to estimate the sizes of some smaller dictionaries. This is an odd use, of course, since there are other, more direct ways to estimate how many different headwords a dictionary contains. But that is one advantage of this exercise: the results of the sampling method can be verified by other methods. Moreover, it minimizes the problems of deciding whether a testee "knows" a word, and there is no need to collect a representative sample of testees.

For this methodological experiment, therefore, we selected three dictionaries: *Merriam-Webster's Collegiate Dictionary* (1993), the *American Heritage Dictionary of the English Language* (1992), and *Stedman's Concise Medical Dictionary* (1987). Since *Webster's Collegiate* is based on *Webster's Third*, we expected that it would contain few words that are not in *Webster's Third*. The *American Heritage* evolved independently, so we expected that it would contain relatively more words that *Webster's Third* omitted. And the medical dictionary, *Stedman's*, was expected to contain many technical terms that were not in *Webster's Third*. In short, we expected these three dictionaries to generate three points on a curve.

We then proceeded to estimate the number of different headwords in each dictionary in two different ways: (i) by the sampling procedure (in each of the three dictionaries we looked up every one of the 434 words on Anglin's first list and counted how many of them occurred as headwords; we then multiplied the number found by 596 [258,601 divided by 434] to derive our estimates because Anglin suggests that each of the 434 sample words represents 596 different dictionary headwords); (ii) by direct counting (we calculated the average number of different headwords per page for a sample of 20 pages, then multiplied by the number of pages in the dictionary). The difference between these two estimates provides an indication of how much the sampling method underestimated the true value.

The results are shown in Table C1. It is apparent that our expectations in selecting these dictionaries were fulfilled. *Webster's Collegiate*, which is based on *Webster's Third*, was underestimated only 7.7% by the sampling

TABLE C1

DICTIONARY STATISTICS: UNDERESTIMATION OF THREE DICTIONARIES

| | DIFFERENT HEADWORDS | | PERCENTAGE |
DICTIONARY	Sampling	Counting	UNDERESTIMATION
Webster's Collegiate......	64,964	70,347	7.7
American Heritage	70,924	86,320	17.8
Stedman's	15,496	33,620	53.9

method; the *American Heritage,* written by different editors and published by a different house, was underestimated 17.8% by the sampling method; and the medical dictionary, *Stedman's,* was underestimated by 53.9%. Discussion of the kinds of words that are in the *American Heritage* and *Stedman's* but not in *Webster's Third* would be amusing, but the point of the exercise has been made: C2 is confirmed.

Since the dictionary-sampling method provides merely a lower bound, it is natural to wonder how good a lower bound it really is in the case of schoolchildren. Unfortunately, in the case of children, we do not have another method for obtaining a more accurate estimate or even for fixing an upper bound, so we cannot make a similar comparison. Consequently, we have no defensible estimate of how good a lower bound Anglin's figures give us. One suspects that they are pretty good—that young children do not know a great many words that are not in *Webster's Third*—but that is merely a belief.

There is one respect, however, in which it seems likely that Anglin seriously underestimated, and that is in the case of inflected words. Note that the dictionary-sampling method does not ignore all inflectional morphology. *Webster's Third* includes an inflected form as a main entry (1) if it is a homograph (if it has a meaning other than its meaning as an inflected form: *pleasing* is an adjective as well as a participle), (2) if it is irregular (*gone, elves*), or (3), according to the explanatory notes at the front of *Webster's Third,* if a regularly inflected form would fall more than 5 inches away from its main entry. This third convention seems to have contributed a few regularly inflected words to Anglin's list. The three conventions together provide enough inflected headwords that he can follow the increasing mastery of inflected forms by older children. But the number of inflected words that are headwords in *Webster's Third* grossly underestimates the number of inflected words in the language and, since most regular inflections are probably mastered in the preschool years, similarly underestimates the number of inflected words that these children probably know. To phrase it in terms of C2, since the children in Anglin's study could recognize many inflected words that do not occur as headwords in *Webster's Third,* Anglin's method seriously underestimates that aspect of their vocabulary.

This again raises the question, Should inflected words be counted when you are trying to estimate the size of a child's vocabulary? If you are interested in the role of morphology in vocabulary growth, as Anglin is, then the contribution of inflectional morphology is an important part of your study (although you should probably study younger children to capture the main effect). On the other hand, if you are interested in the number of root words that a child has mastered, then you will want to exclude inflected words since they can be generated (by rule or paradigm) from the root forms.

But why would you include irregularly inflected words and exclude regularly inflected words? Irregular forms require special learning since they cannot be generated from their root forms, so the rationale might be that you are interested in how much learning the child has done, not in how many words the child knows. But that presupposes more about the word-learning process than we actually know.

Conclusion

It is unfair to criticize an author for not doing something he did not set out to do, and that is not the intent of the following remarks. But Anglin's work, admirable as it is, does not exhaust the varieties of information that children can use in building their vocabularies.

Basic to Anglin's argument is the assumption that lexical knowledge is structured. That is to say, the mental dictionary is not a homogeneous list of concept-utterance pairs that have been memorized by rote. Words are related to one another in many ways, and it is by taking advantage of those relations that children are able to develop their vocabularies so rapidly. In this *Monograph,* Anglin has focused on morphological relations between the utterances, but semantic relations between the concepts can also be useful. Semantic relations are to lexicalized concepts what morphological relations are to lexical utterances. By *semantic relations* we have in mind such relations as synonymy, antonymy, meronymy (part-whole relations), hyponymy or subsumption (subordinate-superordinate relations), and entailments (*kill* entails *die*). Linguists and philosophers could extend this list considerably, but these are enough to make a point.

In the interests of finding new perspectives, consider the following twist on Anglin's project. Suppose you tried to estimate the number of different lexicalized concepts that a person has correctly associated with an utterance. Note that that is not the question that Anglin asked. Anglin estimated the number of different utterances that a person has correctly associated with a lexicalized concept. If there were precisely one concept per utterance and one utterance per concept, this distinction would make no difference. But the mapping between word meanings and word forms in any natural language is notoriously many:many, so the two questions could have rather different answers.

There is no easy way to count lexicalized concepts in a standard dictionary, but imagine that you had a method for doing it. Then, no doubt, you could show a rapid conceptual growth, paralleling the growth in recognizable utterances that Anglin has measured. Then we might ask whether the semantic relations between and among lexicalized concepts contribute to their rapid growth and, if so, how—questions analogous to those that Anglin has asked about morphological relations.

For example, learning synonyms would not count as learning new concepts: a child who had the concept *snake* would not be credited with conceptual growth when she learned about *serpent*. But would a child who knew *red* and *green* be credited with learning one new concept when she learned that red is a *color* and a second new concept when she learned that green is, too? Would a child have to master the concept expressed by *die* before mastering the concept expressed by *kill*? Would a child who knew *dry* and *wet* be credited with a new concept when she learned that they are antonyms? And so on.

We have hypothesized that you have a way of counting lexicalized concepts, so we can assume that you have acceptable answers to such questions. But the simple point is that word meanings come in tightly related clusters, and it is still an open question how the semantic relations among them organize and facilitate the task that children face in mastering the vocabulary of their native language. Anglin's quantitative contribution is impressive in its detail and implications, yet it merely hints at the work that remains to be done.

Anglin closes the *Monograph* with some remarks about the similarity between what goes on when children figure out the meanings of collocations and what probably goes on when children figure out unfamiliar words by reading them in context. So it is appropriate to close this Commentary with some remarks about the consequences of such inductive learning.

Perhaps the most obvious consequence of learning new words from context is that people learn how to use many words that they are unable to define. Yet this is precisely the kind of lexical knowledge that dictionaries communicate least well. For example, when someone learning English as a second language looks up a common word in the dictionary and discovers that it can be used to express any one of N different concepts, the dictionary provides little assistance in determining which of those N concepts is the one most appropriate in any given context. No doubt people are so good at making such inferences that lexicographers have little incentive to encode them explicitly in word books that are already overly long. But, whatever the reason, it is unlikely that conventional dictionaries will be much help in figuring out what *figuring out* consists of.

Anyone interested in words and how they are acquired is well advised to start by looking at the information provided by a good dictionary. But not everything that people know about words will be found there.

References

American heritage dictionary of the English language, 3rd edition. (1992). Boston: Houghton Mifflin.

Di Sciullo, A. M., & Williams, E. (1987). *On the definition of word.* Cambridge, MA: MIT Press.

Merriam-Webster's collegiate dictionary, 10th edition. (1993). Springfield, MA: Merriam-Webster.

Seashore, R. H., & Eckerson, L. D. (1940). The measurement of individual differences in general English vocabulary. *Journal of Educational Psychology, 42,* 14–37.

Smith, M. K. (1941). Measurement of the size of general English vocabulary through the elementary grades and high school. *Genetic Psychology Monographs, 24,* 311–345.

Stedman's concise medical dictionary, 24th edition. (1987). New York: Prentice-Hall.

Webster's third new international dictionary of the English language. (1981). Springfield, MA: Merriam-Webster.

KNOWING VERSUS LEARNING WORDS

Jeremy M. Anglin

I am very grateful to George Miller and Pamela Wakefield for their thoughtful and absorbing Commentary on the analysis of vocabulary growth presented in this *Monograph.* They show clearly how estimates of vocabulary knowledge depend critically on one's definition of a word and, relatedly, on the source from which words are taken in dictionary sampling research. Their methodological experiment reveals in a clever way that even an unabridged dictionary as large as *Webster's Third* (1981) does not define all the words that are included as main entries in other considerably smaller dictionaries, particularly specialized ones such as *Stedman's Concise Medical Dictionary* (1987). Their Commentary also points to several potentially important directions for future research on vocabulary development and suggests mechanisms, other than those stressed in the *Monograph,* that might ultimately help account for the rapid growth of vocabulary knowledge in children.

Miller and Wakefield state that much of what they say is said implicitly if not explicitly in the *Monograph,* but they have put their arguments in an especially clear and interesting way as well as from a somewhat different perspective. And I do indeed agree with much of what they say. In particular, although some researchers may reckon that my estimates of vocabulary size are too high, I agree with their argument that, if one were to adopt their definition of a word and were to be able to figure out a way to estimate all the words children know according to their definition, the resulting estimates would in all probability be even higher than those presented in this study. In my Reply to their Commentary, I want to consider further the implications for estimating children's vocabulary knowledge that would follow from adopting their definition, as well as some others, of what a word is.

Of the questions that motivated the research presented in this *Monograph* (outlined at the end of Chap. III), Miller and Wakefield's comments are primarily but not exclusively concerned with the first ones having to do with how many words children of different ages know. Some readers may find our estimates of the numbers of words known by children of different ages and of the overall rates of vocabulary development to be less interesting than our findings concerning the shifting patterns in terms of the relative contributions made by different word types to vocabulary knowledge and growth during different developmental periods. Nevertheless, others may be quite interested in the former issues, and we felt that they were fundamental ones to address before turning to the more qualitative analyses. Because Miller and Wakefield have focused on these fundamental questions, I will as well below. However, in my Reply, I also want to raise again one of the other sets of questions central to this study, those pertaining to the distinction between knowing words because they have been previously learned and knowing them because they can be constructed or deciphered when the occasion requires it. As discussed in Chapter II, previous researchers have very often taken estimates of children's vocabulary knowledge to indicate how many words they have actually learned, whereas the results of our study suggest that a large proportion of such words may be known or knowable not because they have been previously learned but because they could be figured out through knowledge of morphological rules. Moreover, I believe that, if one were to adopt a definition of *word* such as that proposed by Miller and Wakefield, it would be especially important to clarify what is meant by knowing words, by distinguishing those that have been learned from those that could be deciphered or constructed through the use of rules and other creative processes.

Defining What a Word Is

A point emphasized in the *Monograph* (see esp. Chaps. II and VII) is that one's estimates of vocabulary knowledge will depend critically on one's definition of what a word is. Some researchers have defined *words* in such a way as to lead to estimates of vocabulary knowledge and rate of vocabulary development that are considerably lower than those presented in the current study (e.g., D'Anna, Zechmeister, & Hall, 1991; Dupuy, 1974; Goulden, Nation, & Read, 1990). If one were to adopt other definitions of what a word is, such as that presented by Miller and Wakefield, and if one could develop ways of estimating total vocabulary knowledge using such definitions, one would very likely arrive at higher estimates. The research strategy adopted in the present investigation was to begin by "operationally defining" words as different boldfaced main entry words found in the most recent, largest nonhistorical dictionary of English available when this project was initiated, although in several subsequent analyses attempts were made to clarify what was meant by *words* by subclassifying them into different morphological categories and eventually by attempting to distinguish psychologically basic or learned words from words that are potentially knowable through morphological analysis. Before discussing Miller and Wakefield's definition of what a word is and the implications that adopting their definition might have for estimating children's vocabulary knowledge, it is worth pausing for a moment to consider why we chose to begin by treating as words boldfaced entries in an unabridged dictionary. In particular, I would like to focus on some of the advantages that such an approach holds for researchers interested in conducting empirical studies of vocabulary development such as that reported in this *Monograph*.

One advantage of choosing lexical entries in an unabridged dictionary as one's unit of analysis in studies of vocabulary knowledge, as Miller and Wakefield intimate, is that, not only is what is meant by a word relatively easy to understand, but this approach also draws on the expertise of lexicographers whose business it is to list and define the words of a language in dictionaries. In deciding whether to insert an entry into a dictionary, lexicographers ultimately seek evidence that the term has actually been used sufficiently by members of the linguistic community to be viewed as having entered the language and therefore to merit inclusion. For example, the choice of entries included in *Webster's Third*, the unabridged dictionary used in the present research, was based to a considerable extent on a huge file of several million citations, documented cases in which possible words had been used, usually in written sources. If there was evidence that a potential lexical unit had been used often enough and in sufficiently different contexts, it was included as a word in the dictionary. Thus, although I can see how defining words as boldfaced entries in dictionaries may seem either atheoretical or biased or conservative or liberal to some, there is a rationale to doing so that others may appreciate or even admire: these are words for which there exists evidence that they have entered the language in the sense that they have actually been used by various members of the relevant linguistic community.

A second reason for beginning with this definition of a word in conducting research on vocabulary development, and one that certainly was a factor in our adopting it as a starting point, is that others have done so previously, and the results from some of these studies (e.g., Smith, 1941; Templin, 1957) have suggested an interesting and, indeed, remarkable process of vocabulary development (e.g., Carey, 1978; Miller, 1977; Nagy & Herman, 1987), which is why they are still being discussed extensively in the recent literature. Thus, even though some psycholinguists may feel that words have been defined too conservatively and others that they have been defined too liberally by such researchers, an advantage of adopting this approach while attempting to improve on it is that it is a relatively direct way of establishing the validity of previous findings and of clarifying their implications. This of course was what was attempted in the present study, which is not to say that other, quite different approaches might not also be capable of verifying and illuminating such previous findings (e.g., Nagy & Anderson, 1984).

A third advantage for researchers of accepting as words boldfaced entries in an unabridged dictionary that is important to note is that it allows extrapolation from children's (or adults') knowledge of a representative sample of words taken from it to their knowledge of all the words in the dictionary (as was done in the present study). Thus, by anchoring such research to an authoritative dictionary, it is possible to go beyond the lexicon presented in it to conclusions about the size and general qualitative characteristics of the mental lexicons of children (or adults) in certain ways that would be difficult if one were to define words independently of a dictionary or of some other existing list of the words of a language. For example, estimating how many words might be recognized by an individual on the basis of his or her understanding of those in a sample requires knowing how many are in the population of words being generalized to, and, without some sort of catalog of this population of words, it is not obvious how this could be done.

Thus, there are reasons why for certain purposes researchers might want to choose to define words in terms of the ways lexicographers have in constructing dictionaries. Still, there are certainly other ways of defining words, and no doubt adopting such definitions will affect one's conclusions about the nature of vocabulary development. For example, if one were to define words as monomorphemic free forms (see, e.g., Dupuy, 1974; Goulden et al., 1990), estimates of vocabulary knowledge and rate of vocabulary development would be much lower than those presented in this *Monograph.*

Other possible definitions of what a word is, such as that presented by Miller and Wakefield, would no doubt lead to higher estimates if one could develop a good way of estimating children's total knowledge of words defined in this way. Our estimates of the numbers of main entries from *Webster's Third* known by children at different ages could be viewed as estimates of all the words they know only if one were to define a word as a different boldfaced headword in an unabridged dictionary, as some researchers have. Miller and Wakefield do not question the estimates presented of how many of the quarter of a million different main entry words or so in *Webster's Third* children know. However, the general thrust of their remarks is that, if one were to adopt their definition of what a word is, and if one could devise a way of estimating all the words satisfying their definition that children might know, the estimates would be even higher. Therefore, they argue that our estimates under their definition are rather conservative and should be viewed as lower bounds. In Chapter VII of the *Monograph*, I have discussed how the estimates presented may actually underestimate children's total vocabulary knowledge and how future research would be necessary to reveal to what extent the estimates would increase if knowledge of subentries (including many inflected words), polysemous meanings, homographs, and other words not in *Webster's Third* were studied as well. Consequently, although some researchers will, in all likelihood, feel that our estimates are on the high side, I agree with Miller and Wakefield that they are conservative, particularly if one were to adopt their definition of what a word is, for all the reasons they give.

Miller and Wakefield define a word as "an association between a concept and an utterance that plays a syntactic role" (p. 168). Of course, as they suggest, ultimately their definition of a word would have to be refined somewhat further to distinguish between words and other concept-utterance associations that play a syntactic role. For example, I think that one would want to specify why a lexical compound such as *birthday* would count as a single word whereas a phrase such as *hot day* would not since both would qualify as words under their definition as stated. Differential stress patterns could sometimes be used to distinguish lexical compounds from phrases, as linguists have suggested, but not always. My suspicion is that a refinement needed would add that a word has an inherent unity such that it is not possible to insert another word or morpheme into it without obliterating the word, whereas it is possible to do so in the case of phrases. Thus *hot sunny day* is acceptable, but *birth-sunny-day* is not.

Learning versus Constructing Word Meanings

Let us assume that one could refine Miller and Wakefield's definition of a word to exclude other linguistic units such as phrases that should not be counted as words from those that should (which seems possible) and that a way of estimating children's or adults' total knowledge of such words could be devised (which might be difficult). Then it would follow that the resulting estimates of vocabulary knowledge according to their definition of a word would in all probability be higher than those presented in this *Monograph* and that my estimates should be viewed as "lower bounds," as they argue. Still, in trying to interpret these higher estimates, I believe that it would be important to ask what is meant by "knowing words" and to attempt, as I have in the present study, to distinguish between words that are known because they have been previously learned (i.e., represented in the mental lexicon as distinct entries) and words that are known (or knowable) because they could be deciphered or constructed when the occasion requires it.

Consider inflected words, which Miller and Wakefield identify as the type of word in children's vocabularies most likely to have been substantially underestimated in the present research according to their definition of a word. Although *Webster's Third* includes some inflected words as main entries in the cases outlined by Miller and Wakefield, the majority of such words are included as subentries. Thus, this study, in which only main entries were sampled, is certainly likely to have underestimated children's knowledge of such words. This was confirmed in the two subsequent studies that I conducted with Teresa Alexander and Nancy Malloy mentioned briefly in the *Monograph*. In these investigations, we tested children's knowledge of large samples of both main entries and subentries from *Webster's Third*. The results for main entries were generally consistent with those presented in this *Monograph*. The estimates for total entry vocabulary knowledge (including knowledge of both main and subentries) were substantially higher at each grade level, and it was knowledge of inflected subentry words that contributed most to the increase. Not surprisingly, then, children were found to know many inflected words not included as main entries in *Webster's Third*. However, when the responses of the children to subentry words were coded with respect to whether there was evidence of morphological problem solving, most subentries in general, and inflected words in particular, were coded as revealing such evidence. Thus, although knowledge of subentries increased our estimates of words known substantially, they did not increase our approximate estimates of learned or "psychologically basic" vocabulary nearly as much. We believe that the reason children were able to receive credit for many of the subentry words is that they knew how to figure out their meanings from knowledge of the root forms and the rules of morphology and, in the case of the inflected subentry words, the rules of inflectional morphology in particular.

Consider also the case of the names of cardinal numbers, another interesting example that can be offered both to support Miller and Wakefield's argument and to illustrate how, when considering the words known by children or adults according to their definition of a word or others like it, it would be important to distinguish between those that have been learned and those that could be constructed or deciphered through knowledge of a system of rules. For example, each cardinal number from 1 to 1,000,000,000 has a name. According to the American system of numeration, these names are *one; two; . . . ; nine hundred and ninety-nine million, nine hundred and ninety-nine thousand, nine hundred and ninety-nine; one billion*. These cardinal number names would satisfy Miller and Wakefield's definition of a word—each represents the association between a concept and an utterance, and each plays a syntactic role as a noun, an adjective, or a pronoun depending on the context of its use. Moreover, I believe that compound cardinal number names possess the kind of inherent unity discussed above, which I have suggested they should also have to qualify as words (as distinct from phrases) using the kind of definition offered by Miller and Wakefield. It is possible to produce and to understand each of these "words" and, indeed, all the cardinal number names less than *one trillion*, provided that one has learned (minimally) the names of the integers from *one* to *nineteen, twenty, thirty, forty, fifty, sixty, seventy, eighty, ninety, hundred, thousand, million*, and *billion* (as well as the conjunction *and*), and provided that one has learned the compounding rules according to which cardinal number names are generated. Thus, the learning of as few as 31 basic cardinal number names, one conjunction, and a modestly complex set of rules for compounding would enable the "knowing" of millions, indeed "billions" of words in a nontrivial sense. Yet only a tiny fraction of these words would have to have been actually learned, that is, stored in the mental lexicon as distinct entries.

Informal testing has suggested that some adults and high school students understand how to count into the billions and that some middle- and upper-level elementary school students from the fifth grade on understand how to count into the millions. Thus, a case could be made that some elementary school children know millions of words and that some high school students and adults know billions according to a definition of *word* such as that suggested by Miller and Wakefield. In such cases, it is clear that the dictionary sampling and estimation method used in the present *Monograph* would underestimate their knowledge of cardinal number names because *Webster's Third* lists as main entries only 103 of them (the cardinal number names from *one* to *ninety-nine, hundred, thousand, million*, and *billion*), although it also provides below its definition of *number* a "number table" showing how to generate the cardinal number names. For most adults and children, however, it seems unlikely that they would have actually memorized as unitary wholes many of the number names not listed in *Webster's Third*. Therefore, as in the case of inflected words, it would seem to be especially important here to distinguish those cardinal number names that were actually learned from those that could be constructed or understood through knowledge of the system of compounding rules used to generate them. Although some compound cardinal number names (e.g., *twenty-five*, the number of pennies in a quarter) may have been previously learned by rote, it seems obvious that the vast majority of such names would be produced or understood through knowledge of a system of rules.

Finally, some comments should be made about the issues of polysemy and homography, which, as Miller and Wakefield suggest, would be important to consider in a complete account of vocabulary development. Besides the variety of morphologically defined word types in dictionaries, the most striking feature of them not considered by most previous researchers who have used the dictionary sampling method to answer questions about vocabulary knowledge and development is that, for some main entries, several different meanings or senses are given to define them. This is especially true of root words (as opposed to derived and inflected words, literal compounds, and idioms). Within root words, it is especially true of common or frequently occurring ones (Miller, 1991). Homographs are also sometimes listed and defined, again especially in the case of frequently occurring root words.

Most previous researchers who have estimated recognition vocabulary knowledge have in fact estimated the number of words for which adults or children know at least one meaning. Seashore and Eckerson (1940), Smith (1941), and Templin (1957) ignored polysemy. Moreover, although they counted homographs as separate entries in selecting their sample, credit for knowing such items was given by Seashore and Eckerson if adults could recognize the commonest meaning, and by Smith and Templin if children could identify any single meaning, of any of the set of homographs spelled the same way for each one they selected. Because homographs occur more often for common words, this appears to be the reason their sample was biased in favor of more frequently occurring words (Lorge & Chall, 1963). These researchers did not study the number of different homographs that might be known for such words they selected. Others who have used dictionary sampling methods (e.g., Dupuy, 1974; Goulden et al., 1990) have treated sets of homographs as single items and have also ignored the issue of polysemy.

In the present study, we have also estimated the number and kinds of words for which children know at least one meaning or, in Miller and Wakefield's terms, the number and kinds of utterances that they have associated with a lexicalized concept. In doing so, we viewed the question of the number and kinds of different meanings children might know for the words they can recognize as a related but separable issue, although one that, as discussed in Chapter VII, would be essential to address in future studies to achieve a more complete account of vocabulary development. Such research is important to do but will be challenging. As Miller and Wakefield suggest, identifying the number of different meanings for a given word that would be conceptually distinct for children or adults may not be easy. Unabridged dictionaries, especially for frequently occurring root words, often give as different senses highly related meanings, some of the differences among which are often so subtle that they might not seem that distinct to most people (e.g., Lovell, 1941). For example, many of the senses referred to by Miller and Wakefield for the verb *take* in *Webster's Third* appear to be slight variations of the basic meaning "to gain possession of."

Still, with careful work, it might be possible to go beyond estimates of the number of words for which children know at least one meaning to estimates of the number of different word meanings they know, and such research would, I think, be important if done well. But it would also be important in such research to interpret how the different meanings for a given word are known. In particular, I believe that it would be important to distinguish meanings for a given word that are known because they have been learned as separate sound-concept associations from those that are known on the basis of comprehension of other meanings of them. As noted above, the different polysemous senses for a given word are often semantically closely related, and it seems likely that some of these could be understood (by means of various processes including metaphoric generalization) through knowledge of others.

Similarly, although the meanings of some homographs (e.g., ^1poker, "a metal rod for stirring a fire," and ^2poker, "a game of cards . . .") seem so different that each would probably have to be learned separately, others are quite semantically related, raising the possibility that the meaning of one homograph could be understood through knowledge of the meaning of another. For example, dictionaries often list as separate homographs entries that have closely related meanings but that have been converted into different parts of speech (e.g., ^1help, "to assist," and ^2help, "assistance"). Even young children appear to have some knowledge of the rules of conversion, which preschoolers sometimes overregularize as they do for other morphological rules, producing such constructions as, "I'm going to broom the dust," or "Juice my bottle" (Clark, 1981, 1982; Derwing & Baker, 1986). Thus, the distinction between knowing polysemous meanings and homographs because they have been previously learned and knowing them because they can be deciphered or constructed would be important to consider in such research, just as the related distinction between word learning and knowing words through morphological analysis was in the present *Monograph*.

Conclusion

Only if one were to define words as different main entries in a recent unabridged dictionary (as some researchers have done implicitly or explicitly) could the estimates presented in this *Monograph* be construed as being of all the words children know. If not, they should be viewed simply as estimates of all of the roughly quarter of a million different main entry words lexicographers chose to include in *Webster's Third* that are known by children. Other definitions of *word* would no doubt result in different estimates of all the words children know, some lower and some higher. If one were to adopt Miller and Wakefield's definition of a word and were to be able to devise ways of estimating children's total vocabulary knowledge having done so, the estimates would in all probability be higher, as they argue. But many of the additional "words" credited (e.g., inflected words, cardinal number names) would likely be known (or knowable) in the sense that they could be constructed or deciphered through knowledge of rules, not because they had been previously learned.

The estimates for how many words children have actually learned under their definition of *word* would also likely be somewhat higher than those presented in this *Monograph* for "psychologically basic" vocabulary, particularly if one counted the learning of different polysemous meanings and homographs as separate instances of word learning. However, the differences between such estimates and those generated by the current study for learned vocabulary would not be as large as those for known or knowable words.

If anything, adopting Miller and Wakefield's definition of a word or others like it would serve to strengthen the conclusion that vocabulary development is a remarkable process and one that we need to understand better. Ultimately, under the present view, this will require greater insight into the processs by means of which children learn words and commit them to long-term memory and those underlying the acquisition and use of rule systems and other creative procedures that enable them to construct and decode the meanings of words that they have not previously learned.

References

Carey, S. (1978). The child as a word learner. In M. Halle, J. Bresnan, & G. A. Miller (Eds.), *Linguistic theory and psychological reality*. Cambridge, MA: MIT Press.

Clark, E. V. (1981). Lexical innovations: How children learn to create new words. In W. Deutsch (Ed.), *The child's construction of language*. London: Academic.

Clark, E. V. (1982). The young word maker: A case study of innovation in the child's lexicon. In E. Wanner & L. Gleitman (Eds.), *Language acquisition: The state of the art*. New York: Cambridge University Press.

D'Anna, C., Zechmeister, E., & Hall, J. (1991). Toward a meaningful definition of vocabulary size. *Journal of Reading Behavior*, **23**, 109–122.

Derwing, B., & Baker, W. (1986). Assessing morphological development. In P. Fletcher & M. Garman (Eds.), *Language acquisition* (2d ed.). New York: Cambridge University Press.

Dupuy, H. (1974). *The rationale, development, and standardization of a basic word vocabulary test* (DHEW Publication No. HRA74-1334). Washington, DC: U.S. Government Printing Office.

Goulden, R., Nation, P., & Read, J. (1990). How large can a receptive vocabulary be? *Applied Linguistics*, **11**, 341–363.

Lorge, I., & Chall, J. (1963). Estimating the size of vocabularies of children and adults: An analysis of methodological issues. *Journal of Experimental Education*, **32**, 147–157.

Lovell, G. D. (1941). Interrelations of vocabulary skills: Commonest versus multiple meanings. *Journal of Educational Psychology*, **32**, 67–72.

Miller, G. A. (1977). *Spontaneous apprentices: Children and language*. New York: Seabury.

Miller, G. A. (1991). *The science of words*. New York: Scientific American Library.

Nagy, W., & Anderson, R. (1984). The number of words in printed school English. *Reading Research Quarterly*, **19**, 304–330.

Nagy, W., & Herman, P. (1987). Depth and breadth of vocabulary knowledge: Implications for acquisition and instruction. In M. G. McKeown & M. E. Curtis (Eds.), *The nature of vocabulary acquisition*. Hillsdale, NJ: Erlbaum.

Seashore, R. H., & Eckerson, L. D. (1940). The measurement of individual differences in general English vocabularies. *Journal of Educational Psychology, 31,* 14–37.

Smith, M. K. (1941). Measurement of the size of general English vocabulary through the elementary grades and high school. *Genetic Psychology Monographs, 24,* 311–345.

Stedman's concise medical dictionary, 24th edition. (1987). New York: Prentice-Hall.

Templin, M. (1957). Certain language skills in children: Their development and interrelationships (Institute of Child Welfare, Monograph Series No. 26). Minneapolis: University of Minnesota Press.

Webster's third new international dictionary of the English language. (1981). Springfield, MA: G. & C. Merriam.

CONTRIBUTORS

Jeremy M. Anglin (Ph.D. 1970, Harvard University) is associate professor of psychology and currently chair of the Developmental Psychology Division at the University of Waterloo. His research interests include language acquisition and cognitive development. Several of his recent studies have focused on lexical, semantic, and conceptual development during childhood. He has previously been a consulting editor for the *Monographs of the Society for Research in Child Development* and has served on the editorial board of *Child Development*. He is the author of *The Growth of Word Meaning* and of *Word, Object, and Conceptual Development* and the editor of *Beyond the Information Given: Studies in the Psychology of Knowing*.

George A. Miller (Ph.D. 1946, Harvard University) is a cognitive psychologist at Princeton University.

Pamela C. Wakefield (B.S. 1982, Upsala College) is a member of the research staff at Princeton University.

STATEMENT OF EDITORIAL POLICY

The *Monographs* series is intended as an outlet for major reports of developmental research that generate authoritative new findings and use these to foster a fresh and/or better-integrated perspective on some conceptually significant issue or controversy. Submissions from programmatic research projects are particularly welcome; these may consist of individually or group-authored reports of findings from some single large-scale investigation or of a sequence of experiments centering on some particular question. Multiauthored sets of independent studies that center on the same underlying question can also be appropriate; a critical requirement in such instances is that the various authors address common issues and that the contribution arising from the set as a whole be both unique and substantial. In essence, irrespective of how it may be framed, any work that contributes significant data and/or extends developmental thinking will be taken under editorial consideration.

Submissions should contain a minimum of 80 manuscript pages (including tables and references); the upper limit of 150–175 pages is much more flexible (please submit four copies; a copy of every submission and associated correspondence is deposited eventually in the archives of the SRCD). Neither membership in the Society for Research in Child Development nor affiliation with the academic discipline of psychology are relevant; the significance of the work in extending developmental theory and in contributing new empirical information is by far the most crucial consideration. Because the aim of the series is not only to advance knowledge on specialized topics but also to enhance cross-fertilization among disciplines or subfields, it is important that the links between the specific issues under study and larger questions relating to developmental processes emerge as clearly to the general reader as to specialists on the given topic.

Potential authors who may be unsure whether the manuscript they are planning would make an appropriate submission are invited to draft an outline of what they propose and send it to the Editor for assessment.

This mechanism, as well as a more detailed description of all editorial policies, evaluation processes, and format requirements, is given in the "Guidelines for the Preparation of *Monographs* Submissions," which can be obtained by writing to the Editor designate, Rachel K. Clifton, Department of Psychology, University of Massachusetts, Amherst, MA 01003.